Public Opinion and Twentieth-Century Diplomacy

New Approaches to International History

Series Editor:

Thomas Zeiler, Professor of American Diplomatic History, University of
Colorado Boulder, USA

New Approaches to International History covers international history during
the modern period and across the globe. The series incorporates new
developments in the field, such as the cultural turn and transnationalism, as
well as the classical high politics of state-centric policymaking and diplomatic
relations. Written with upper level undergraduate and postgraduate students in
mind, texts in the series provide an accessible overview of international, global
and transnational issues, events and actors.

Published:

Decolonization and the Cold War, edited by Leslie James and Elisabeth
Leake (2015)
Cold War Summits, Chris Tudda (2015)
The United Nations in International History, Amy Sayward (2017)
Latin American Nationalism, James F. Siekmeier (2017)
The History of United States Cultural Diplomacy, Michael L. Krenn (2017)
International Cooperation in the Early Twentieth Century,
Daniel Gorman (2017)
Women and Gender in International History, Karen Garner (2018)
International Development, Corinna Unger (2018)
The Environment and International History, Scott Kaufman (2018)

Forthcoming:

The International LGBT Rights Movement, Laura Belmonte
Canada and the World since 1867, Asa McKercher
Reconstructing the Postwar World, Francine McKenzie
The First Age of Industrial Globalization, Maartje Abbenhuis and Gordon
Morrell
Global War, Global Catastrophe, Maartje Abbenhuis and Ismee Tames

Public Opinion and Twentieth-Century Diplomacy

A Global Perspective

Daniel Hucker

BLOOMSBURY ACADEMIC
LONDON • NEW YORK • OXFORD • NEW DELHI • SYDNEY

BLOOMSBURY ACADEMIC
Bloomsbury Publishing Plc
50 Bedford Square, London, WC1B 3DP, UK
1385 Broadway, New York, NY 10018, USA
29 Earlsfort Terrace, Dublin 2, Ireland

BLOOMSBURY, BLOOMSBURY ACADEMIC and the Diana logo are trademarks
of Bloomsbury Publishing Plc

First published in Great Britain 2020
This paperback edition published 2022

Series design by Catherine Wood

Cover image: The Big Three. British Prime Minister David Lloyd George (1863–1945)
right, American President Woodrow Wilson (1856–1924) centre, and French Prime
Minister Georges Clemenceau (1841–1929) at the Versailles Peace Conference at
the end of World War I, June 1, 1919. (© Hulton Archive/Getty Images)

A catalogue record for this book is available from the British Library.

A catalog record for this book is available from the Library of Congress.

ISBN: HB: 978-1-4725-2488-1
PB: 978-1-4725-2282-5
ePDF: 978-1-4725-2716-5
eBook: 978-1-4725-3309-8

Series: New Approaches to International History

Typeset by Deanta Global Publishing Services, Chennai, India

To find out more about our authors and books visit www.bloomsbury.com
and sign up for our newsletters.

Contents

Acknowledgments

I have worked on the topic of public opinion for many years, and it continues to dominate my research and teaching. A debt of gratitude is thus owed to all those who have encouraged me on this path over the previous years (too many to mention), and to the cohorts of students that I have taught along the way for their blend of insight and indulgence. This particular book was written on the invitation of the series editor, Tom Zeiler, so a special thanks must go to him and, indeed, to Anthony Adamthwaite for first suggesting my name for the project. Several years have passed since this original invitation, so I must express my gratitude to several members of the editorial team at Bloomsbury for their enduring patience. In particular, I would like to thank Claire Lipscomb, Maddie Holder, and Dan Hutchins.

More recently, I was fortunate enough to be involved in a fascinating conference on the topic of public opinion hosted at Bath Spa University in June 2018, so I would very much like to thank David Coast and Laura Stewart, the organizers of that conference, for their invitation to give a keynote address. This proved to be a great help as I completed this project, a much-needed reminder that public opinion history was vital and important.

Equally important has been the supportive and friendly atmosphere provided by colleagues within the Department of History at the University of Nottingham. It is a privilege to work alongside so many esteemed scholars, and I am fortunate, indeed, to count many of them as friends. Finally, I would like to thank family and friends (as ever) for their love and support.

Abbreviations

AABN	Anti-Apartheids Beweging Nederland
AAM	Anti-Apartheid Movement
ABC	American Broadcasting Company
ACCESS	American Coordinating Committee for Equality in Sport and Society
ACOA	American Committee on Africa
AFSC	American Friends Service Committee
AKZA	Aktiekomitee Zuidelijk Afrika
ALSC	National African Liberation Support Committee
ANC	African National Congress
AP	Associated Press
BBC	British Broadcasting Corporation
BSE	Bovine spongiform encephalopathy ("mad cow" disease)
CAAA	Comprehensive Anti-Apartheid Act
CAO	Committee of African Organizations
CARIS	Campaign Against Racialism in Sport
CBS	Columbia Broadcasting System
CCCA	Comité Contre le Colonialisme et l'Apartheid
EC	European Community
EEC	European Economic Community
EU	European Union
HART	Halt All Racist Tours
IAAM	Irish Anti-Apartheid Movement
IDATU	Irish Distributive and Administrative Trade Union
IFOP	Institut français d'opinion publique
IOC	International Olympic Committee
IPB	International Peace Bureau

IPU	Inter-Parliamentary Union
KZA	Komitee Zuidelijk Afrika
LEP	League to Enforce Peace
MACV	U.S. Military Assistance Command, Vietnam
MCC	Marylebone Cricket Club
MOBE	National Mobilization Committee to End the War in Vietnam
NBC	National Broadcasting Company
NZRFU	New Zealand Rugby Football Union
PRWM	Polaroid Revolutionary Workers' Movement
SANE	National Committee for a Sane Nuclear Policy
SANROC	South African Non-Racial Olympic Committee
SAONGA	South African Olympic and National Games Association
SASA	South African Sports Association
SDS	Students for a Democratic Society
STST	Stop the Seventy Tour
TANU	Tanganyika African National Union
TUC	Trades Union Congress
UDC	Union of Democratic Control
UKIP	United Kingdom Independence Party
UN	United Nations
USIA	United States Information Agency
WILPF	Women's International League for Peace and Freedom
WSP	Women Strike for Peace

Introduction

International (or diplomatic) history has proven to be unusually inattentive to public opinion. As E. M. Carroll noted in his 1931 study of French public opinion prior to the Great War: "Historians of international relations have rarely concerned themselves in detail with any phase of public opinion," its "intangible character" putting them off almost as much as the lack of "satisfactory conclusions" that can be drawn.[1] This can be attributed to the traditional contours of the discipline, favoring as it does a "top-down" methodology to the history of international relations that focuses on the "great men," the statesmen, politicians, and diplomatists who are considered central to the diplomatic process. In addition, the evidential base that the discipline has traditionally relied upon is strictly empirical, pursuing a Rankean approach to historical study. In its earliest guises, the discipline of "diplomatic" history maintained a very rigid approach that focused on the nation-state as the key political actor, emphasizing throughout the *Primat der Aussenpolitik*.[2] Changes came when the narrowly defined "diplomatic" history morphed into something more inclusive and holistic that was labeled "international" history.[3] Attentive to broader disciplinary shifts, diplomatic history was influenced by the *Annales* school, as well as scholars pursuing Marxist, economic, or anthropological approaches, and later by the postmodern "turn," all of which encouraged them to consider the less obvious determinants of foreign policy. As Patrick Finney has argued, the transition from "diplomatic" to "international" history was much more than a negligible semantic shift: it marked a crucial turning point after which historians of international relations were attentive "not only to diplomacy, but also to economics, strategy, the domestic sources of foreign policy, ideology and propaganda, and intelligence."[4]

In spite of this, public opinion remains a relatively underscrutinized aspect. Explaining this neglect is not too difficult. "International" history remains wedded to an empirical approach that prioritizes the archival record, and the archives of foreign ministries (and other governmental departments) and the people that populated them in particular. The evidential base is then chiefly formal, diplomatic correspondence and memoranda, steeped in the stiff and formal language of the rational and dispassionate realm of foreign policymaking. To be sure, historians have always engaged with personal and informal source materials, including private correspondence, personal diaries and memoirs, in which practitioners are more likely to acknowledge the more intangible and emotional factors affecting their policymaking. Yet, even when references to "public opinion" in such sources (and indeed in more formal governmental sources) are more abundant, they are often abstract and opaque. It is also unclear where these perceptions of public opinion came from, and more difficult still to prove definitively any direct causal link between traces of public opinion and official policy decisions. For a discipline so attached to an empirical methodology, this uncertainty and ambiguity is disconcerting.

Developments in public opinion research, especially efforts to make the process of gauging opinion more scientific and thus "accurate," have only exacerbated this uncertainty. Given the slippery nature of "public opinion" as a concept, the need to grasp it more accurately assumed an added urgency by the turn of the twentieth century once it was recognized as a genuine and important factor in foreign policymaking. This contributed to the creation and rapid growth of the modern polling industry, using carefully calibrated and rigorously researched sampling and polling techniques in an effort to accurately define that most elusive of categories—public opinion. These allegedly "scientific" and "objective" mechanisms have resulted in opinion polls becoming the favored source of information about public opinion, held to be far more reliable than the multitude of other sources that provide only a fragmented and potentially subjective picture at best. For historians working on periods for which no opinion poll data is available (and this is most historians given that poll data is only widely available for the post–Second World War period, and even then confined to countries in the developed world) this is problematic. As one historian has noted: "The historian of opinion who builds on opinion polls may possibly be building on sand, but his foundations are certainly on a different sort of material from those historians of earlier periods."[5] That said, whether poll data is available or not, the historian of public opinion must engage with even more fundamental but no less perplexing questions: How can one define public opinion and, once defined, how can one ascertain what influence it had on diplomatic policymakers?

Defining Public Opinion

Public opinion history is always fraught with challenges. The terminology is contentious, it is methodologically demanding, and conclusions as to its impact are frequently speculative. Although the term itself—"public opinion"—is ubiquitous and widely evoked, it defies easy definition. An instinctive response would be that "public opinion" is simply the opinion of the public, the man or woman on the street, the "ordinary" people, or the manifestation of a "general will." It is not unusual for analyses of public opinion to eschew definitions entirely, simply taking it as a given that public opinion exists and that everyone knows (and largely agrees) as to what the term denotes. Not much interrogation of the term is needed before such easy assumptions begin to unravel. One of the founders of the Mass Observation organization in Britain, Tom Harrisson, demonstrated this in a 1940 article entitled simply "What is Public Opinion?" Noting how the term "has become vague and ambiguous through abuse and misuse," Harrisson insisted that a more accurate understanding of "public opinion" was required, beginning with an acknowledgment that various "levels" of opinion existed. "When we talk about public opinion," he wrote, "we should mean the top level in this great conglomeration of private opinions."[6] Harrisson was acknowledging how, instead of there being a single, unitary, and homogenous public opinion, there existed in reality a great plurality of individually held private opinions, only some of which (the "top level" opinions) contribute subsequently to a composite "public opinion" capable of reaching and influencing policymakers.

This goes some way to providing a satisfactory working definition of "public opinion," similar to that articulated by V. O. Key in the 1960s, whereby public opinion comprises those "opinions held by private persons which governments find it prudent to heed."[7] As Adam Berinsky has observed more recently, Key's definition is "expansive" and allows a distinction to be drawn between the "strongly formed, crystallized opinions of citizens" that elites must respond to and the "lightly held beliefs and transient preferences" that policymakers can usually (though not always) overlook.[8] This is an important distinction, but it is equally important to note, as Harrisson did back in 1940, that other factors influence the emergence of "top level" opinion. "Public opinion," he suggested, "is what you will say out loud to anyone." Hence opinions only assume the character of being "strongly formed" or "crystallized" when individuals are brave enough to articulate them publicly, or simply when a critical mass of individuals succumb to "group think," preferring to conform by echoing dominant opinions that might not necessarily be held in private. A further distinction is also required, as even these publicly articulated opinions must become "published opinion" in order to have any meaningful impact, and this "published" opinion is inevitably mediated by various media channels (Harrisson highlighted the press, the BBC, newsreels, and parliamentary debates). The emergent "public opinion" that permeates the consciousness of policymaking elites can thus be considerably detached from any real or authentic public opinion. As Harrisson put it: "The Press and Parliament version of public opinion is frequently miles away from 'real public opinion,' let alone private opinion."[9]

On the one hand, this is deeply problematic for the historian of public opinion, precluding the possibility of ever determining accurately a genuine "public opinion" at any given time. On the other hand, it can liberate the historian, making the discovery of *genuine* public opinion less important than the discovery of a public opinion that genuinely *mattered*, insofar as it had an impact on political elites. This is not to say that a perceived public opinion will always be an inaccurate reflection of the genuine public sentiment. Yvon Lacaze's definition is useful here, describing public opinion as "a collective phenomenon, a reflection and affirmation of a dominant position within a social group."[10] How public opinion is perceived—based on those opinions that are expressed publicly and in published form—might be quite far removed from genuine popular sentiment, but it might, equally, arise from it and thus mirror it relatively accurately. In reality, it will usually lie somewhere in between, being both reflective of a genuine and organic conglomeration of opinions and one that will necessarily be simplified, distorted, and amplified by processes of mediation. To be sure, identifying how elites perceive and respond to public opinion is difficult. Even when available sources provide clear traces of elite perceptions of public opinion (as they frequently do), the "opinion" that emerges is often diverse, fluctuating, and sometimes contradictory. In this sense, elite perceptions of public opinion mirror the uncertainties and vicissitudes of the concept itself, as exposed plainly within the abundant literature that strives to make sense of it.

Even where the historian succeeds in identifying the dominant representations of public opinion that pervaded the policymaking milieu, establishing whether they had any discernible impact on policy choices is problematic. Conclusive "smoking gun" evidence is rarely found in the archives, meaning that historians struggle to *prove* anything about public opinion's influence. Demonstrable facts (insofar as such things can be said to exist) are replaced by supposition, suggestion, and intimation. Correlation is most certainly not causation, but it is often the most historians have to work with. A movement in perceived public opinion that correlates with an equivalent movement in policy does not *prove* a causal link, but if compelling, it merits attention. Accepting this allows historians to focus on recreating (and explaining) how and why certain dominant expressions of a collective public opinion emerge, and teasing out comparisons with the evolution of foreign policy. To do this, the historian must first pinpoint what Harrisson labeled the "top level" opinions. How is this to be done? What sources should be consulted? What is the archive of public opinion? Ultimately, the "archive" of public opinion history is a constitutive element in the construction of public opinion in the first instance. That is, the historian must use the very same sources that were used at the time, the sources through which a plurality of privately held opinions morphed into something more manageable, a smaller number of collective opinions articulated more vocally and frequently. If public opinion was understood *at the time* to be those opinions communicated in certain petitions, pamphlets, demonstrations, newspapers, radio broadcasts, television programs, or opinion polls, then historians can justly use the same sources as evidence. The public opinion that emerges may not reflect accurately the views and opinions held privately by individual citizens, but it will be very close to the public opinion identified, perceived, and responded to by those in power. It is this public opinion, and arguably this public opinion alone, that assumes the role of historical actor.

For historians of the twentieth century, the process of "recreating" the climate of opinion should be easier than for historians of earlier eras. This is due to both the greater abundance of sources and the greater awareness of public opinion's importance, resulting in ever-more-sophisticated attempts to locate and define it. The twentieth century dawned with an expanding franchise and the emergence of a golden age of journalism (at least in the West) rendering the voting (and thus influential) public more numerous while simultaneously being represented by a popular press that took extremely seriously its role as a "fourth estate." As the century progressed, interest in public opinion grew and a rudimentary polling industry emerged in the United States, spreading to Europe by the late 1930s. At the same time, new media (most notably radio, but also cinema and, soon enough, television) provided new mechanisms for reflecting, assessing, and also shaping the mood of the listening and watching public. Public relations also grew in prominence, prompted by both commercial imperatives and the apparent ability of Europe's dictators to shape and mold a pliable public opinion in their image. The polling industry grew exponentially after the Second World War, while television steadily began to eclipse radio and even the printed press as the dominant medium through which the public garnered information about world events. Although the internet began to challenge television's dominance by the century's close, the Rubicon had not yet been crossed. Still, the World Wide Web was the culmination of twentieth-century processes of globalization that combined to make the world an ever-smaller place and ensuring that more people in more places were aware of global events and thus in a position to venture an opinion about them. Indeed, it is unsurprising that a concept of a "world" or "international" public opinion was evoked throughout the century, as will be shown at various junctures in the chapters that follow.

The changing landscape of public opinion indicators over the twentieth century was, as the following pages will demonstrate, something that policymaking elites took very seriously, even if explicit references to it feature only sporadically in the evidential base. But even if the archives provide little conclusive evidence of how policymakers understood and internalized representations of public opinion, a plurality of sources can help historians recreate the broader social, political, and cultural landscape in which their policy choices were made. An effort to recreate the broader landscape is something that international historians, in particular, have been reluctant to make, at least until relatively recently. Back in 1981, Pierre Milza noted how the insights gleaned from a variety of other disciplines—notably sociology, anthropology, ethnology, and social psychology—were yet to be embraced by international historians despite having been used (very profitably) for many years by medieval historians, as well as historians of the modern era concerned with culture, society, and religion.[11] This is, as noted above, beginning to change. The postmodern and cultural "turns" have certainly led to a reconfiguration of the discipline, and more recent moves toward "emotionalizing" international history will lend these developments further impetus. Nevertheless, more work needs to be done. That international historians are somewhat behind the curve makes it particularly urgent that they do more to understand and appreciate public opinion's rightful place as a key determinant of foreign policy.

Public Opinion in Historical Context

The need for international historians to take public opinion more seriously is accentuated when one considers how the concept has a long history as a recognized political actor. Long before the dawn of the twentieth century, those in positions of power and authority had identified public opinion as a force to be reckoned with. The ancient Greeks were certainly attentive to it and recognized its importance. Thucydides accounted for public opinion in his *History of the Peloponnesian War*, one of the earliest "diplomatic" histories, demonstrating clearly that the ancient Greeks were both aware of and responsive to the apparent demands and wishes of the vox populi. Pericles is a noteworthy example of an Athenian politician who demonstrated an awareness of the importance of public speech and publicity.[12] The ancient Greeks also grappled with debates about public opinion that continue to rage today. Plato's conception of the public was rather paternalistic, suggesting that knowledgeable elites must educate the people, whereas Aristotle was more positive, seeing public opinion as an expression of prevailing attitudes and norms that must necessarily inform governance. As will be shown in subsequent pages, these seemingly conflicting conceptions of public opinion, and the uneasy way in which they would often cohabit, would remain just as prominent well into the twentieth century and beyond.

The Romans too were attentive to the public mood, their technological advances facilitating the more rapid dissemination of information and thus augmenting an awareness of the power of "news" in cultivating and shaping an "enlightened" public opinion. Most Roman scholars gravitated toward Plato's articulation; Cicero, for example, claimed: "Sic est vulgus: ex veritate pauca, ex opinione multa æstimat."[13] Such a paternalistic view of public opinion continued into the medieval period. As John Durham Peters maintains, the feudal lord alone constituted the "public" in medieval Europe, representing "the public symbol of the glory and honor of the social whole."[14] Nonetheless, despite a relative dearth of sources, some scholars have insisted that the conception of a medieval *consensus* was "synonymous with the prevailing body of traditional opinion."[15] Machiavelli also emphasized the importance of the "public voice and fame" when it came to choosing men for public office, evoking public opinion as the composite agglomeration of numerous individual opinions, the control of which is but one function of statecraft. For Machiavelli, public opinion was susceptible to manipulation, but only a reckless prince would believe that it could be ignored with impunity.[16]

By this time, although public opinion was considered worthy of attention, it was still understood largely as an unruly mass in need of control and coercion by an assertive, strong, and paternalistic leader. This was challenged as a notion of a powerful and influential public opinion grew in prominence alongside the intellectual and philosophical trajectories of the Enlightenment. It certainly ushered in a transition whereby public opinion was conceptualized as a progressive force rather than a regressive and unruly mass. This new conception reflected ideas articulated previously by Machiavelli and subsequently by Thomas Hobbes, but drew most heavily on the philosophy of Locke, Montesquieu, and Jean-Jacques Rousseau. John Locke's seventeenth-century theory of governance, stressing the "law of opinion," has been interpreted as the first positive appraisal of public opinion since Aristotle.[17] To be sure, Locke went further than Machiavelli and Hobbes in affording public opinion a more direct and consensual role in the processes of governance, helping to establish the conviction that political legitimacy rested in the consent of the governed.[18]

For Montesquieu, the notion of an *esprit général* was essential, an opinion shared and developed by Rousseau and his famous conceptualization of the *volonté générale*. This "general will" amounts to a collective expression of a community opinion capable of influencing policymakers who must be both aware of it and prepared to act in its interests and on its behalf. There are striking synergies here with what Bauer terms "the prototypes of the *Volksgeist* of the German romantic schools," being "rough approximations of public opinion" as might be understood in an era of proto-nationalism and emergent models of mass citizenship.[19] Rousseau might have foregrounded the "general will" as the basis of legitimate governance, but his reading of public opinion was in many ways still "pre-modern." In his *Nouvelle Héloïse* he contrasted public opinion, which was equated with vain prejudices, with the more balanced and stable "morality."[20] This was a notion shared by Jacques Necker, Louis XVI's finance minister, who was among the first to popularize the term "public opinion." Necker equated public opinion with emotion and sentiment rather than intelligence and rationality. Nevertheless, he recognized the need to appease a French public growing increasingly agitated by economic mismanagement. It has been suggested that Necker's "great contribution to the study of public opinion was not so much what he wrote about its power but rather his important innovation of publishing fiscal statements (*compte rendu*) so that the merits and faults of government policy in this field could be appraised in public." Necker was unwilling to yield power to the people, but he was demonstrably more attentive to its wishes.[21] Simply acknowledging that a public opinion *existed* and that it might need to be *appeased* was a tangible demonstration of the impact of Enlightenment thought. It is difficult to dispute that such conceptions of public opinion contributed to the ideological currents that would underpin both the American and French revolutions.

But even prior to these revolutions it was clear that the impact of the printing press, in conjunction with ever-growing literacy rates and the emergence of a coffeehouse culture in Europe and North America, was profound. In pre-revolutionary France there was no equivalent to the British Parliament that could claim to speak on behalf of the public, hence the idea of a "general will" being propagated by the *philosophes* was based less on a tangible manifestation of opinion and more on an abstract composite of rumor, hearsay, and speculative gossip permeating the urban coffeehouses and salons. European coffeehouses dated back to the mid-seventeenth century, soon becoming important centers of news gathering and dissemination, as well as hubs for broader social and political debate. When a young Louis XVI noted that "I must always consult public opinion; it is never wrong," he was acknowledging implicitly what Jürgen Habermas has famously termed the "public sphere," which was rooted in this new cultural environment.[22] Not only had public opinion assumed an unprecedented power and influence by the nineteenth century but it had also become firmly embedded in the philosophical and intellectual climate of the era. For Jeremy Bentham, opinion served a critical function in establishing accepted societal norms that conditioned public and political behaviors. Echoing Bentham, John Stuart Mill contended that legislative laws were only needed when the "laws of opinion" (drawing from Locke) proved inadequate.[23]

Public opinion's emergence as a prominent factor in European politics owed a great deal to the recent and rapid growth in literacy. "A closed and restricted public," noted Hans Speier, "gradually developed into an open one, enlarging both its size and its social scope as illiteracy receded."[24] A more recent study notes simply that the concept of "the public" grew out of Enlightenment ideas "and the many important social transformations that took place in the late nineteenth and early twentieth centuries in Europe."[25] As Susan Herbst insists, these ideas would continue to inform political thinkers throughout the nineteenth century and beyond. "The independent voice of the public," she reasons, "had emerged never to be entirely silenced again, no matter the authoritarian intentions of a leader."[26] The latter point is crucial, indicating that even dictators must be alert to the wishes of the public; indeed, the very legitimacy and authority of a dictatorial regime is contingent on popular support, or at the very least a convincing façade of such support. Of course, astute dictators could ensure that the type of pluralistic "public sphere" imagined by Habermas does not exist, but this does not preclude the existence of public opinion. The importance of opinion is recognized implicitly by dictatorships through their efforts to control it; Mussolini, for example, organized mass rallies in 1935 intended to showcase popular support for Italy's invasion of Abyssinia, in so doing creating an "official" public opinion that did not necessarily correlate with the more genuine expressions of opinion noted by police and Fascist Party reports.[27] Ultimately, Mussolini was unable to mold Italian public opinion even by summer 1940; as Italy entered the war on the side of Nazi Germany, public sympathies appeared to lie squarely with the Western democracies.[28] A similar pattern was evident in Nazi Germany where even the power and sophistication of Joseph Goebbels's propaganda machine could not prevent the façade of consensus that had supported Nazi foreign policy from breaking down in the aftermath of the Wehrmacht's defeat at Stalingrad.[29]

In a sense, the genie was out of the bottle. Even prior to the twentieth century, political, intellectual, technological, and cultural shifts had combined to reveal to the public the power and influence that they wielded. In addition, the public's ability to project its opinions, both individually and collectively, grew exponentially. The media is critical here, and the centrality of the media within any discussion of public opinion's impact on diplomacy will become apparent in the subsequent pages. If "news" had been important from the days of ancient Greece, through the Roman Empire and into the medieval era and beyond, it assumed an unprecedented significance toward the end of the early modern period. Developments in the printing press during the sixteenth century were pivotal in fomenting a "news" industry. The early 1700s, for example, saw the emergence of influential "moral weeklies" like *Tatler* (1709) and the *Spectator* (1711) that came to represent and shape the views and opinions of an expanding middle-class readership.[30] This readership mushroomed over the next three centuries, and newspapers and magazines inevitably proliferated in an effort to meet a growing demand. Newspaper readership in Europe grew from 2.5 million in 1713 to over 16 million by 1801, and the reading public's appetite for news increased as a result. News of diplomatic adventurism—and wars in particular—was devoured. As James Van Horn Melton has remarked, "more than any other kind of event, war aroused public opinion and stimulated the growth of political journalism."[31] As the public relied almost exclusively on the press for information about far-flung ventures, so the power and authority wielded by these publications grew. One London pamphlet from 1761 claimed that "the political principles of most Englishmen are entirely under the influence of pamphlets and newspapers."[32]

As the modern age commenced, an awareness of "public opinion" as a significant and impactful concept was firmly established. The term had become, as Van Horn Melton notes, "common currency in political discourse," and it was becoming clear that British parliamentarians saw themselves as "beholden to it."[33] A driver of this conviction was what Jeremy Black has termed a "wider social, cultural and intellectual shift," resulting in "information" trumping "received wisdom" in importance, and an expansion of the "political nation" to include a burgeoning reading public whose influence on policymakers was both tangible and growing.[34] By the close of the nineteenth century, it seemed that public opinion had become not only a fixture in the political and popular lexicon but also an important political actor in its own right. Its role extended into matters of foreign policy and diplomacy. "Once the importance of public opinion was discovered as a new factor in international relations," wrote Hans Speier in 1950, "it became tempting on moral as well as on expediential grounds to utilize it."[35] In the early nineteenth century, the British statesman George Canning considered public opinion "a power more tremendous than was perhaps ever brought into action in the history of mankind." Klemens von Metternich, by contrast, believed any public oversight of diplomacy to be dangerous, and thus described Canning as "a malevolent meteor hurled by divine providence upon Europe." Despite Metternich's protestations, it would be the more positive conception of public opinion that gained traction as the nineteenth century progressed. Viscount Palmerston, for example, deemed public opinion "stronger than armies" and capable of prevailing over "the bayonets of infantry, the fire of artillery and the charges of cavalry."[36]

By the nineteenth century, the power ascribed to public opinion was clearly apparent, even if, on occasion, it was exaggerated intentionally to justify policy choices. "Public sentiment is everything," proclaimed Abraham Lincoln in 1858: "With public sentiment, nothing can fail; without it, nothing can succeed."[37] In 1860 he suggested that public opinion "settles every question" in the United States, and that any legitimate, sustainable policy must "have public opinion at the bottom."[38] In 1861, Britain's prime minister Palmerston told a Russian envoy that "there are two great powers in this country, the government and public opinion; and that both must concur for any great and important steps" to be undertaken.[39] Public opinion's growing purchase on all aspects of political life was not without its discontents. Indeed, the more disparaging conceptions of public opinion as fickle, unstable, and emotional were never far from the surface. By the late nineteenth century, many public intellectuals began to conflate public opinion with a rowdy and disorderly mass, a notable example being Gustave Le Bon's *The Crowd* (1895). For Le Bon, the "crowd" provides individual members of a society with an anonymity that allows and encourages them to act with more reckless abandon than they might normally do, while also providing an environment in which ideas could spread like a contagion. In this sense, the crowd is akin to a body of people united by shared emotional experiences.[40]

As John Carey suggests, Le Bon's notion of the crowd is overwhelmingly pejorative and pejoratively gendered: "They [crowds] are extremely suggestible, impulsive, irrational, exaggeratedly emotional, inconstant, irritable, and capable of thinking only in images—in short, just like women."[41] As the power of the "people" grew, so there emerged, among some sections of the European intelligentsia, a backlash. Friedrich Nietzsche insisted that "the great majority of men have no right to existence, but are a misfortune to higher men."[42] The derision with which many looked upon the "masses" helps explain why so many public intellectuals in the late nineteenth and early twentieth centuries were intoxicated by eugenics.[43]

But even more moderate political thinkers were worried by the fickle nature of a public that might be co-opted for pernicious ends. De Tocqueville expressed concern lest public opinion, given its growing influence on American politics, might morph into some form of domestic tyranny. John Stuart Mill expressed similar apprehensions, evoking a public opinion comprising of "the masses," susceptible to tyranny and the rule of an "overwhelming majority."[44] This negative reading of public opinion's influence was influential but not unanimous. It ran concurrently with the more positive portrayals of public opinion that characterized the Progressive Era in the United States. The veteran British statesman, James Bryce certainly held that public opinion wielded a greater influence in the United States (a country he knew well) than it did in Europe. "The United States," he wrote, "more than any other country, are governed by public opinion, that is to say, by the general sentiment of the mass of the nation, which all the organs of the national government and of the State governments look to and obey."[45]

By the dawn of the twentieth century, these two divergent interpretations of public opinion existed simultaneously. The year 1899 provides a clear example of this, being the year of both the first Hague Peace Conference and the outbreak of the Second Boer War in southern Africa. The former appeared to demonstrate how public opinion could advance progressive causes, in this case disarmament and the codification of the laws of war. The British peace activist William Evans Darby lauded the Hague conference for "furnishing a new illustration of the power of public opinion," while his French colleague Frédéric Passy felt sure that governments would eventually succumb to "the pressure of public opinion."[46] However, the Boer War erupted just weeks after the Hague conference ended, and this projection of British power and militarism was welcomed initially with a wave of patriotic fervor on the part of the public. As James Thompson notes: "Historians dating the strange death of the liberal public have recurred repeatedly to the impact of popular enthusiasm for the Boer War."[47] A similar pattern would be repeated in 1914, the wave of popular enthusiasm for war (in all countries) demonstrating that a pacific public opinion would not instinctively act to restrain bellicose politicians and diplomatists. Nonetheless, not all hope was lost. Public opinion might be malleable, and it might even, in 1914, have been too easily whipped into a warlike frenzy by the press and politicians, but this could be interpreted as evidence that it could be manipulated for more altruistic and selfless purposes in the future. The popularity of Woodrow Wilson's "Fourteen Points" showed the possibilities, as hopes were aroused that an educated and informed public would play a vital constitutive role in underpinning the new world order that must, necessarily, emerge from the ashes of the war.[48]

The Public Opinion/Foreign Policy Nexus

The failure of the League of Nations, the subsequent horrors of the Second World War, and the postwar failure to adhere completely to the lofty war aims of the Allies all combined to undermine the early twentieth-century conviction that public opinion would operate consistently as an altruistic force in international affairs.[49] Although it was starting to be recognized as a pivotal factor in foreign policymaking, there were significant concerns that its effects might be deleterious. As Chapter 1 will explore, the hopes and aspirations that the horrors of the Great War would usher in an era of "new" and "open" diplomacy with public opinion at its heart soon dissipated. The Paris Peace Conference, rather than marking the first genuinely open international forum, reverted, instead, to the old diplomatic methods of secrecy and realpolitik. More troubling, perhaps, was the realization that public opinion had contributed to this disappointing outcome. Rather than exercising a moral pressure on warlike statesmen to embrace new diplomatic norms, public opinion had, at least in part, encouraged them down the road of national self-interest. Hence the idea resurfaced that the public was incapable of contributing positively to diplomacy. This was a viewpoint articulated influentially by Walter Lippmann in 1927: "We must assume that a public is inexpert in its curiosity," he wrote, "intermittent . . ., slow to be aroused and quickly diverted." That public opinion was a fickle and unreliable observer of foreign affairs was taken as a given, interested in foreign policy issues "only when events have been melodramatized as a conflict."[50] Lippmann stressed that relying on public opinion as a governing force in diplomacy was foolhardy. "When public opinion attempts to govern directly," he averred, "it is either a failure or a tyranny."[51]

Lippmann's disparaging model of public opinion gained further traction after the Second World War, unsurprisingly, given the recent examples of dictatorships directing and manipulating their own publics to support the most insidious objectives. As Jean-Jacques Becker has noted, the use of propaganda had taken hold during the 1914–18 war, and would be used even more energetically and perniciously thereafter, marking a transition from an era in which public opinion triumphed to one where the "manipulation of public opinion" prevailed.[52] Dictators were not alone in seeking to exploit public opinion's vulnerability to manipulation. Early public relations gurus like Edward Bernays were convinced that opinion could be "moved, directed and formed," although not necessarily for injurious purposes.[53] Indeed, Bernays was inspired by Ferdinand Tönnies's contention that the task for the "higher strata of society—the cultivated, the learned, the expert, the intellectual [is to] inject moral and spiritual motives into public opinion. Public opinion must become public conscience."[54] The need to educate an ill-informed public also featured in Gabriel Almond's important contributions in the 1950s. He asserted in 1956 that the "mass public, fed by the mass media, is generally uninformed about national security policy issues," and tends to respond to elite-driven cues "with moods." The consequences are potentially catastrophic: "Often public opinion is apathetic when it should be concerned, and panicky when it should be calm." Although Almond remained optimistic that a more attentive and knowledgeable public was "increasing in size," more needed to be done to cultivate it.[55]

Within the academy, an "Almond–Lippmann consensus" thus took hold, maintaining that public opinion had a chiefly deleterious impact on foreign policymaking. The message for those who devised diplomatic policy was that they should either ignore public opinion or take the necessary steps to engineer a public opinion in support of their policies. Throughout the twentieth century the idea persisted that public opinion could be weaponized in pursuit of diplomatic strategies, an idea that really took hold in the context of the Cold War (the growing prominence of public diplomacy during this period attests to this). A 1949 book published on behalf of the American Council on Foreign Relations entitled *Public Opinion and Foreign Policy* took this issue very seriously. Lester Markel noted in the book's introduction that "no American program, no plan for world order, can succeed unless it has the full support of public opinion, both at home and abroad." This meant not only that policymakers should be attuned to the wishes of the public but also that the public themselves, being too often ignorant and prejudiced about aspects of foreign affairs, must be better educated and directed.[56] The extent of Nazi control of German public opinion was still fresh in the memory, and a conviction was also germinating in the early Cold War that Stalinist Russia was more adept than the Western democracies in using public opinion as "a powerful instrument of national policy."[57] For Markel, the United States needed to be more proactive in utilizing "propaganda" (or "information" for want of a less problematic or loaded label) to advance their policy objectives. To do so, he ascribed considerable importance to the "three great moulders of public opinion—the *government*, the *press* and *citizen groups*."[58]

Markel's prescription was clearly rooted in the notion that public opinion, at least as regards foreign affairs, was as the Almond–Lippmann consensus maintained: an open book, generally ignorant, often indifferent, but invariably susceptible to gusts of emotion that made it an unsuitable driver of diplomatic strategy and policy. As Douglas Foyle reminds us, this consensus propagated the view that "a largely ignorant public opinion on foreign policy reacted in an emotional rather than reasonable or rational manner, which in turn led to higher attitude volatility."[59] This view of public opinion remained prominent into the 1970s, when, in an influential contribution, Bernard C. Cohen contended that policymaking elites (at least in the United States) were largely oblivious to public opinion; indeed, he cited one US State Department Official's appraisal: "To hell with public opinion . . . . We should lead and not follow."[60] Many Cold War practitioners of diplomacy were equally dismissive of the public. George Kennan compared it to "one of those pre-historic monsters with a body as long as this room and a brain the size of a pin."[61] Hans Morgenthau was adamant that the diplomatic realm should be immune to the pressures and whims of the public, insisting that "the rational requirements of a good foreign policy cannot from the outset count on the support of a public opinion whose preferences are emotional rather than rational."[62] Kennan and Morgenthau represented, as a recent study insists, the "cynical view" common to foreign policy realists "eager to insulate the intricacies of foreign policymaking from what they saw as an unsophisticated and emotional public."[63] But, like many of the dogmas of the early Cold War, the Almond–Lippmann consensus would be shaken substantially by the repercussions of the war in Vietnam.

The Vietnam War, and its immediate aftermath, prompted a reappraisal of the public opinion/foreign policy nexus. Scholars began to contend that the American public's response to that conflict was entirely prudent, opposition to the war growing in tandem with its escalating financial and human costs. Ergo, rather than being characterized as an emotional entity subject to irrational "moods," the public was reconceptualized as stable and rational, responding to events in a reasonable and judicious way. Stemming from this, a new consensus emerged by the end of the twentieth century that the public was, for the most part, a pretty prudent observer of foreign affairs.[64] As Ole Holsti commented, this invalidated "the earlier consensus about public impotence."[65] This is not to say, however, that the public was now considered sufficiently educated about issues of foreign affairs to take ownership of them. Rather, as Kertzer and Zeitzoff contend, it was now held that while the public might often "lack knowledge" about complex foreign policy issues, it does not "lack principles." These principles can be defined as liking victory and success, disliking inconsistency, favoring multilateralism, and preferring clearly defined foreign policy aims rooted in core values.[66] Similarly, while the public *does* obtain most of its knowledge and information of foreign affairs from "élite-based cues" (whether governmental or the media), these cues "only tell part of the story." For Kertzer and Zeitzoff, the public is "more resistant to elite manipulation" than the previous consensus would suggest, and even if there remains a risk of public consent being "manufactured," this is just as likely to emanate from fellow citizens as it is from a pliant media parroting elite opinions, especially in an atomized era of social media.[67]

Although the rather contemptuous model of public opinion conveyed by the Almond-Lippmann consensus no longer holds water, it seems that the projection of an entirely "prudent" and "rational" public must also be questioned. At the very least, the public continues to exhibit volatility when articulating opinions about foreign policy issues. Simply put, some aspects of foreign affairs rouse public interest where others do not. On the one hand, this suggests that the public possesses agency. As John Mueller asserts, "The public not only substantially sets its own agenda, particularly in the case of war, but it can be quite selective, and often rather unpredictably so."[68] If, as Mueller claims, the public "sets its own agenda," and is not dictated to by the media, what role does the press actually play? Mueller's answer is that the press places items "on the shelf" from which the public selects those that it considers the most salient. The Ethiopian famine of the mid-1980s, for example, only really piqued public interest in the United States after NBC gave it a platform in October 1984.[69] The NBC coverage was, itself, prompted by Michael Buerk's famous report from Ethiopia that was aired in the UK by the BBC, and ultimately shown by 425 separate broadcasting organizations to a global audience of 470 million people.[70] Crucially, Buerk's broadcast was *not* the first occasion that the Ethiopian famine had permeated the Western news. The media had already put the topic on the shelf, but it was only by late October that, as Mueller puts it, the public "put it on the agenda and demanded the magnification."[71]

In the modern world of atomized media content, where the days of dominant news channels reaching vast audiences appear to be in the past, how certain issues will be placed "on the shelf" is unclear. It is evident nonetheless that some stories, and certainly some images, *can* still permeate a global public consciousness; the distressing picture of the drowned Syrian toddler, Alan Kurdi, which spread globally in late 2015, certainly resulted in a (tragically ephemeral) evoking of compassion in the West for the plight of the migrants.[72] More recently, the photograph of the bodies of Óscar Alberto Martínez Ramírez and his 23-month-old daughter, Valeria, who had drowned in the Rio Grande, went viral, prompting much soul-searching about the plight of migrants and the way in which the United States should respond.[73] It is beyond the scope of this book to venture into the increasingly complex media environment of the twenty-first century and its impact on the relationship between policymakers and the public. Suffice to say, as Susan Herbst remarked in 2011, that the already "uncontrolled flow of ideas and signs" of the twentieth century made it very difficult to identify an organic, genuine "public opinion," and this challenge is only exacerbated in the contemporary context of increasingly varied and polarized expressions of opinion.[74] The following chapters, therefore, are simply a preliminary effort to navigate the intersection of public opinion and diplomacy as it developed through the twentieth century.

Aims and Objectives

This book provides an introduction to this intersection by considering five distinct case studies. Chapter 1 looks at the impact of public opinion in 1919, and British public opinion in particular, on policies pursued at the Paris Peace Conference. Chapter 2 shifts attention across the channel by analyzing how French public opinion affected that country's diplomatic response to the Nazi menace, from Hitler's coming to power in 1933 to the outbreak of war in September 1939. Chapter 3 traces the impact of American public opinion on the prosecution of war in Vietnam, while Chapter 4 examines the role of public opinion within the global anti-apartheid campaign, and how much this contributed to the end of white-minority rule in South Africa. The final chapter considers the topic of European integration in the final few decades of the twentieth century, assessing how far European public opinion was a driver of or an impediment to this process. The broadly chronological approach will facilitate a systematic appraisal of how public opinion's role in the foreign-policymaking process shifted over the century. It will account for different conceptions of public opinion, the different mechanisms by which public opinion found expression, and the extent to which a variety of different policymaking elites responded to it. The chosen case studies also provide a degree of geographical breadth although, because of the limitations of sources and existing literature, they are necessarily Western-centric. This focus, though regrettable, is necessitated by the fact that most public opinion scholarship emanates from these countries.

Chapter 1, though ostensibly about British public opinion in 1919, is actually more far-reaching. As will be demonstrated, 1919 represented the culmination of ideas and conceptions of public opinion that had been fermenting for many years, certainly since the late nineteenth century, and not least the growing conviction that public opinion—on an international scale—was becoming an increasingly important diplomatic actor that would almost certainly work in pursuit of progressive and peaceful causes. The chapter highlights how public opinion's ability to influence policymakers had assumed unprecedented levels in an era of rapidly expanding literacy and a concomitant rise in a popular press that nourished an increasingly news-hungry public. It reflects too on the growing public demand for diplomatic openness and transparency (in so doing, speaking to more well-known debates about the transition from "old" to "new" diplomacy), the dilemmas and tensions that this posed in the frenetic and tense context of the Paris Peace Conference, and the ways in which policymakers responded to these new realities.

By focusing on French public opinion during the 1930s, Chapter 2 charts further how advances in technology affected the public opinion/foreign policy nexus. Newspapers remained important, but the interwar years saw the rapid emergence of cinema newsreels and radio as prominent sources of public information about foreign affairs. In addition, the later 1930s saw the first use of opinion polls on European shores, including early polls conducted in France. The chapter also attends to the growing use of propaganda, and with it the often unfavorable comparisons that were made between the allegedly "decadent" democracies and the more dynamic dictatorships, the latter proving (arguably) more adept at controlling and harnessing popular opinion in support of their agendas. And there is a historiographical imperative for this case study, as public opinion features prominently in the influential "decadence" interpretation of France's 1940 defeat, demonstrating how the concept of public opinion can be used and abused in the construction of dominant historical narratives.

Public opinion has been used in just such a way to fashion a narrative that helps explain America's defeat in Vietnam, as will be unpicked in Chapter 3. The suggestion that public opinion, by turning against the war, contributed to the political decision to pull out of Vietnam before American objectives were secured is as seductive as it is contentious, and therefore deserving of closer interrogation. The evolution of technology will again feature prominently, looking in depth at the far more widespread use of opinion polls as well as considering the role of television (noting how Vietnam has been termed the first "television war"). The role of the media is central to this chapter, addressing arguments that an irresponsible media, through its reckless and inaccurate reportage of events in Indochina itself, not to mention the succor and legitimacy that it lent to the domestic anti-war movement in the United States, was chiefly responsible for ensuring that an otherwise winnable war was lost. The vexing question of whether the media *leads* or *reflects* public opinion is thus particularly prominent.

Chapter 4 considers the role of public opinion as a more genuinely international actor, assessing how far it was able to erode the legitimacy of the white-minority government in apartheid-era South Africa. It explores the ability of transnational citizen activists to coordinate and execute methods of protest beyond the normal channels of diplomatic interaction, bypassing governments and international organizations to showcase the growing power and purchase of an international public. The use of sanctions, divestment, and sporting and cultural boycotts kept the issue of apartheid in the public spotlight, even when many Western governments were eager, for reasons of Cold War expediency, to avoid upsetting the Pretoria regime. Technology played a part here too, especially in the 1980s when the anti-apartheid movement was at its height. Satellite television helped to cultivate the sense of anti-apartheid activism constituting a genuinely "global" movement, to the extent that it became a veritable "brand" that chimed with the sensibilities of an increasingly consumerist public.

The final chapter considers the role of public opinion as the postwar process of European integration evolved, bringing the analysis to the very end of the twentieth century and beyond (the centrality of public opinion in the current Brexit debates is impossible to ignore). This chapter charts how public attitudes toward the European project evolved from a "permissive consensus" to a more skeptical and questioning position as the processes of integration transcended the original economic objectives and morphed into something that assumed a distinctly political and cultural dimension that, in turn, began to impinge on national sovereignty. Ergo, the chapter explores the particular challenges for politicians and diplomats who are pursuing the creation of a supranational organization, given that public opinion (and the media in which it finds expression) remains stubbornly national. The difficulties in cultivating a European "public sphere," or simply creating a European media framework in which a "European" identity might take hold, are instructive given the current crisis of legitimacy that the European Union is experiencing.

The overriding aim of this book is not to provide a definitive assessment of public opinion's influence on diplomacy throughout the century. It is also not intended to have the final word on any of the specific case studies under scrutiny. Instead, it seeks to show how public opinion is both an acknowledged but also an underscrutinized actor in foreign affairs. There *is* an abundant scholarship on the foreign policy/public opinion nexus, but this emanates almost exclusively from the disciplines of political science, international relations, and media and communications studies. The history of this nexus has been afforded too little attention by professional historians. It is hoped, therefore, that this book will encourage scholars and students alike to pay more attention to public opinion in its historical context. Nobody would deny that public opinion *exists*, or that the label "public opinion" refers to something real and tangible. In addition, few would contend that it has *no* influence on the course of diplomacy (although the extent of this influence can be debated). Assessing it may be difficult, and extrapolating definitive conclusions more difficult still, but these difficulties must not stop us from trying.

British Public Opinion and the 1919 Paris Peace Conference

Assessing the influence of British public opinion on that country's diplomacy at the 1919 Paris Peace Conference is no easy task. As a point of departure, a focus on one individual is beneficial. This individual is not David Lloyd George nor any of the other politicians or diplomats who represented Great Britain in Paris (although these individuals will feature prominently throughout the chapter). Instead, it is prudent to foreground the veteran liberal MP and statesman, James Bryce. Bryce is relevant here for three reasons. First, he was interested, academically and politically, in the concept of public opinion, and had written on the topic substantially. Second, Bryce was a pivotal figure in British wartime thinking about the shape that a postwar order should take and the role that public opinion would play within it. Finally, his closeness to (and knowledge of) the United States is helpful in better understanding the hold that the League of Nations "idea" had on the British public, especially given the project's largely Anglo-Saxon roots. Moreover, Bryce's particular interest in public opinion took shape in his voluminous analysis of the "American Commonwealth" first published in 1888, and discussed in the introduction to this book. For Bryce, America was *the* country in which the power and purchase of public opinion was most evident.[1]

Bryce viewed public opinion as positive, considering it "on the whole wholesome and upright."[2] He was, nonetheless, cognizant that opinion was vulnerable to manipulation for political or commercial ends. Public opinion, he averred, "is also made."[3] While acknowledging this risk, Bryce remained confident that an authentic opinion would always prevail over a manufactured one. Although journalists could, to an extent, "lead" public opinion, they are compelled to reject positions that fail to resonate with the reading public; they are, after all, answerable to proprietors who want their content to chime with the prevailing winds of popular opinion for the purposes of circulation and revenue. In this sense, Bryce was typical of a generation of men who viewed the growing sovereignty of public opinion without fear or trepidation. Instead, he celebrated public opinion's emergence as one of the foundations of American greatness.[4] Was this, though, an instance of American exceptionalism? Could British public opinion be similarly trusted to act in benign and beneficent ways? Based on some of Bryce's comments during the 1914–18 war, the answer to the latter question would seem to be "no." He was certainly concerned that the press could whip the public into an anti-German frenzy that would preclude the creation of a just and sustainable peace when the current war ended. In January 1917 he declared himself "surprised and alarmed at the power which the press has shown." "If public opinion means the press," he continued, "parlous indeed is our condition."[5]

Bryce's views are important because he was the key figure around which the so-called "Bryce Group" coalesced, a collection of politicians and intellectuals whose ideas did much to create the foundations of the postwar League of Nations. Given his connections with the United States (his last diplomatic post prior to retirement was as ambassador in Washington from 1907 to 1913), it was natural that pro-League initiatives emanating from the two countries would dovetail. When, in 1916, President Woodrow Wilson publicly espoused support for the League to Enforce Peace (LEP), Bryce was delighted. Hitherto, suggested Bryce, pro-League advocates like himself had been reluctant to put their schemes before the British public, fearful of being labeled defeatists who sought a premature peace before Prussian militarism had been eclipsed. Wilson's adhesion to the project, he suggested, prepared the ground well, focusing the public's attention on a postwar settlement.[6] Bryce might have been concerned that the press would have a deleterious impact on British public opinion, but recognized that the greater impetus for pro-League publicity could be exploited to shape opinion more favorably. It was in this context that the Bryce Group's proposals were made public in April 1917, just after America's intervention in the war. Although economic and military sanctions were included in the scheme, there was no formal mechanism for their application, hence the enforcement of League judgments would rely chiefly on enforcing a delay, in the hope that this would allow wiser counsels to prevail rather than rushing headlong into conflict. As Sakiko Kaiga has noted, the group's proposals thus relied, at least in part, on "idealistic devices such as the moral force of world public opinion."[7] As Bryce himself put it in the 1915 draft: "The public opinion of the world would surely prove to possess a greater force than it has yet [shown] if it could but find an effective organ through which to act."[8] Wilson expressed consistently the same sentiment. His address to the plenary session of the Paris Peace Conference in February 1919 stated emphatically that his proposed League relied "chiefly upon one great force, and that is the moral force of the public opinion of the world."[9]

Public opinion was, from the start, central to the League of Nations project. But before a League could even be established, the victorious Allied powers had to settle the terms of peace with their vanquished adversaries, notably Germany. A League of Nations capable of fulfilling the aspirations of those who had long worked toward such an end (including the Bryce Group) was contingent upon the delivery of a stable and equitable peace. The shape of this peace was contingent on the public opinion within the victorious powers that would dominate the diplomatic maneuverings in Paris. And the public *would* be watching; the conference itself was subjected to an unprecedented level of public and journalistic scrutiny. "There were swarms of newspaper correspondents from every part of the world clamouring for copy," recalled Lloyd George: "All the eyes of the world were concentrated on this great assembly of the nations."[10] The received wisdom about public attitudes within the "Big Three" is well known. French opinion demanded the imposition of harsh terms on Germany. American opinion was more sympathetic toward the vanquished powers, but keen to retreat into an isolationist shell, unwilling to commit to Europe's future and thus undermining the League project from its inception. Within this dominant, if rather crude and simplistic narrative, British opinion is held to hold the middle ground, not as vindictive as the French but not as lenient as the Americans; less concerned with constructing a watertight European security system than France, but more committed (if only due to geographical necessity) to Europe than the United States. As this chapter will reveal, Britain's position during the Paris deliberations was not always consistent. Focusing on the role of British public opinion is instructive, demonstrating how the inconsistencies of Britain's diplomacy during this frenetic period did, at least in part, mirror the vicissitudes of public sentiment at home.

Anticipating the Paris Peace Conference: The Role of Public Opinion

When the First World War ended and attention turned to the construction of a postwar order, it was widely held that public opinion would play a far greater performative role in international affairs than it had hitherto. The folly of the 1914–18 war, like the folly of the alliance system and arms races that preceded it, had seemingly resulted from the methods of "old" diplomacy, secret treaties, and maneuverings undertaken by politicians and diplomats who were led by sensationalist newspaper proprietors and ruthlessly capitalistic arms manufacturers rather than the public. The postwar era was an auspicious moment for ushering in a "new" and "open" diplomacy, foregrounding public opinion. In Britain, groups like the Union of Democratic Control (UDC) argued explicitly for greater democratic oversight and accountability, a stance echoed by other pressure groups such as the Women's International League for Peace and Freedom (WILPF). These ideas permeated the highest political echelons; numerous schemes devised during the war years concerned with erecting a new world order were equally upbeat about the future influence and power of public opinion in shaping a sustainable peace.

Woodrow Wilson was the most prominent exponent of a "new" diplomacy in the immediate postwar period, making him a hugely popular figure in the war-ravaged Europe that had suffered most from the "old" diplomatic norms of the past.[11] Wilson came to personify the hopes and aspirations that many European citizens harbored in late 1918 and early 1919, convinced that the horrors of the recent conflict must mean that the "war to end all wars" had been precisely that. A new world order, with Wilson's Fourteen Points at its center, seemed the most practical way of ensuring that a "new" diplomacy would prevail. This optimism was very much a product of its time. Wilson himself was a man of the Progressive Era, and largely shared the conviction that public opinion was a progressive force. The more public opinion was empowered, the more beneficent would be its influence, especially if directed thoughtfully and prudently by well-meaning political leaders. As J. Michael Hogan reminds us, Wilson's conception of public opinion was a fusion of progressive optimism and the "more cynical view of public debate and mass persuasion" that would dominate the public relations and advertising industries that flourished into the 1920s.[12] The cynical dimension of Wilson's take on public opinion should not be overstated. Like many of his contemporaries, Wilson was convinced that public opinion was a force for good; he simply recognized that it needed to be well informed and properly directed. Indeed, in outlining the fundamental contours of a postwar League in a speech on July 4, 1918, he asserted that "what we seek is the reign of law, based upon the consent of the governed and sustained by the organized opinion of mankind."[13]

Wilson's conception of public opinion thus reflected broader trends that had been evident for several decades. In the late nineteenth and certainly into the early twentieth century, many individuals and organizations began to recognize the power of public opinion and its potential influence on diplomacy. Its moral influence was accentuated repeatedly, as demonstrated within the multifaceted international peace movement. The late nineteenth century witnessed the birth of the International Peace Bureau, itself emanating from a series of international peace congresses intended to facilitate the transnational discussion and dissemination of anti-war and anti-militarist ideas. At the same time the Inter-Parliamentary Union was formed, an attempt by like-minded parliamentarians, cutting across national borders, to ensure greater parliamentary (and, ergo, greater public) control over foreign policy and diplomacy. The two Hague Peace Conferences in 1899 and 1907 demonstrated that this citizen activism was genuinely influencing policymakers, and although their outcomes were disappointing, hopes grew that a more enlightened and educated public opinion would soon exercise a restraining hand on belligerent and warlike politicians. Education was pivotal, especially within the newer, American-based organizations that emerged in the early twentieth century, notably the Carnegie Endowment for International Peace and the World Peace Foundation. They shared with Wilson a conviction that public opinion *could* be a progressive force, but it needed guidance.

The outbreak of war in 1914 was clearly a blow to those aligned to the peace movement, and the prevalence of so much jingoistic and patriotic sentiment when war came dented people's faith in public opinion's tendency to choose peace over war. But the arguments that some within the peace movement made in the early stages of the First World War —that the war itself would be the best advert for their cause—were not without merit. As the conflict dragged on and as the human (and financial) cost became ever-more-difficult to bear, public opinion began to shift. By the close of the war, it was clear that the people—particularly but not exclusively in combatant countries—were tired of conflict, distrustful of those that had allowed it to happen, and determined to avoid a repetition. There was also a sense that the people had been hoodwinked, compelled to support a war that nobody really understood, and that, had they been better informed and aware of the facts, they would have acted to prevent. It is thus unsurprising that many of the schemes and suggestions formulated during the war itself with a view to planning for a lasting postwar peace positioned public opinion as a focal point. In short, an idea that had been fermenting for several years matured between 1914 and 1918. An educated, informed, and empowered public opinion would henceforth act as a necessary restraint on bellicosity, rendering wars between nations if not obsolete then certainly less likely. This conception of an empowered popular opinion dovetailed with other, broader idealist impulses, many of which—open diplomacy, democratization of foreign policy, and so on—would soon become indelibly associated with Woodrow Wilson.

The growing purchase of public opinion in the aftermath of the Great War era was the subject of an influential study by Arno Mayer in the 1950s. This period, suggested Mayer, saw new "forces of movement" reconfiguring diplomacy.[14] Ideologically, Wilsonianism and Leninism came to the fore, both sharing a belief in "the infallibility of public opinion," assuming that the "people" were "equipped with sufficient reason and rationality to enable them to judge and support an enlightened foreign policy."[15] Mayer's thesis is only partially convincing. After all, even among those groups and individuals advocating the democratization of foreign policy, it was rarely assumed that the public was *already* adequately informed and educated. Instead, influential and well-informed individuals must educate and enlighten the public. In short, the public first needed to be *led*, only then could it *lead*. Others have criticized Mayer for a lack of ideological balance. Marc Trachtenberg contends that Mayer too easily and unquestioningly condemns the right as "selfish, vindictive, [and] intransigent" while the left is lauded for its promotion of "healthy" Wilsonianism.[16]

Trachtenbergs's criticism is not without merit, as the "healthy" Wilsonianism was always more popular in intellectual circles than it was with the wider public. As E. H. Carr wrote in 1936, the intellectual has a crucial role to play "as the leader of public opinion," but once the ideas they espouse become divorced from "the political thinking of the man in the street" they lose their practicability and are relegated to the utopian "world of prophecy."[17] As the war came to an end, and in its immediate aftermath, the twin currents of popular sentiment and intellectual reasoning appeared to converge around a pro-League mindset that (albeit briefly) appeared anything but prophetic or utopian. The League idea was a central facet of Allied war aims from as early as 1914, gaining traction after Wilson publicly endorsed the LEP in 1916, and growing further once America joined the war in April 1917.[18] In Britain, prior to this, the Bryce Group began contemplating a postwar world, balancing pragmatic discussions of systematizing the use of collective military force against more idealistic conceptions where a "world public opinion" would provide a moral imperative for peace.[19] Certainly, many of the ideas that would soon become synonymous with Wilsonianism were visible in liberal and radical circles where, as Henig notes, ideas and plans for a postwar international society were "well-advanced" by 1918, not least within the ranks of the UDC. Some in Britain went further, advocating not a Wilsonianism vision of a binding agreement between separate sovereign states but something resembling a "super-state," under the control of the people rather than national governments.[20] But few (if any) politicians and diplomats countenanced for one moment the prospect of a superstate.[21]

This apparent divergence between idealistic pressure groups and realistic diplomats must not be overstated. In actuality, there was a noticeable symbiosis between the pragmatic, realist approaches and the idealism of the various advocates of internationalism. As Glenda Sluga insists, although internationalism has been routinely "tainted as utopian in ways that nationalism, regardless of its content, has not," in reality "the national and the international remain entwined."[22] With regard to British thinking about a postwar settlement, this means that one must not see the two approaches as being diametrically opposed and thus irreconcilable. Many of the schemes forwarded for constructing a new world order not only sought to reconcile the idealist with the realist but also genuinely believed that such a reconciliation was possible. The potential role of public opinion was one area where the two sometimes converged. The Bryce Group believed that public opinion would *eventually* play a crucial role in underpinning any future international order, but currently it was not equipped to do so. Substantial education was required in the meantime. As Kaiga concludes, the Bryce Group relied on three assumptions about public opinion: first, that the people were inherently peaceful; second, that any lingering warlike spirit could be eliminated through education; and third, that an "adequately informed, instructed, and mobilized popular opinion would suffice to prevent future wars."[23] Not everyone was as sanguine as Bryce about public opinion performing a beneficent role. Goldsworthy Lowes Dickinson was so disillusioned by the British public's jingoism and warlike fervor during the early part of the war that he became "desperately pessimistic about the future of all civilisation," even doubting "whether it is worthwhile preaching to the insane."[24]

Nevertheless, most proponents of a League emphasized strongly the performative role of public opinion. League enthusiasts in all countries shared a conviction that its legitimacy would be guaranteed by an overwhelming degree of public support.[25] As Georges Scelle put it, the League should be "the daughter of public opinion, released from the guidance of ill-intentioned shepherds, and aware of her own strength."[26] The Bryce Group's 1915 proposals stated clearly that a postwar international organization must be created "through which that great body of international public opinion which favours peace may express itself." In this sense, public opinion would provide a corrective to those elites who pursue wars "in pursuit of selfish interests or at the bidding of national pride."[27] Simultaneously, Wilson's escalating wartime prominence heartened many in

Britain who were intoxicated by his rhetoric of liberal internationalism. Even in the midst of a 1918 general election campaign that appeared to confirm the British public's desire to punish Germany severely, evidence of more idealistic impulses was abundant. Many individuals and organizations, particularly those of a liberal persuasion, were keen to maximize the publicity value of President Wilson's impending trip to Europe. Bryce wrote to Wilson directly to express his satisfaction that the American president was coming to Europe "to join in settling the greatest and most difficult series of problems statesmanship has ever had to deal with," noting how many in Britain were energized by Wilson's "warm interest" in the subject of a postwar League.

Examples of British public enthusiasm for Wilsoniasm are not hard to find. The Carlisle Women Citizens' Association wrote to Wilson on December 4, 1918, hoping that their appeal, "coming from the women of your mother's native town, will have an especial interest." "No better appeal and stimulus could be afforded to a body of newly emancipated women," they continued, than a presidential visit to their town, an opportunity to showcase "the highest idealism and the wisest statesmanship."[28] The British section of the WILPF also wrote to Wilson that month, assuring him that he had on his side the "might of a great people and the right of internationalism," but warning the president of "the Old-World forces against you," which grew stronger with each passing day. They were confident, nevertheless, that the simultaneous growth of popular sentiment "in favour of the New-World principles which you alone among statesmen have fearlessly expressed" would overcome these pernicious forces.[29] As Margaret Macmillan has put it so eloquently, Wilson "kept alive the hope that human society, despite the evidence, was getting better, that nations would one day live in harmony."[30]

The conviction that public opinion would henceforth play a pivotal role in the democratization of foreign policy was not without its discontents. As Bouchard remarks, there was, among politicians and diplomats, a natural reflex against this, challenging the easy assumption that, because greater democratization works domestically, it would, ipso facto, work equally well in the international domain.[31] Still, a dominant impression had emerged by the immediate postwar period that the future would hinge increasingly on public opinion. Back in 1916, the former US Secretary of State, Elihu Root, insisted that postwar diplomacy must reflect "the principles of popular government" and that the will of the people had assumed the role of a "great new sovereign that is taking charge of foreign affairs."[32] If the 1919 deliberations in Paris were to be the first meaningful examination of this "new" diplomacy in practice, domestic political issues in Britain would first play a critical role in establishing what the British public wanted. After all, in the spirit of a "new" diplomacy of democratized foreign policy, this "great new sovereign" would necessarily dictate policy.

Lloyd George was very much a man of his era, mindful of the impact of mass communications on the relationship between governments and those they governed. More particularly, Lloyd George viewed the press as the essential conduit through which this increasingly complex relationship could be managed. The war, which brought forth considerable advances in propaganda, had taught some valuable lessons as to how governments could handle the press via a formal apparatus and personal contacts. The premier's personal staff essentially cultivated what the newspaper baron Lord Northcliffe considered (pejoratively) an "astute but unscrupulous press bureau" with the sole intention of managing the risks posed by an unfettered and uncontrolled press.[33] This was not simply cynical political expediency; Lloyd George accepted that governments *had* to be more accountable to the public. The government had demanded huge sacrifices from the British people during the war; in its aftermath, especially given the vastly extended franchise, democratic virtue necessitated that the government be attentive to the public's wishes. This also extended to the domain of foreign policy.[34]

Lloyd George's fixation on the press was unsurprising. Newspapers remained the most influential means of mass communication. Mediums that would proliferate in the later interwar period, such as cinema newsreels and radio, were still in their infancy. Other sources of public opinion that had been prominent through the "long" nineteenth century—notably the platform and petition— were not superfluous by 1918–19, but had been usurped by newspapers that were becoming more affordable and more widely read within an increasingly literate public sphere. With this in mind, Lloyd George read and annotated newspapers voraciously, particularly the *Manchester Guardian* and *The Times*, but also using his staff to keep him abreast of coverage in other British papers and even the European and American press. This is not to say, however, that he felt powerless in the face of any potential press onslaught. As Michael Graham Fry has commented, Lloyd George was convinced that the press could be "seduced, even used, if one were not excessively squeamish." Careful and prudent management of the press, especially the cultivation of influential proprietors and editors, could be used to both harness support and undermine political adversaries.[35]

But British opinion in the immediate aftermath of war was animated by considerable anti-German sentiment. As Martin Ceadel has noted, British peace activists were disconcerted by "the public's vindictive mood as soon as the war was won."[36] "Make the Hun pay" was a common slogan in Britain and, although Lloyd George maintained that any "sense of revenge" or "spirit of greed" should not trump principles of justice, he was subjected to considerable pressure by the Northcliffe press, which accused him of being pro-German.[37] Northcliffe, who had finished the war as Director of Propaganda, used his newspapers (specifically *The Times* and the *Daily Mail*) to make the issues of punishing the Kaiser, extracting hefty reparations from Germany, and the treatment of enemy aliens, the key battlegrounds of the 1918 general election. This irritated Lloyd George, who had intended to campaign on predominantly domestic issues. The prime minister's first election speech, in Wolverhampton on November 23, focused on home affairs, but he felt compelled in his second address, in Newcastle on November 29, to foreground foreign policy, in particular German war crimes and the reparation issue. As Fry remarks, the rhetoric altered accordingly: "A just peace became a 'sternly just peace,' a 'relentlessly just peace.'"[38] His speech in Bristol on December 10 was perhaps the most forceful of all, stating that Germany must pay "in full if they have got it," assuring his audience that "we can expect every penny" that was in Germany's capacity to pay.[39] The premier was consistently careful to add this caveat—that any reparations figure must be within and not beyond Germany's capacity to pay—but the caveat was a less pugnacious soundbite than the talk of paying "every penny."

Given this climate, and the prevalence during the 1918 election campaign of slogans like "Hang the Kaiser," Patrick Cohrs praises Lloyd George for maintaining a relatively level head, despite acknowledging that the Welshman "did not shy away from capitalising on widespread anti-German sentiment."[40] William Mulligan strikes a similar tone, suggesting that the prime minister could not ignore the "vindictive impulses" of the electorate but always did so with a realist's eye on Germany's capacity to pay. Yet, even accepting Lloyd George's successful balancing act, Mulligan concludes that the overall tenor of the 1918 election campaign steered the British government toward a more punitive approach that would culminate in the Versailles Treaty itself.[41] The well-known demand to squeeze Germany "until the pips squeak" *was* played upon by the Lloyd George coalition during the campaign, their final manifesto stating explicitly that they would "Punish the Kaiser" and "Make Germany Pay."[42] The prime minister demanded on December 5 that the "arch criminal Kaiser" be tried for "high treason against humanity." As Zara Steiner remarks: "The demand for retribution and restitution swept the country." Every candidate opposing a harsh peace was defeated.[43] The pressure on Lloyd George to adopt a more vengeful stance did not emanate from the press alone. His cabinet colleague (and future foreign secretary) George Curzon had visited Paris in the immediate aftermath of the Armistice, advising Lloyd George on his return to take seriously the French suggestion that the Kaiser be put on trial. British public opinion, he insisted, "will not willingly consent to let this arch criminal escape by a final act of cowardice."[44]

It is notable that no UDC member was returned to Parliament in the 1918 election, suggesting that their more lenient approach to the forthcoming peace deliberations failed to resonate with a prevailing public mood of vindictiveness. But this latter sentiment was ephemeral. By early March 1919, the American Commission was reporting that British public opinion—as conveyed by the press—was now "calling for a policy which will relieve the acute conditions in Germany." At the same time, the British public appeared to maintain that any postwar League must avoid being a victor's association (omitting Germany and Russia), which would ultimately render the European continent "an armed camp"; only the *Morning Post* maintained a stridently anti-German outlook.[45] In this sense, Margaret Macmillan is correct in asserting that "public opinion, that new and troubling element, was no help." The British public wanted the Kaiser hanged in late 1918, but their stance had softened considerably within a handful of months.[46] Already, it seemed, the influence of the "great new sovereign" on foreign affairs was proving to be problematic. Little surprise, therefore, that writing shortly after the conclusion of the Paris Peace Settlement, Walter Lippmann's influential portrayal of a fickle, emotionally volatile, and "bewildered public" would take hold.[47]

1919: Peacemaking in Paris

The British delegation arrived in Paris in 1919 with two similar proposals for a League of Nations, the "Cecil Draft" (itself underpinned by the work of Alfred Zimmern and the recommendations of the Phillimore Committee) and Jan Smuts's *The League of Nations: A Practical Suggestion*. These schemes retained many of the central tenets of Wilson's conception of a League but stripped back some of the president's idealism to the extent that the resultant League has been seen as amounting to "an expansion of the concert of Europe."[48] That the British political and intellectual establishment had spent so long and invested so much energy in formulating detailed plans for a durable postwar settlement based on some kind of League is significant in itself. It demonstrates that politicians and diplomats had to pay at least lip-service to ideas and conceptions of a "new" and "open" diplomacy that had, for several years and decades captured the imagination of an increasingly well-educated public sphere.

Wilsonian rhetoric clearly struck a chord with a broad cross section of world opinion, and even permeated the realm of foreign-policymaking elites. Sir Maurice Hankey, British Cabinet Secretary and very much an "old school" diplomat, carried a copy of Wilson's Fourteen Points with him throughout the Paris deliberations, considering it the "moral background" to the entire enterprise.[49] In addition, Lloyd George's private secretary, Philip Kerr, was a keen advocate of "new" diplomacy, while other prominent and influential liberal figures including Milner and Churchill supported the League idea, albeit with caveats intended to maintain Britain's military and imperial prestige. On the other side of the coin lay the "unreconstructed" advocates of "old" diplomacy, notably Conservatives like Lord Sydenham, Leopold Amery, and Sir Henry Wilson.[50] Whether apostles of the new diplomacy or unreconstructed adherents of the old, it was clear that public opinion could not be ignored, a reality true not only for Britain but also for all countries represented in Paris. As Steiner has put it, the "future architects of the peace remained sensitive to the public mood," in contradistinction to those who assembled little over a century earlier in Vienna. Unlike the statesmen of 1815, those gathered in Paris in 1919 were mostly elected representatives, answerable to their publics, subjected to ever-more-intense press scrutiny, and increasingly conscious of a growing demand for "the peoples' voice [to] be heard in the corridors of power."[51]

Paris became, for the first half of 1919, the epicenter of the world. The peacemaking process aroused massive public interest across the globe, but it was not just journalists flocking to France to witness and report on events. As Macmillan reminds us: "Votes for women, rights for blacks, a charter for labour, freedom for Ireland, disarmament, the petitions and petitioners rolled in daily from all quarters of the world."[52] Myriad expressions of public opinion resulted in a cacophony of noises and pressures that would surely have bewildered many of the veteran statesmen gathered there, men more familiar with the significantly less frenetic norms of the "old" diplomatic methods. Most of the countries represented were democracies, answerable (at least to an extent) to their publics and thus necessarily attentive to the potential electoral repercussions of maladroit foreign policy decisions.[53] In this context, Paris might not have been, as Steiner suggests, the best choice of venue, the "heated atmosphere, fanned by the excesses of the Parisian press . . ., hardly conducive to reasoned deliberations."[54] Indeed, it was only because of the obduracy of the French premier, Georges Clemenceau, that the negotiations took place in the French capital, overruling Lloyd George's preference for Geneva.

The most widespread interpretation of the "Big Three" at Versailles is that Clemenceau sat at one extreme (agitating for the most punitive terms to be imposed on Germany), Wilson at the other (favoring a lenient settlement), with Lloyd George positioned somewhere in between. An analysis of the political and journalistic rhetoric of the day does suggest that French public opinion was more inclined than British and American opinion to favor the use of force to uphold the League, just as it was more hostile to the idea of complete disarmament.[55] But this interpretation has been challenged, Marc Trachtenberg contending that the British were the main "stumbling block" preventing a moderate settlement as Lloyd George, under pressure from domestic opinion to ensure a harsh settlement, demanded higher reparation figures than those being sought even by the French. Even as the public's vengeful mood dissipated, the British premier appeared intent on extracting substantial indemnities, the apparent mildness of the Fontainebleau Memorandum marking no real change in Britain's stance on reparations, which remained "as unbending as ever."[56]

Lloyd George's ambiguity reflected a public opinion that was far from homogenous. After all, the prime minister was, as Macmillan reminds us, a "consummate politician" who was well aware of the public mood, telling his colleagues on Christmas Eve 1918 that the British people would abhor "the continuance of a state of affairs which might again degenerate into such a tragedy." They might want to punish Germany, but they also wanted a viable and sustainable peace, hence it was essential that the forthcoming conference produce a League of Nations. Less clear was how far the British public would go to give the League the power necessary to ensure compliance with its decisions. Did they support a firm, British military commitment to the League, or were they satisfied, instead, that a more nebulous form of moral suasion would suffice?[57] At the opening Plenary Session of the Conference on February 14, 1919, Wilson clearly prioritized the latter. As he had earlier told a meeting of the League of Nations Committee on February 10, his conception of a League was predicated on the "court of public opinion," because this, rather than any more tangible legal and military mechanisms, would be both more "effective" and "more powerful."[58]

This has long been held up as the single biggest failing of Wilson's creation, both at the time and since. Former foreign secretary Lord Hurd has asserted that Wilson's belief that the mobilization of world opinion was sufficient to dispense with military or even economic sanctions constituted the "weakest point" of his entire agenda.[59] At the time, this solution was considered satisfactory to many in Britain who wanted to create a League, but all the while avoiding the kind of entangling military commitments that would give it teeth. There was a degree of consistency in how British officialdom interpreted the ultimate sanction that would underpin the League, a consistency that ran through the schemes of Cecil and Smuts and was embraced subsequently by Balfour and Lloyd George. In short, public opinion *was* this sanction, assuming its power and potency by a League-enforced period of delay in the event of any international controversy, allowing tempers to cool and wiser counsels to prevail.[60] Cecil himself proclaimed that "the great weapon we rely on is public opinion," while Balfour claimed that the League's power emanated not from battleships and armies, but from "delay and publicity and public opinion."[61]

Nevertheless, a fear was crystallizing that the future peace and stability of Europe might be hindered rather than helped by squeezing Germany until the pips squeaked. It was not long after this that the seeds of what would become a dominant interpretation of the Versailles settlement (at least in Great Britain and the United States) were sown, attributable in no small part to the publication in December 1919 of John Maynard Keynes's *The Economic Consequences of the Peace*. This book—an immediate bestseller that has remained in print ever since—helped to establish a narrative whereby the excessive severity of the settlement was attributed to French vindictiveness and the final settlement was deemed deeply unfair to Germany.[62] But, although some of the warlike passions so much in evidence during the khaki election did start to subside, sections of British opinion continued to "press for a vindictive peace," notably the *Daily Mail*. Concerned that the British government may now accept a compromise settlement with a concomitant reduction in reparations from Germany, this paper unleashed a campaign in late March 1919 against any perceived capitulation.[63] This campaign had an effect on the public. For many in Britain, Germany *had* still lost the war, and Germany and its Allies must shoulder the burden of responsibility and guilt. As the American Commission's intelligence reports suggested, sections of the right-wing British press were becoming noticeably more belligerent, even proclaiming the country "ready to march on Berlin to enforce the peace terms."[64]

Although this more vengeful spirit was not widespread, that it existed at all spoke to just how divided British public opinion was during 1919. Satisfying a divided public is no easy task, and as the peace treaty dealing with Germany neared completion, criticism emanated from all quarters, and by no means just those who lamented its alleged leniency. Robert Cecil warned Lloyd George in late May that "large sections of English and American opinion are very uneasy over the terms of the Draft Treaty." This growing disenchantment, he suggested, reflected a belief that "the Treaty is out of harmony with the spirit, if not the letter, of the professed war aims of the Allied and Associated Governments," meaning not only Wilson's Fourteen Points but also Lloyd George's expression of British wartime objectives in his Caxton Hall speech of January 5, 1918. Convinced that the war had been waged with a view to establishing a durable peace, the British people had coalesced around a pro-League mindset and were now concerned that the proposed peace terms were "an unsound basis" on which such a League could be constructed. In fact, Cecil even suggested that the "Hang the Kaiser" rhetoric of the khaki election "was largely the outcome of the desire that the disturbers of peace should be adequately penalised."[65]

Bouchard notes how advocates of a durable peace, from Britain, France, and America, who had invested so much time and effort in furnishing politicians and diplomats with detailed schemes and propositions, were left bitterly disappointed by the League that was emerging by spring 1919. The politicians, he remarks, had infused "a dose of reality" into the League idea that moved it away from some of the idealistic impulses that had shaped much of the early agenda.[66] To be sure, groups like the UDC were unhappy, and this discontent would find an echo elsewhere, notably in the ranks of the Women's International League. At the same time (and particularly on the British right), the prospect of an entangling continental commitment was troubling. In this regard, the League that emerged—predicated more on a moral rather than a physical sanction— was a satisfactory outcome, even if it irritated the French.[67] At least there *was* a League, and this at least offered something tangible to cling to, even for those who had wished for more. Indeed, the British public's support for the League throughout the 1920s and well into the 1930s suggests that the disappointment felt in spring 1919, arising from its apparent imperfections, did not translate into a loss of public confidence or support. In fact, the opposite happened, as there followed a concerted effort to create the necessary structures to promote League activities, particularly among the youth, seeking to imbue young minds with the "spirit of Geneva."[68]

Indeed, Harold Temperley, a delegate to, and subsequent historian of, the Paris Conference, tried to reassure those who felt that the public had been marginalized throughout the treaty-making process by reminding them that it was provisional and subject to modification. "Opportunity is now thus provided," he wrote, "for the public opinion of the world to act upon the documents drawn up at Paris, and even at this early stage it is seen that some parts will not long survive the criticisms that have been directed upon them."[69] Nevertheless, the publication of the treaty prompted considerable unease among those who had anticipated Wilsonian idealism taking hold. Several members of the American delegation resigned in protest at the apparent abandonment of these idealistic impulses. Some British participants vented a similar unhappiness. "We came to Paris confident that the new order was about to be established," lamented the Foreign Office's Harold Nicolson, "we left it convinced that the new order had merely fouled the old. We arrived as fervent apprentices in the school of President Wilson; we left as renegades."[70] The impetus for the "new order" that Nicolson was evoking had apparently emanated from public opinion, yet the same public opinion—as expressed in the vindictively anti-German tropes that characterized the 1918 "khaki election" and the right-wing press campaign of spring 1919—contributed to an outcome that was more attuned to the old diplomacy than the new. The terms presented to the Germans via the June 16 ultimatum were harsh. A broken, angry, and demoralized Germany eventually acquiesced. The final treaty was signed, with much fanfare, in the Hall of Mirrors at Versailles, on June 28, 1919.

Publicity at Paris: "Open" Diplomacy and the Management of the Press

If Lloyd George, throughout his political career to date, seemed attentive to the growing power and purchase of the press (albeit for his own ends), he was less sanguine about openness when it came to the diplomatic proceedings in Paris in 1919. As Fry reminds us, Lloyd George conceived of democratic diplomacy not as "open covenants openly arrived at but deliberating in private and submitting the results to public judgment." In short, diplomats could not go about their delicate business under the relentless glare of an attentive public and an intrusive press. To do so would result in a peace manufactured by "public clamour" when what was required, he argued, was a peace engineered by prudent statesmen capable of rising above a noisy and volatile public.[71] For Sir George Riddell, the newspaper proprietor who was tasked with liaising between the press and the British delegation at the Paris Peace Conference, the prime minister's consistent refusal to countenance greater publicity and openness was symptomatic of his increasingly autocratic methods. Despite his best efforts to keep the press apprised of developments at the conference, and in spite of frequent leaks to the press from numerous quarters, Riddell bemoaned how there had been "no systematic issue of information" resulting in the machinations of the Council of Four being "shrouded in mystery." Inevitably, the public became uneasy, but Lloyd George remained unrepentant, his attitude, according to Riddell, "that of a benevolent autocrat: 'I will decide what is for your good and will see that you get it.'"[72] In his memoirs, Lloyd George maintained that the public received what information it needed: "Nothing was withheld from the public which it was imperative they should know."[73]

This unwillingness to embrace completely "open" diplomacy at Paris may also have stemmed from Lloyd George's irritation at press criticism of him and his government prior to the conference getting under way. He later claimed that his decision to call a general election in 1918 was an effort to silence the "active and persistent campaign of criticism" in the British press directed toward his government. "If this sniping went on during the Peace Conference," he claimed, "it would give the impression to the representatives of the Allies that the British people were not behind the British Government." This, in turn, would weaken Britain's bargaining position in Paris, just as (in Lloyd George's opinion) the American position had been weakened by Wilson's electoral "disaster" in the November 1918 mid-terms. As a result, Wilson's "occasional threats to appeal to American opinion, when he did not get his way at the Conference, conveyed no real menace."[74] Unlike Wilson, Lloyd George benefited from an election victory that, as he put it, resulted in the British delegation traveling to Paris "with the full authority of the nation behind it." For the prime minister, this was a mandate to simply go to Paris and get on with the diplomacy without any further and unnecessary press intrusion.

Lloyd George was soon disabused of the belief that his election victory would quieten press criticism. Arguably, his reluctance to embrace genuinely "open" diplomacy in Paris exacerbated press attacks, a perceived deficit of information serving only to irritate journalists and editors. It had been widely hoped that the age of "new" diplomacy would ensure that these deliberations would be open and accountable, exposed to the full glare of the world's press. The apparent progress made over the two Hague Peace Conferences heightened these aspirations: the 1899 meeting had excluded the press, but the 1907 meeting, though falling short of allowing the press unfettered access, was considerably more transparent.[75] In 1919, as Temperley recalled: "An army of pressmen had come to Paris, and the attention of the whole world was concentrated on the Conference." This "army" of journalists demanded complete access to the deliberations, and managing these expectations was difficult. After all, as Lloyd George recalled, the consensus among the diplomatists was that unconstrained press access to the deliberations "would interfere materially with our efforts to reconcile differences and to arrive at a common understanding."[76] Despite the commitment to "open" diplomacy in his Fourteen Points, Wilson was, from the start, maneuvering toward a solution that would (he hoped) satisfy both the journalistic demand for openness and the diplomatists' demand for secrecy. Having thought "a great deal lately about the contact of Commission with the public through the press," Wilson concluded that the American Commission in Paris should "hold a brief meeting each day and invite the representatives of the press to come in at each meeting for such interchanges of information or suggestions as may be thought necessary."[77]

A January 1919 meeting of Allied representatives to discuss the issues of publicity engineered a similar solution. Wilson, doubtless aware of his popular association with a "new" diplomacy predicated on openness and accountability began by claiming that "he did not know how it would be possible for him to defend privacy for the meetings of the full Conference except on unusual occasions." He proposed a compromise—amended slightly (cosmetically rather than substantively) by Balfour and Lloyd George which read:

> The representatives of the Allied and Associated Powers have given earnest consideration to the question of publicity for the proceedings of the Peace Conference. They are anxious that the public, through the Press, should have the fullest information compatible with safeguarding the supreme interest of all, which is that a just and honourable settlement should be arrived at with the minimum of delay.[78]

The statement went on to assert that because the proceedings were "far more analogous to the meeting of a Cabinet than to those of a legislature," and given that nobody supposes that the former should ever be conducted in public, the same should hold true in this situation. Wary that too much publicity would arouse distrust and suspicions on all sides, the peacemakers were keen to stress that this "necessary limitation" did not mean that they underrated the "importance of carrying public opinion with them in the vast task by which they are confronted." On the contrary, they were adamant that the public would be the ultimate arbiter of their success or failure: "They recognize that unless public opinion approves of the results of their labours they will be nugatory."[79]

Despite these restrictions, Temperley noted how "the sheer volume of people involved in the Council of Ten discussions made leaks to the press inevitable and impossible to prevent."[80] To be sure, given the volume of journalists in attendance, it was simply impossible to prevent information (whether accurate or not) from seeping out. Robert Cecil, the British delegate at Versailles in charge of negotiations for a League of Nations, noted in his diary in early January how he had spoken with a journalist from *Le Matin* and "authorised him to say that the British people were strongly in favour of a League of Nations." Cecil confessed, however, that he was "not very clear as to what was meant by that expression."[81] Cecil's diary reveals frequent discussions with journalists, predominantly British, French, and American, indicative not only of the degree of press interest in the proceedings but also the apparent willingness of the assembled diplomats to relay information. He initially seemed to treat these press interactions as something of a game, but there were soon signs of a tightening grip on press coverage. When cross-examined by some English journalists on February 6, Cecil could only respond that "we had been told not to say anything at present," while adding that he "would see what I could do for them."[82]

The peacemakers were becoming more attentive to the need to keep the press under control or simply out of the loop. By the time the Council of Four came to dominate the proceedings at Versailles, it was clear that one of Wilson's Fourteen Points—removing diplomacy from the private sphere—had been discarded in deference to the old-fashioned practice of private meetings behind closed doors.[83] This prompted unease in Britain; the American Commission noted in early April 1919 how British newspapers were attacking "the secrecy with which the Big Four have surrounded their deliberations." Indeed, by mid-April, it was noted that British public opinion is "more than ever annoyed over the secrecy of the methods of the Council of Four," an irritation clearly permeating Parliament, as evidenced by "the petitions to Lloyd George and Clemenceau from their respective legislative assemblies."[84] The growing proclivity for secrecy not only irked parliamentarians but also seemed to stretch to some of the delegates in Paris. Cecil even complained directly to Lloyd George, lamenting that he felt "rather uncomfortable, partly because like the British public I don't know what is going on."[85]

The parliamentary petition bemoaning the lack of transparency compelled the prime minister to respond in the House of Commons. In his speech on April 16, Lloyd George went on the offensive, bemoaning the press and its "silly talk about secrecy" and proclaiming: "No Peace Conference ever held has given so much publicity to its proceedings." He was equally forceful in asserting that his actions in Paris had been entirely faithful to the spirit of both his wartime speeches and his election pledges.[86] The prime minister also seized the opportunity to launch an excoriating attack on Northcliffe, accusing him of "diseased vanity," dismissing *The Times* as a "threepenny edition of the *Daily Mail*," and decrying the "kind of trash" that had filled such papers over the previous weeks.[87] This politicking in the press, he suggested, seeking to portray dissension among the

Allies that simply did not exist, was both irresponsible and not in the public interest. As far as Lloyd George was concerned, the British people simply wanted a good peace with the least delay possible.[88] In response, the *Daily Mail* labeled the prime minister "a spoiled child" unable to stomach legitimate criticism without giving an infantile retort.[89] *The Times* also attacked Lloyd George for indulging in "false analogies and cheap rhetorical effects," and insisted that they would ignore his criticisms and "maintain by honest and fearless publicity what it conceives to be the highest traditions of British journalism."[90]

The campaign that emanated from certain sections of the rightist press (notably Northcliffe's *Daily Mail*) from late March 1919, accusing Lloyd George of being too pro-German and too soft on the reparations question, certainly exasperated the prime minister. Northcliffe, doubtless bitter that he was given no official role at the Paris Conference (the press liaison position being taken by Riddell), responded to this snub by appointing a "dedicated enemy" of Lloyd George, Wickham Steed, as editor of *The Times*. Steed duly went about launching the press attacks that had spurred the prime minister's astonishing retort in the House of Commons.[91] Had Lloyd George brought this on himself? According to Temperley, the Northcliffe campaign was typical sensationalist journalism, and it took hold and resonated with sections of the British public only because of the inadequate information provided via official channels. The substance of earlier deliberations of the Council of Ten meetings was leaked frequently to the newspapers, ensuring that the press and public felt better informed, but the Council of Four discussions were conducted in almost total secrecy. In the absence of official information, rampant press speculation was rife, making it difficult for the reading public to differentiate between truth and falsehoods.[92]

To be sure, by late March there were clear indications that the press (and quite possibly, therefore, the public) was becoming frustrated, partly at the apparent lack of progress in Paris but mostly at the lack of information. By March 24 Riddell noted that "feelings of dissatisfaction were growing" and that the government should expect "a general attack by all sections of the press." In a bid to alleviate this, Riddell urged the need for greater publicity.[93] He reminded Lloyd George that the entire world "is asking for peace," that "all eyes are turned to Paris," and that the general public "do not understand the delays." Lloyd George retorted that Riddell's job was to "get the papers to be more reasonable," expressing anger that the press appeared to overlook the "gigantic task" that the peacemakers were attempting to accomplish. Riddell was unmoved, suggesting that criticisms would dissipate if more information was provided. "They deal with the facts as they know them," he said. "The Conference is too secretive."[94]

But this level of secrecy seemed to be what the diplomats desired, allowing them to avoid making any firm public commitments prior to the final treaty being signed. This was particularly true of Lloyd George. Asked by Riddell whether the terms of the draft peace should be disseminated publicly, the prime minister's response was unambiguous. "No, certainly not!" he replied. "They will be handed to the Germans when they come to Versailles. If the terms were published beforehand, the position of the German Government would be made impossible. The terms might lead to revolution." Furthermore, Lloyd George insisted that any newspaper that failed to adhere to this arrangement would face punishment.[95] One of the American delegates, Henry White, offered an alternative explanation for Lloyd George's aversion to publicity, attributing it less to potential repercussions in Germany, and more to the potentially deleterious impact it might have on British opinion. In White's appraisal, Lloyd George was animated by the not unreasonable fear that "there will be a very strong opposition to it from more quarters than one in England." White also noted that Clemenceau shared his British counterpart's reticence, fearful lest the terms of the treaty prompt "strong protests" in France, notably from the socialists.[96] Nevertheless, Clemenceau soon acquiesced to Wilson's demand for more openness, leaving Lloyd George isolated and resulting in a compromise whereby the press could publish a summary of the terms to be put to the Germans.[97]

The British press welcomed this development. Indeed, representatives of British papers had petitioned the peacemakers on May 2, arguing "that it is essential in the interests of the Allied people that accredited correspondents of the Allied Press should be admitted when the Peace Terms are handed to the Germans, so that an adequate report of the proceedings may be supplied to the public." They got their way, but still had to overcome consistent obstacles. As Riddell remarked, they had had to fight "inch by inch," the default position of the "autocratic" diplomats being that "they like to work in secret and to tell the public just as much as suits their purpose."[98] Nevertheless, the full glare of the modern media was in evidence when the various diplomatists arrived at the Trianon Palace Hotel on May 7, 1919, received by a throng of reporters, photographers, and cameramen. Riddell noted how "the combined whir of the cinema cameras was almost equal to that of a small aeroplane." Inside, a handful of correspondents, including a handful from Germany "who looked gloomy and ill at ease," were witness to the formal proceedings.[99] Where the Germans were uneasy, the Big Three appeared happy with their work. Frances Stevenson noted that everyone was pleased with the terms, especially as "there is no fault to find with them on the ground that they are not severe enough."[100]

For the Germans, though, the severity of the terms came as a shock given the expectations engendered by the rhetoric of Wilson's Fourteen Points.

After the Germans had tabled their counterproposals, there remained considerable unease among the Allied and associated powers as to how the final peace would be received. During a discussion at the Quai d'Orsay on May 29, France's foreign minister, Stephen Pichon, was adamant that French public opinion would demand that Germany adhere strictly to the terms imposed, while Cecil intimated that the British public would be uneasy with the treaty as a whole, demanding "considerable changes."[101] Politically, the proposed treaty was criticized from multiple directions in Britain, some abhorring its alleged leniency, others unhappy with its apparent harshness. Once again, British opinion was divided. Walter Long, the Unionist First Lord of the Admiralty, assured Lloyd George that the British people were overwhelmingly positive in their appraisal, and most of all thankful to the prime minister for his tireless efforts. Even so, as Fry notes, this encouraging news did not dovetail with other indicators of opinion, notably some alarming by-election defeats.[102]

The final settlement with Germany was clearly imperfect, but this did not prevent a huge degree of press interest at the official signing of the Versailles Treaty in the Hall of Mirrors on June 28. In keeping with the treatment of the press throughout, the whole process was, as Riddell remarked, "badly arranged" from the journalists' point of view, with too little space being provided for them.[103] The presence of these legions of journalists and photographers testified to the global public interest in the diplomatic proceedings and their outcomes. This interest, in turn, only intensified the sense that the Versailles settlement was, as Zara Steiner has described, "a bundle of compromises that fully satisfied none of the three peacemakers."[104] Little surprise, therefore, that press criticism of the settlement continued to find free expression, much to the chagrin of many of those involved in its creation. Several weeks after the Peace Conference had concluded, Lloyd George's bitterness at what he labeled the impatient and "unreasonable" journalists in attendance had not diminished.[105] He claimed in his memoirs that the persistent grumbling of the "disaffected press" was little more than a minor irritant, as politicians and diplomats remained confident that such expressions "had no support in any quarter that counted."[106]

Nonetheless, he was clearly affected by it, recalling how a "retinue of papers," led by *The Times*, maintained "a cross fire of criticism and innuendo" throughout the conference, resulting in everything that was "said and done at the Peace Council [being] distorted or disproportioned." Lloyd George blamed Northcliffe for this constant barrage of criticism and disaffection, describing his attitude as "that of an extremely angry man" who was convinced that "unappreciative and envious politicians" had overlooked his substantial wartime service by selecting Riddell rather than himself to take charge of press liaison.[107] The press had certainly proved to be a troublesome element in the proceedings, a new and unfamiliar actor in diplomacy. Simply ignoring the press, or even trying to marginalize it, was counterproductive; efforts to do so in Paris in 1919 only increased unease and suspicion on all sides. In addition, the press had a powerful argument at its disposal: it claimed to speak for "the people" and in an emergent era of "new" and "open" diplomacy, public opinion was being widely vaunted as the "great new sovereign" in foreign affairs. In short, policymakers had to be more accountable and open to the press in order to be more accountable and open to the public.

Underpinning the notion of a "new" and "open" diplomacy was the conviction that public opinion would be a progressive force for good, restraining bellicose and vindictive statesmen and thus ensuring that the postwar peace (and the new world order that would emerge from it) reflected a magnanimous spirit of international concord and goodwill rather than nationalistic grievances and self-interest. At times, the public *did* exhibit these tendencies, but not consistently. The public was all-too-frequently fickle and inconsistent, rarely (if ever) speaking with a single voice, and often mediated by the press in such a way as to distort the reality. Diplomats in Paris in 1919 struggled with two things above all: first, reconciling the demands of a "new" diplomacy with their instinctive predilection for the methods of the "old"; and, second, the need to reflect the wishes of their publics, finding ways of ascertaining what "public opinion" actually was, and responding to it accordingly.

Conclusion

This chapter began with a discussion of James Bryce, the veteran British diplomat who was both a keen advocate of a League of Nations and a cheerleader for the power of public opinion. Bryce's appraisal of the 1919 settlement was emphatically downbeat. He wrote to Elihu Root that it sacrificed "future peace to present exigencies" and would prove to be "a short-sighted policy sure to bring retribution." Bryce remained convinced that the resultant terms were not attuned to the wishes of the British public, suggesting that "public opinion here, which does not like to express itself (especially in its want of information) regrets the present terms of peace being imposed upon Germany and Austria, as constituting no real peace, but providing material for future troubles.

'Quantula sapientia regitur mundus!'"[108] Bryce's critique targeted the politicians and diplomats, and, in so doing, largely absolved the public of any complicity. This chapter has suggested, however, that public opinion contributed (however inadvertently) to the imperfections of both the peace treaty and the resultant League of Nations. The public mood *was* unstable and fluctuating, a vengeful anti-German sentiment cohabiting with a desire to deliver a magnanimous peace rooted in the progressive principles of a "new" diplomacy. The failure in 1919 to reconcile these two demands was recognized by scholars writing during the Second World War, anxious that these errors not be repeated. E. H. Carr, for example, described the situation in 1919 as the consequence of a "characteristic war-time blend of stupidity and vindictiveness with high-minded idealism and unbounded faith in a near approach of the millennium."[109]

In the midst of an even more destructive war, it would have been tempting to ascribe the current conflict to the failure of those in 1919 to resolve the previous one adequately. R. B. McCallum wrote in 1944 that the British public's unease with the harsh treatment of Germany at Versailles (an unease which only grew after the publication of Keynes's book) was weaponized by German propaganda, especially under the Nazis, allowing it to be used to legitimize and normalize the appeasement of Germany in the interwar years.[110] It could be argued further that the perception of Versailles as "harsh" owed much to the fact that the statesmen had, in 1919, resisted demands for a "new" and "open" diplomacy. As Ruth Henig reminds us, the "skilled and cynical practitioners of Old Diplomacy" had successfully resisted the move toward not only an "open" diplomatic method but also the pursuit of disarmament and the solidification and tightening of collective security mechanisms. For Henig, the "inevitable result" of this was "the outbreak of the Second World War."[111] But this was by no means obvious at the time. Indeed, despite the disappointment evident in more vocal pacifist circles, the British public's response to the 1919 settlement was generally positive. The American Commission, having monitored the response to the settlement in the British press, suggested that the overwhelming majority of the country greeted the peace treaty "with approval." Even the Conservative press, it was noted, which had just recently grown twitchy lest the final arrangement be too lenient, considered the outcome "more favorable than it had hoped."[112]

Despite its imperfections, the League of Nations would go on to become an article of faith for many in interwar Britain. As E. H. Carr later noted, the British public's "profound faith" in the League was equivalent to a "religious phenomena."[113] Public demand for a League was crucial in ensuring that one even emerged in 1919, but suggested further that the public's aspirations had begun to outrun the diplomatic possibilities. This was certainly the view taken by Harold Nicolson in the 1930s, as the revisionist powers were exposing cruelly the League's impotence. The inclination to blame the crises of the 1930s on the imperfections of both Versailles and the League was, according to Nicolson, unfounded, as it was "the spirit and not the letter" of Versailles that was the problem, not least its false promise of ushering in a "new" diplomacy.[114] He lamented how the public now viewed the professional diplomatist with distrust, seeing them as "a member of an exclusive caste, detached from the main currents of public opinion, ignorant of economics, speaking several foreign languages with an exquisite accent, and as such unworthy of confidence." The public's demand for a "new" diplomacy, where the people were sovereign and able to overrule the self-interested bellicosity of the professional diplomat, was premature; universal peace, remarked Nicolson, would take centuries to accomplish, and, in the meantime, the "pacifist" countries can only restrain militarist states through militarism itself.[115] Above all, Nicolson resented the apparent public desire to see all diplomacy conducted under the full glare of publicity. Complex diplomatic negotiations required secrecy, and the clamor for openness introduces an "appalling reality" into the foreign-policymaking process.[116]

Nicolson's pessimistic assessment reflected the gloomy context of the mid-1930s when he was writing, and his criticism of public opinion should not detract from the more beneficent influence it exerted in 1919. As Carl Bouchard insists, what is most notable about the public discourses surrounding the League idea, both during the war and in its immediate aftermath, is that the public *could* speak intelligently about issues of peace and war, and that their opinions about a new world order were not inconsequential. Throughout the war, politicians evoked consistently the "new power of public opinion."[117] Hopes had been high that this public opinion would always be a force for good, and that public oversight of diplomacy would reduce the likelihood of war in the future. Nevertheless, an examination of British public opinion's influence on policy at the Paris Peace Conference demonstrates that these hopes were misguided and arguably naïve. At times, the public pushed the government in pursuit of a magnanimous peace and a progressive new world order based on internationalism and openness. On other occasions, the public demanded a vindictive peace that apportioned blame and extracted massive indemnities from the vanquished. All the while, it was unclear just how far the press and politicians were able to manipulate public opinion, or simply claimed to be speaking on its behalf. These uncertainties would encourage efforts over the remainder of the twentieth century to both gauge opinion more accurately and control it more effectively.

French Public Opinion and 1930s Appeasement

In 1940, writing after France had succumbed to the Wehrmacht, an American journalist Edmond Taylor sought to explain France's collapse. Having served from 1933 to 1940 as head of the Paris bureau of the *Chicago Tribune*, Taylor's was an eye-witness account of the fall of France. His conclusion was stark and uncompromising. "French democracy collapsed," he insisted, "because democratic morale between 1934 and 1940 dropped steadily lower, while anti-democratic morale rose steadily higher."[1] On the surface this conclusion chimes with the well-known "decadence" thesis that soon became the dominant historical narrative employed to explain 1940. Indeed, other accounts penned during the Second World War (notably Cecil Melville's *Guilty Frenchmen* and André Géraud's *Les Fossoyeurs*) offered excoriating appraisals of France's inability to confront the Nazi menace.[2] At the same time, the Vichy regime was happy to evoke a morally bankrupt Third Republic that needed replacing. In the immediate postwar period, France's shortcomings were ascribed not only to the political and military leadership but also to the nation at large. Marc Bloch's *L'étrange défaite*, published posthumously in 1946 (Bloch having been executed by the Nazis in 1944), set the tone, evoking a deeper malaise that undercut France's ability to fight the Germans effectively.[3] Bloch's account was soon supplemented by a handful of early histories of the Third Republic. For Maurice Baumont, the Maginot Line was emblematic of a decadent France that had been "reduced to the defensive."[4] Two of the foremost French practitioners of international history in the postwar era, Pierre Renouvin and Jean-Baptiste Duroselle, penned similar interpretations in which the decadent democracies struggled against the more dynamic dictatorships.[5] Duroselle would later publish his seminal *La décadence*, a hugely influential account that consolidated the decadence thesis.[6] Duroselle acknowledged that the French people were "resolute" when war came, but claimed nonetheless that the very coming of war was "the first defeat" for a profoundly pacific people.[7]

This allusion to the "people" demonstrates the centrality of public opinion to an emplotment of French defeat in which the absence of moral fiber is paramount. Eugen Weber's scathing account, *The Hollow Years*, concluded that isolated acts of "bravery, initiative or foolhardiness" during the battles of 1940 were too little too late following "years of indecisiveness and intellectual idleness, [and] anachronism among the leadership." For Weber, poor leadership was but one symptom of a wider malaise afflicting the entire country. The masses too were culpable; Weber evoked a crisis of "public morality" whereby an advanced nation like France found itself in "an advanced state of decay."[8] Yet, as Edmond Taylor noted, when Édouard Daladier took France to war in September 1939, there were few signs of disunity despite a palpable lack of enthusiasm. In Taylor's account, the French public accepted war in 1939, and did so with a considerable degree of cohesiveness and unity. This did not mean that they were *ready* for it; in the background lurked a "horror of war" that morphed into despair when the moment came. This left Taylor perplexed, struggling to reconcile an apparent willingness to fight with an intense anxiety as regards the potential repercussions. The unity and sangfroid of September 1939 was, suggested Taylor, "almost incomprehensible" given the French people's overwhelming aversion to war.[9]

To explain this paradox, Taylor employed terminology that sits comfortably within a conventional "decadence" narrative: "apathy," "absence of enthusiasm," "uncertainty of aim," "lack of initiative," "paralyzing red tape," "sheer neglect," and so on. But these negative traits of the late Third Republic should not be attributed to a helplessly and hopelessly divided public opinion. Instead, Taylor blamed poor leadership and the cumulative effects of a "demoralized democracy" since 1934.[10] The social and political fault lines of 1930s France are well known: the agitation of the Stavisky scandal; the violent events of *6 février* 1934; the failure of collective security (especially vis-à-vis Italy's 1935 invasion of Abyssinia); the troubled Popular Front experiment with its concomitant industrial unrest and latent threat of civil strife; the reverberations of the Spanish Civil War; the confused response to the 1938 Munich Accords. All of this contributed to a process that would culminate in the "unavoidable catastrophe" of a war in 1939 for which it was difficult to arouse enthusiasm. "Nous n'avons pas fait la guerre, nous avons glissé dans la guerre" (We have not gone to war, we have slipped into it) was, noted Taylor, a "characteristic verbal expression" in September 1939.[11] To a degree, this verdict adheres to the trajectory of a declinist, "decadence" narrative, rooted in a peculiarly French intellectual tradition of conceptualizing their history through the prism of crisis and renewal. Still, there have been many efforts, certainly since the 1970s, to subvert this orthodoxy, positioning France's response to the events of the 1930s more sympathetically within the broader structural context of diplomatic, economic, and military constraints.[12] The seductiveness of the declinist narrative owes much to a scaffolding of vocabulary that collapses when scrutinized more closely. "The morally-couched criticisms of interwar France," insists Robert Young, "are so often ignited with familiar verbal wormwood: rot, malaise, paralysis, corruption, dishonesty, blindness, indifference, defeatism and, the favourite, decadence."[13]

Although these revisionist efforts have done much to undermine the "decadence" thesis, the narrative retains, as Philip Nord insists, a "measure of plausibility."[14] In particular, explaining away France's defeat as the culmination of a national "decline" had political uses, legitimizing the promise of national "renewal" offered by both Philippe Pétain's Vichy regime and the *France éternelle* evoked by Charles de Gaulle. How far French democracy was, to use Taylor's phrase, "demoralized" remains unclear. The Jewish novelist, Irène Némirovsky, prior to being sent to her death at Auschwitz, suggested that the French people had grown "tired of the Republic as if she were an old wife." For Benjamin Martin, however, those responsible for the Republic's demise were the political leaders who "lacked courage and failed the nation they led."[15] This view echoes Taylor's 1940 claim that a "lack of moral courage on the part of democratic leaders" contributed to the situation the country found itself in by 1939–40.[16] Nord provides a slightly different interpretation, insisting that the Republican tradition persisted in France during the 1930s, even when it often "looked like an also-ran in a race dominated by fascists and communists."[17] Although Nord sees the 1940 defeat as a military event rather than an inevitable outcome of national decline, he acknowledges the fragility of the late Third Republic. France was certainly a troubled nation in the 1930s, unsure of itself and its place in the world. As Jean-Louis Crémieux-Brilhac noted in his magisterial study of French opinion in 1940, France had been a "divided" nation throughout the 1930s, its diplomatic responses conditioned by a domestic context of "political struggles, social tensions, a barely functioning institutional structure, economic stagnation, anxiety and self-doubt."[18]

Inherent within this depiction is the notion that France, as an entire nation, was paralyzed by anxiety, contributing to a wider social and cultural malaise that undermined France's foreign diplomatic strategy. In spite of this, Crémieux-Brilhac is adamant that the French people were ready for war in September 1939, though they did not want it.[19] Even so, the suggestion that public opinion in

France contributed to the Republic's defeat in 1940 retains considerable lustre. It was first articulated in the heated atmosphere of the 1940s, immediately following France's collapse. Charles Micaud's 1942 book *The French Right and Nazi Germany* took no prisoners in comparing public opinion in France (and to a lesser extent Britain) unfavorably to that in the dictatorships. "A well-controlled and therefore apparently united public opinion," he wrote, "was a tremendous asset in the hands of the dictators, while the divisions and strife in the democracies were a major element of weakness."[20] Although the intimation that the dictators benefited from almost total mastery of domestic opinion is questionable,[21] there was a perception at the time (and subsequently) that public opinion in the "decadent" democracies lacked the dynamism and discipline that characterized Nazi Germany and fascist Italy. This chapter focuses not on the dictatorships but the democracies, and specifically 1930s France, scrutinizing how democratic diplomats and statesmen often struggled to come to terms not only with the fascist menace but also with the demands of an increasingly articulate, voluble, and influential public sphere. It will show that representations of public opinion, at different junctures, both stymied and facilitated a firm and equivocal response to the fascist challenge.

Gauging Public Opinion: The Press

In one crucial respect, at least, little had changed since the immediate aftermath of the Great War: newspapers were still considered the paramount indicator of the public mood. This remained the case despite the rapid emergence and proliferation of new mediums of communication, notably radio, but also cinema (and hence the cinema newsreel) and, toward the end of the 1930s, the advent of opinion polling in Europe. Political elites initially viewed these new mediums with suspicion. Diplomats in this era—in France no less than any other country—were invariably men of a certain age, class, and social background, hardly constituting the kind of social environment in which change would be embraced readily. Little wonder, then, that France's veteran ambassador in London remarked in 1938, that the early opinion polls in Britain were of interest only insofar as their results corroborated what could be gleaned by "the permanent barometer of opinion that is the press."[22] Charles Corbin's focus on the press was by no means uncommon and entirely unsurprising. As will be shown, the power of cinema and radio was only beginning to be recognized by the 1930s, while opinion polls were not routinely undertaken in the Third Republic until the establishment, toward the end of 1938, of the *Institut français d'opinion publique* (IFOP). Prior to this, opinion was only gauged via sporadic administrative reports, occasional straw polls, and the usual mechanisms of elections. On a day-to-day basis, politicians could rely only on those institutions that claimed to speak "for" the public, including pressure groups, trade unions, political parties, and, most of all, the popular press.[23]

Newspapers thus remained the preferred medium for interpreting and gauging the public mood, and in France there existed a plethora of publications—national and provincial, daily, weekly, and monthly—reflecting all shades of opinion. The French newspaper industry had expanded rapidly during the Third Republic, reflecting wider trends of improving literacy rates, lower costs of print production, the impact of the telegraph in facilitating the speedier relay of newsworthy stories, and the ease and speed with which papers could be distributed nationwide. As Raymond Kuhn has noted, the daily print-run in France in 1870 was under one and a half million; by 1914, this had risen to just under ten million.[24] What Claude Bellanger has termed the "golden age" of the French press benefited from a governmental attitude predicated on facilitating freedom of both publication and enterprise.[25] Prior to 1914, few steps were taken to control the press, and it was only with the Great War that a more direct form of state intervention was deemed necessary. The legacy of this tighter wartime regulation was that the interwar French press was akin to a cartel, with restrictions placed on the number of pages permitted per issue, the size of the pages themselves, and the overall cost of the newspaper. Attempts to challenge the cartel were fiercely repressed and invariably unsuccessful.[26] When seeking explanations for France's defeat in 1940, it is unsurprising that many contemporaries—and subsequent historians—have identified a stagnant and corrupt press as contributing to a wider malaise and "decadence" that afflicted the very core of the Third Republic.

The Great War was also a catalyst for the greater professionalization of journalism in France, the *Syndicat National des Journalistes* being established in 1918. In this more professional era, the role of the newspaper was changing. According to Auguste de Chambure, writing in 1914, where newspapers in the nineteenth century were "the incontestable master of public opinion," the press had evolved into something akin to educators by the turn of the twentieth, providing information to a more self-aware and self-conscious public.[27] As this new "information age" progressed, the pre-1914 expansion of the French press plateaued but, by 1939, there were still five and a half million provincial newspapers being printed daily, with Parisian papers attaining similar figures.[28] Although this equated to a slight rise in the overall number of papers printed, it represented a decline in the number of newspapers per 1,000 French inhabitants, and certainly compared unfavorably to the continued growth of the press in Britain (where, by 1939, nearly 20 million papers were printed daily compared to just 11 million in France).[29]

Indeed, the number of genuinely "popular" titles (those that sold over one million copies) was reduced, and many of the prominent "grande presse" papers of the pre-1914 period experienced sizable drops in readership. *Le Journal*'s circulation fell by 50 percent in the interwar period, while *Le Matin* and *Le Petit Journal* experienced drops of closer to 80 percent.[30] This was due partly to wartime impediments to nationwide distribution, which had benefited some provincial titles whose popularity grew in the interwar period. By 1939, half of the ten biggest selling French newspapers were provincial titles—*Ouest-Éclair* (Rennes), *La Petite Gironde* (Bordeaux), *L'Écho de Nord* (Lille), *La Dépêche de Toulouse*, and *Le Réveil du Nord*—although none of these journals could get close to the circulation figures of the two largest Parisian papers (both *Paris-Soir* and *Le Petit Parisien* sold well over a million copies by 1939).[31] The popularity of certain newspapers was also attributable, at least in part, to the changing nature of the medium itself. In interwar France, as elsewhere, newspapers began to shift away from serious politics and toward newer and more glamorous aspects, including fashion, sport, gossip, and, of course, photography.[32]

Nonetheless, this transition was less pronounced in France than elsewhere. *Paris-Soir* was practically alone in seeking to emulate the style and appearance of the British tabloids but enjoyed unparalleled success as a result. When Jean Prouvost bought it in 1930, circulation stood at barely 60,000; by 1939 it had reached well over a million.[33] For the most part, however, French newspapers retained the more serious appearance and approach of the nineteenth-century press. While British newspapers became less politicized in the interwar years, their French equivalents remained, as Chalaby puts it, "directly involved in political struggles."[34] As a result, the social and political fissures that defined 1930s France were played out daily in the press. As d'Almeida and Delporte remark, the press—in combination with the more recent mediums of cinema and radio—acted as a mirror to the "profound social and political mutations of interwar France."[35] The potential threat of foreign powers seeking to use French newspapers to undermine the Republic was also recognized. *L'Humanité*, for example, took great delight in using Russian archives to demonstrate a degree of complicity between the government of Tsarist Russia and certain French newspapers ahead of the First World War . Somewhat ironically, *L'Humanité* itself was censured for being little more than a French mouthpiece for the Kremlin, while into the 1930s the Popular

Front government became increasingly concerned that the German and Italian regimes were exploiting rightist French journals to disseminate propaganda. In these fast-moving times, it was apparent that the media—and newspapers in particular—were still viewed by politicians and diplomats as a potentially decisive means for not only ascertaining but also manipulating popular opinion.

This was especially true of those French newspapers that were overtly representative of specific political interests, if not the biggest selling "populist" titles (notably the two newspapers with the largest circulations by the end of the 1930s, *Paris-Soir* and *Le Petit Parisien*, both of which were predominantly neutral when it came to politics). Elsewhere, the press was heavily politicized and inevitably rather polemical, and may, perhaps, be considered as a valuable echo of the public mood. By the turn of the 1930s, certain prominent journals reflected particular political affiliations. One of the ramifications of the 1919 electoral reforms was that greater political emphasis would henceforth be placed on parties rather than individuals, a development reflected in the press. Small circulation papers that had previously served the interests of individual deputies were rapidly usurped by (considerably fewer) large circulation papers that ostensibly conveyed a party's political position.[36] On the far-left, the communists were represented by *L'Humanité* (and later *Ce Soir*), while trade unionists were represented by *Le Peuple*. On the extreme right, *L'Action française* was undoubtedly influential, a valuable mouthpiece for Charles Maurras and his monarchist and anti-parliamentary movement.

Elsewhere, the weekly *Gringoire* lurched increasingly toward the far-right as the 1930s progressed, while *Je Suis Partout* followed a similar course—not least in espousing a virulent anti-Semitism—culminating in an overtly collaborationist stance during the Second World War. *Le Petit Journal* also represented the extreme right, being used after 1937 for propaganda purposes by Colonel De La Rocque, while *Le Matin* and *Le Jour* exhibited similar proclivities. The socialist SFIO was represented by *Le Populaire*, while the Radical Party had, among others, *L'Œuvre*, *L'Ère nouvelle*, and *La République*. The moderate right was also amply represented, notably by titles such as the *Écho de Paris*, *L'Époque*, *L'Intransigeant*, and *Le Jour*, while *Le Figaro* represented a more moderate monarchist line and *Le Temps* was a centrist paper widely viewed as the quasi-official mouthpiece of the French foreign ministry, the Quai d'Orsay. Other interest groups were also catered for. *La Croix* and *L'Aube* were prominent Catholic journals, while countless other titles represented specific interest groups or constituencies of opinion, not to mention glossy titles based on photojournalism (e.g., *L'Illustration*) and satirical journals like the *Canard enchaîné*.

Although an extensive number of newspapers were available in 1930s France, few achieved anything equating to a genuinely "mass" circulation, and those that got close were demonstrably less political. In addition, estimates of circulation figures often reveal a discernible drop toward the end of the decade.

Circulation of selected French newspapers (1939):

Newspaper	Circulation
Paris-Soir	1,739,584
Le Petit Parisien	1,022,401
Le Journal	411,021
L'Ouest-Éclair	350,000*
L'Humanité	349,587
La Petite Gironde	325,000*
Le Matin	312,597
L'Echo du Nord	300,000*
Ce Soir	262,547
La Dépêche de Toulouse	260,000*
L'Œuvre	236,045
Le Réveil du Nord	200,000*
Le Jour-Echo de Paris	183,844
Le Petit Journal	178,327
Le Populaire	157,837
La Croix	140,000*
L'Intransigeant	134,462
Le Figaro	80,604
L'Epoque	80,000*
Le Temps	68,556
L'Action française	45,000*
Le Peuple	16,000*
L'Aube	14,000*
L'Ordre	12,000*
L'Ere nouvelle	4,000*

*Denotes an estimate where actual figures are not available.

All figures taken from Pierre Albert, "La presse française de 1871 à 1940," in Bellanger et al, *Histoire générale de la presse française*, tome III, p. 511, p. 604.

The figures above, from 1939, reveal a substantial decrease from mid-decade. Chalaby has suggested that, in 1936, the circulation of *Le Petit Parisien* was 1,400,000, compared to the figure of just over one million cited above. Among those papers that adopted a more far-right opinion as the decade progressed, a decline in sales was even more pronounced; Chalaby estimates that *Le Matin* sold 680,000 copies daily in 1936, *Le Petit Journal* 225,000 copies, and *L'Action française* 200,000 copies. Albert's figures for 1939 show a marked drop for all three titles, indicative, perhaps, of a public disenchanted by fractious political debate, or simply beguiled by exciting new mediums—such as radio and cinema newsreels—for their regular dose of news and information.

Whatever the reasons, both contemporary policymakers and subsequent generations of historians have succumbed to the temptation to view French newspapers—in all their political diversity—as a relatively accurate mirror of the public mood. However, as Pierre Albert warns, even a heavily politicized press, like that of the French Third Republic, could not simply shape the opinions of its readership, hence the historian has a "thankless task" in seeking to elucidate its precise influence on public opinion. This influence is confused further by the fact that newspapers, in order to be economically viable, were susceptible to control and coercion from interested financial parties.[37] Unlike in Britain, where the press had become subject to market forces compelling newspapers to favor populism over political content, the cartel-like nature of the French press left it highly susceptible to political interference. The use of newspapers to act as a mouthpiece for a particular political agenda raises the issue of "media capture," defined by Bignon and Flandreau as efforts made by government, politicians, and corporate interests to "extract personal benefits from controlling newspapers."[38]

Such corruption was nothing new; prior to the Great War, the Third Republic's permissive attitude toward press freedom had resulted in newspapers relying heavily on the political and financial spheres for funding and finance. As Chalaby notes, the government used the press to "protect its interests," parties used it to "publicise their opinions," and politicians to "promote their careers." Many prominent newspapers also received monies from foreign countries, including prominent titles like *Le Temps*, *Le Matin*, and the news agency Havas. It has been suggested, therefore, that the French press was not only corrupted by French political and corporate interests but also vulnerable to bribes from the Italian, Greek, Spanish, Soviet, and Nazi governments.[39] Concerns arising from such "media capture" feature prominently in the wider historiography of interwar France; Marc Bloch famously apportioned part of the blame for France's 1940 defeat on a corrupt media, a view echoed in subsequent years by prominent historians such as Jean-Noël Jeanneney.[40] With regard to public opinion, this cultivated a residual representation of a divided, fractured, and decadent society that contributed to France's diplomatic responses to the fascist threat.

Gauging Public Opinion: Emergent Mediums

Various attempts *were* undertaken throughout the 1930s to restrict the pervasiveness of internal and external corruption of the French press, illustrating how policymaking elites were conscious of the potentially harmful ramifications of unwelcome propaganda on a malleable and vulnerable public opinion. There was a growing awareness in all Western countries during the interwar period that public opinion was not only a factor that had to be accounted for in the decision-making process but also one that was susceptible to manipulation, as was being demonstrated by France's totalitarian neighbors. New mediums, notably radio, could be harnessed for such purposes. Jeanneney has identified four instances during the decade that illustrated emphatically the effective use of radio by authoritarian regimes. First, in the early years of the 1930s, the Japanese had installed loudspeakers in public spaces throughout occupied Manchuria in order to broadcast publicly their propagandistic message. Second, the Nazis had used broadcasts in Austria to undermine the Dolfuss government ahead of his assassination in 1934 and continued to air pro-German messages up to the 1938 Anschluss. Third, in response to the imposition of League sanctions following Italy's invasion of Abyssinia, Mussolini sanctioned the use of radio broadcasts in ten languages (including Arabic and Turkish) across North Africa and the Levant in a bid to undermine British and French colonial authority in these regions. And, finally, Franco won the "radio propaganda war" during the civil war in Spain, enjoying greater control of the airwaves in Spain and parts of North Africa than his Republican adversaries.[41]

Radio sets had become increasingly affordable by the 1930s, resulting in more people, in all Western countries, becoming regular listeners. France was no exception, with the number of radio sets increasing from 5,000 at the end of the 1920s to over 5 million by the end of the 1930s.[42] During the 1920s, radio was largely the domain of the amateur enthusiast, and the French government was initially content to allow private enterprise a free hand in the development of the medium. However, as the power and reach of the radio became more apparent, successive French governments sought to take greater control of the airwaves, resulting in an industry that was neither predominantly commercial (as was the case in the United States) nor predominantly state-sanctioned (as occurred in Britain with the dominance of the BBC). In 1923 an early attempt at regulation ostensibly gave the French state complete control of the airwaves, but in reality, licenses were given to private stations allowing them to continue broadcasting.[43] In 1926 the *ministère des postes, télégraphes et téléphones* was established, but given that private radio stations had taken root in the preceding years, it proved impossible to establish a state monopoly. A law was passed in 1928 limiting the total number of permitted radio stations to 26, to be divided fifty-fifty between public and private enterprises.[44] As Raymond Kuhn has remarked, this resulted in a "coexistence of both private and public radio stations operating at the local and regional levels."[45]

The staggering growth of radio during the 1930s soon alerted politicians to its potential to reach a wider public. A pivotal moment in the history of French radio came during the 1932 legislative elections, when the premier André Tardieu broadcast an electoral speech over the airwaves for the first time. In the eyes of Tardieu's leftist opponents—notably the socialist Léon Blum—this appropriation of radio was both shameless and cynical, leading to the insistence that the platform provided by radio be available to all parties in subsequent election campaigns.[46] At the same time, the 1930s witnessed greater efforts by the French authorities to control the airwaves, especially the public stations which, after 1933, were funded by a license fee rather than advertising. Control over the dissemination of news was increasingly seen as a matter of national importance, especially in light of the events of February 1934. At the time, only 15 percent of the French population were radio listeners, still too little, notes Cécile Méadel, to have a discernible impact on events as they unfolded. Nevertheless, the ideologically motivated battles on the streets of Paris on February 6, 1934, provided an early example of radio "news" being relied upon as a source of information.[47]

This new medium was quickly recognized as being potentially dangerous. On February 4, the interior minister, Eugène Frot, installed a censor to work alongside the Parisian radio journalists in an effort to water down the information that would be relayed.[48] Clearly, the potential of radio to unsettle and inflame public opinion—or even exacerbate tensions within opinion that already existed—was acknowledged. It also played a part in stoking fears of what the "next" war might look like, emphasizing the potential horrors of aerial bombardment. Radio, according to Crémieux-Brilhac, "played its part in the pacifist concert" in the mid-1930s by giving a "primetime" platform to pacifist intellectuals like Georges Pioch and Henri Pichot.[49] At the same time, the 1936 elections (which ushered in a Popular Front administration) were the first in which radio was genuinely politicized. Furthermore, in the early weeks of the Popular Front government, a distributors' strike caused a brief hiatus in the supply of newspapers. Denied their usual source of news, the French turned to the radio.[50] With regard to matters of foreign affairs and diplomacy, radio came of age in France at the end of the decade, especially once Édouard Daladier became the president of the council in April 1938. Daladier, though not a "natural" on the airwaves, nonetheless recognized its potential to reach the masses. Throughout his premiership he would take to the air on numerous occasions, chiefly to overcome domestic fissures and to galvanize a previously fractured French populace behind a more robust foreign policy. It is unsurprising that Daladier soon assumed a reputation as the "homme de radio."[51]

Another form of media worthy of consideration is the cinema, and particularly the cinema newsreel. France was, of course, a pioneer in the motion picture industry, and newsreels had appeared routinely in French cinemas since the early twentieth century, companies like "Pathé-Journal" and "Société Léon Gaumont" at the forefront.[52] It is important to note, too, that cinema attendance rose substantially between 1934 and 1938, one estimate suggesting an increase in ticket revenue of 45 percent (largely at the expense of theater)[53], indicating how more and more French people were exposed to this new medium. At the same time, in spite of these technological advances, the old-fashioned expression of opinion that was the popular demonstration remained prominent in 1930s France, especially on the political left. As Jessica Wardhaugh reminds us, the left was wedded to the notion of militant working people functioning as a collective, constituting a "rational crowd"; the political right, by contrast, was more suspicious of what might be considered an unruly and emotionally volatile mob.[54] Advocates of a Popular Front were certainly keen to use "the crowd" as an expression of the popular will. Carefully orchestrated demonstrations, both in Paris and in the provinces, were a staple of the early Popular Front, participation affording the demonstrators a voice and a platform as well as a sense of community and belonging, where the "gesture of the raised fist was a symbol of resolution and unity."[55]

Of course, such popular and collective expressions of opinion were not always positive or benign. The Popular Front government that came to power in 1936 was immediately undermined by industrial action and factory occupations, exacerbating fears in rightist circles of communist infiltration and possible revolution. This febrile atmosphere of ideologically driven partisan hostility was only heightened in July when civil war erupted in Spain. Although it would be an exaggeration to claim that France was on the cusp of its own civil war, the risks of more severe and violent civil strife were not entirely fabricated.[56] In terms of representations of public opinion, this *would* have influenced policymakers. Industrial unrest, demonstrations on the street, the visibly politicized and partisan nature of much of the French press—all were manifestations of the *volonté générale* that could not fail to permeate the consciousness of those in power. Indeed, the fear of a civil war erupting in France played a pivotal role in Léon Blum's decision to adopt a policy of non-intervention in Spain.[57] Mass action, or the broader role of the crowd, was not limited to political demonstrations and industrial action, nor to the rituals associated with particular dates (May 1, July 14, November 11, etc.). It also manifested itself more spontaneously, as shown by the vast crowds that gathered in Paris in 1938 to welcome Daladier back from Munich, lining the streets from Le Bourget to the War Ministry. Where other, more politically oriented gatherings were overwhelmingly male, the crowds in late September 1938 were notable for the prominence of women; Daladier was particularly struck (and certainly not unmoved) by the number of young mothers thrusting their babies toward him as his car passed.[58] The number of densely attended religious services through September 1938 was another indication of how far the French public was animated by the growing threat of war as the Sudeten crisis intensified.[59] Another spontaneous expression of popular opinion was the crowd that gathered to welcome Neville Chamberlain to Paris in November 1938, the prominent participation of women again arousing comment.[60]

But if this manifestation of opinion seemed to indicate support for Chamberlain's energetic pursuit of appeasement, responses to Italian claims for "Tunis, Corsica, and Nice" in late November were suggestive of a desire to embrace firmness. Britain's ambassador to Paris, Sir Eric Phipps, reported an amusing procession of Sorbonne students marching along "the Boulevard St. Michel shouting for Sardinia, 'Venice pour nos amoureuses' and Vesuvius."[61] Similarly, French ministers including Jean Zay and César Campinchi feared that Parisians might take to the street to protest the visit to the capital, in early December 1938, of Joachim von Ribbentrop for the signing of the Franco-German Declaration.[62] The prominent journalist Geneviève Tabouis recalled the "rather amusing" police preparations for the German foreign minister's visit, the authorities fearing that the "people might be hostile," and might even subject Ribbentrop to physical assault.[63] In the aftermath of Munich, it seemed, French opinion was divided but increasingly exhibiting a lack of patience with the methods of the dictators.

These diverging expressions of popular opinion coincided with a general strike called by French trade unionists for November 30, but a firm governmental response saw the industrial action end in failure.[64] Daladier's uncompromising stance toward the strikes was a further example of his determination to convey a different image of France to that which had prevailed for much of the 1930s, replacing discord and unrest with unity and hard work. To this end, the *Président du Conseil* harnessed the media, not only the radio and newspapers but also newsreels to reach both a domestic and international audience. Themes of imperial grandeur and French military preparedness were designed to reassure an anxious public, while themes of French resistance to Italian territorial demands and the solidification of Franco-British amity were used to project an impression of French resolve and trustworthiness overseas.[65] A notable example of how France's military capabilities were lauded was an award-winning 1938 Pathé documentary, commissioned and funded by the government, called "Somme-nous défendus?" the answer to the question posed being an emphatic "yes."

These more positive motifs also cropped up in some of the more popular feature films of the late 1930s. Although pacifist-tinged films like *La Grande Illusion* (1937) and *Paix sur le Rhin* (1938), or films depicting social fragmentation and decadence like *Le jour se lève* (1939) or *Le règle du jeu* (1939) are better known today, it was often films with more upbeat messages of military might (e.g., *Le Double Crime sur la Ligne Maginot* (1937), and *Trois Artilleurs au Pensionnat* (1937)) and imperial prestige (including *L'Appel du Silence* (1936)) that performed most impressively at the box office.[66] This is not to say, however, that the impact of these films was uniformly positive. Elizabeth Grottle Strebel suggests that they helped to "foster a certain complacency, a Maginot mentality," the government-sanctioned films in particular presenting "a highly romanticised view" of military realities. "In every possible way," she concludes, "French cinema of the period contributed to a defeatist mentality, to a psychological acceptance of the Munich agreement and to the 1940 defeat." Charles Rearick offers a similar, albeit less dogmatic assessment, noting how, in spite of the plethora of films that sought to reassure an anxious public, "the French did not come together in a patriotic *union sacrée*" in 1940.[67]

Such verdicts, however, fail to account for the clear movement of public opinion away from appeasement and toward firmness in the post-Munich period. This evolution in public sentiment was seized upon by Daladier in his efforts to augment governmental control of radio, cinema, and the printed press via a series of decree laws in 1939. In July 1939, he had even initiated the creation of a propaganda ministry.[68] Though not without controversy, these actions had results. By ensuring that the French people accepted war in 1939, and ensuring further that a solidified Franco-British entente was in place when war came, Daladier deserves credit for overseeing a "revival" of positive and upbeat representations of French opinion. To be sure, political and press opinion in Britain increasingly "applauded the French people for choosing unity and discipline over petty squabbling and insubordination."[69] That French opinion endorsed the direction of Daladier's policies—both domestically and internationally—can be adduced from the few polls conducted by the IFOP prior to the Second World War. Though 57 percent of respondents in October

1938 approved of the Munich Accords (only 37 percent disapproved), some 70 percent still indicated that France and Britain must henceforth resist any further demands from Nazi Germany. Questions posed by the IFOP about foreign affairs between Munich and the summer of 1939 indicated growing popular support for firmness; in July, 76 percent stated that France should forcibly resist any German attempt to seize Danzig. The poll results—though fragmentary and sometimes even contradictory—confirm a considerable movement of French opinion toward a policy of resisting Hitler. As Christel Peyrefitte concludes, the price to be paid for this movement was war, and the respondents to the polls knew it.[70]

France in an Era of Fascist Expansionism

The 1930s was, for France, a particularly turbulent decade, both domestically and internationally. At home, the country was hit hard (albeit quite late) by the economic repercussions of the 1929 Wall Street Crash, which compounded further existing political and social tensions. The broader ideological struggle between left and right that was affecting the entire continent was pronounced in France, played out most clearly in the tumultuous events of *6 février 1934*. Pitched battles in the streets of Paris between partisans of the far-right *Ligues* on the one side and card-carrying communists on the other illustrated graphically the domestic schisms afflicting the nation as a whole. The Stavisky scandal was seized upon by a sensationalist press to stoke further these domestic fires, which inevitably had repercussions in the political sphere. French governments came and went throughout the 1930s, successive premiers struggling to hold together for a long a cohesive and lasting administration. Newspapers were frequently mobilized for political ends, creating a febrile atmosphere of disunity and mutual suspicion. The economic impact was considerable, as persistent industrial unrest hampered production and dislocated industry. When the British journalist, Alexander Werth, described in 1935 a "France in ferment," few observers would have disagreed.[71] Another foreign journalist, the American William Shirer, returned to Paris in early 1934 to find that "rancour and intolerance poisoned the air."[72]

The social dimension cannot, of course, be understood in isolation from the tumultuous diplomatic developments that accompanied them. In particular, the advent of the Nazis in Germany was an enormous concern to a country that had spent the previous fifteen years trying to shore up its security against its "hereditary enemy." After all, under Hitler, German intentions were made clear; a Conseil Supérieur de la Guerre note warned in August 1933 that the Nazi government had "scarcely hidden its desire to return to the policies of expansion . . . and to establish hegemony over Europe, [and that it would] impose its will with a policy of force . . . as soon as it has gained clear military superiority."[73] France's fixation on security was an area of consensus in an otherwise fractured society, but there was less unity when it came to the issue of disarmament. The rightist press—from moderate journals to those espousing far-right positions— uniformly rejected any reduction of French armaments without enhanced security guarantees first being obtained, a stance echoed in the political sphere. Indeed, only the socialists and communists advocated unconditional disarmament. As Thomas Davis has remarked, the violent infiltration of a pro- disarmament rally in the Trocadéro by the far-right illustrated the strength of feeling on that side of the political fence.[74]

Some in France simply hoped that the Nazi problem would disappear as quickly as it had arisen,[75] but it soon became apparent that Hitler's presence would not be ephemeral. In this context, the French people demanded "*sécurité*" more than ever. French politicians were certainly afforded little latitude when negotiating at the Geneva Disarmament Conference. The British noted in August 1933 that the then-premier Édouard Daladier "was bound by the whole force of French parliamentary and public opinion [which] requires him either to produce a stormproof disarmament convention or to take steps to maintain French superiority in arms. For French opinion there is no via media between these two courses."[76] Yet, initially, the French public appeared relatively sanguine about developments across the Rhine. On the one hand, the people were preoccupied with domestic economic concerns and political scandals, while the preceding German governments of Von Papen and Von Schleicher had already awakened the French to a revived militarist spirit in Germany.[77] But Hitler was different. Germany walked out of both the Geneva Disarmament Conference and the League of Nations with much fanfare in October 1933, in the process transforming an ominously troubling situation into a decidedly dangerous one. Could a divided France muster a meaningful response? If so, how far was this diplomatic response conditioned by popular opinion?

After all, French concern with security against Germany was heightened after Hitler came to power, and was by no means confined to political and military circles. Robert Soucy's analysis of French press reactions to Hitler's first two years in power show that the brutality of Nazism *was* made abundantly clear across newspapers of all stripes. Soucy suggests that this alienated many in

France who might otherwise have succumbed to fascist ideology, thus (in part) explaining why French fascism itself lacked the degree of purchase experienced in some other countries.[78] Soucy acknowledges that the French press, beholden as it frequently was to financial backers or particular political agendas, cannot be taken as a marker of "public opinion," but contends that whilst newspaper readers "were not passive recipients of a newspaper's ideology," they were not "immune" to the messages conveyed.[79] Messages pertaining to the Nazi peril assumed an added urgency in 1935 as the Führer's efforts to subvert the Versailles order became more daring. On March 16, Berlin announced formally that rearmament would commence, including the introduction of conscription allowing for a standing peacetime army of 550,000 men. This development naturally alarmed the French, but there was no immediate articulation of fury or fear. As Alexander Werth remarked, the announcement prompted "more annoyance than surprise."[80] Indeed, clandestine German rearmament had been going on for some time, and the French knew it—Hitler was only doing so more brazenly.[81] Furthermore, responses were conditioned by ideological alignments. The communist Maurice Thorez was adamant that France's response must *not* include extending the duration of their own military service. "We cannot allow anything that might lead the French working class into a war under the guise of defending democracy against fascism," he insisted, claiming that they would use all means at their disposal to campaign against the imposition of an "imperialist war."[82] Such statements exposed the French to charges of pacifism and appeasement: writing in *Le Temps*, Wladimir d'Ormesson lamented the "monstrous alliance . . . of the die-hard pacifists [on the French left] and the most extravagant Prussian militarism. Ten million human lives and western civilization will pay for it."[83]

The growth of Germany's military potential was exacerbated further by the signing in June 1935 of the Anglo-German Naval Agreement (allowing for a sizable expansion of Germany's naval prowess) and, earlier in the year, Germany's public announcement of the existence of an already strong and rapidly growing Luftwaffe. For many in France, and not just those on the political left, these developments increased the allure of a potential arrangement with Soviet Russia. But, while a possible alignment with Russia was diplomatically and militarily expedient, it was fraught with difficulties. Jean-Baptiste Duroselle has identified four strands of French public opinion as the nation contemplated an arrangement with Moscow. First, the communists unsurprisingly endorsed an unconditional *rapprochement*; second, the pacifist left embraced an alliance if only for pragmatic reasons; third, the moderate right distrusted the Soviets but hesitatingly acknowledged the realist arguments for an alliance given events in Germany; and fourth, the right-wing *irréconciliables* remained staunchly and dogmatically hostile. Louis Barthou, who had replaced Daladier as president of the Council, was, suggests Duroselle, attentive to the public mood, conscious that "a vast majority" supported a rapprochement with Russia. Public opinion did not force his hand, contends Duroselle, but it certainly encouraged Barthou in the direction of the Franco-Soviet Pact.[84]

France not only looked to the Russians for enhanced security against Germany but, in 1935, also had an arrangement of sorts with the Italians and the British courtesy of the Stresa Front. For the French right, unsettled by the prospect of a Soviet alignment, this offered a more palatable response to the Nazi menace. *Le Temps* was effusive in praising Stresa for confirming the "absolute solidarity" of Paris, London, and Rome, while *Le Petit Parisien* applauded the "impression of calm power."[85] Stresa was, however, a short-lived effort to revive the troika of Locarno guarantors. Almost immediately it was undermined by France's diplomatic flirtation with Soviet Russia, Britain's unilateral decision to negotiate the Anglo-German Naval Agreement, and Italian adventurism in Abyssinia. The latter had a profound impact on public opinion. Details of the Hoare–Laval plan (which amounted essentially to giving Italy two-thirds of Abyssinia) were leaked to the Parisian press on December 9, provoking partisan press and popular responses and ultimately leading to the fall of Pierre Laval's government.[86] These events did little to reassure a French public that was already becoming increasingly nervous about the international climate. It was clear by 1936 that the initial uncertainty that had marked French public reactions to the advent of German Nazism had morphed into an acute and growing anxiety. In March, Hitler undertook his next gamble by remilitarizing the Rhineland, in flagrant contravention of the terms of Versailles and the spirit of Locarno. Diplomatically, France's response was of almost legendary passivity. How far should governmental timidity be ascribed to a "pacifist" population? Did a French public unready for war and unwilling to fight really dictate such a muted reaction?

It has been contended that French passivity in response to the Rhineland remilitarization can be explained, in large part, "by a pacifist sentiment, more or less avowed, that had permeated almost every section of opinion."[87] Of course, France's response was also conditioned by military and strategic calculations, chief of staff Maurice Gamelin warning that any such action must be undertaken *either* under the auspices of the League *or* in conjunction with the other Locarno guarantors (Italy and Great Britain).[88] Even if these considerations were paramount, French public opinion offered little imperative to pursue an alternative course. Duroselle contends that this episode occasioned a rare display of French public unity, the French people being uniformly "amazed and frightened," their attitude encapsulated by the slogan "Above all, no war!"[89] This unanimity can be attributed to a brief juxtaposition of "pacifist" sentiment on both sides of the political spectrum. Many on the political left were animated by a traditional, doctrinal pacifism, and while the events of 1936 challenged these convictions, they were still widely held at the time of the Rhineland incident. At the same time, there was a move toward what Charles Micaud has labeled a "neo-pacifism" on the political right, less a doctrinal opposition to war and more a pro-appeasement mindset rooted in anti-communism.[90] Julian Jackson is right to warn against oversimplification, as this did not mean that the right became anti-war while the left gravitated toward bellicosity: "Both sides were now divided," concludes Jackson, and particularly the left.[91]

It is vital to avoid seeing the public and press reaction as being uniformly in favor of passivity. Sections of the press presented a more upbeat appraisal of France's overall strategic position. The *Dépêche de Toulouse* even portrayed the Rhineland remilitarization as a setback for Germany, at the same time seeking to celebrate France's military potency.[92] Nonetheless, an allegedly pacifist public provided a convenient scapegoat for France's submissiveness. One contemporary politician recalled in his memoirs that the "immense majority" of public, press, and parliamentary opinion was opposed to a forcible response to the Rhineland remilitarization, with most French people simply thinking that German troops were merely returning to German territory.[93] For both the French and the British, it was convenient to attribute their diplomatic meekness, at least in part, to the anti-war sentiment of the people they represented. At the same time, each blamed the other when justifying their passivity to their publics. As Richard Davis contends, both London and Paris were "only too willing to present their ally to their public opinion as the ones who had made it impossible to adopt a policy of firmness."[94] For the French, the Rhineland incident further highlighted the prevalence of domestic discord. "Rather Hitler than Blum" was a common refrain on the French right during March 1936 and would continue to be heard during the election campaign that culminated in the formation of a Popular Front administration headed by the socialist Léon Blum, in May. And before this, in January 1936 when debating the ratification of the Franco-Soviet Pact, most rightist deputies voted against, because, as Jackson puts it, "their growing fear of Communism in France was starting to dilute their hereditary suspicion of Germany."[95]

France's political polarization also affected their response to the civil war in Spain. Logically, France's Popular Front government should support the democratically elected *Frente Popular* administration across the Pyrenees, yet Blum opted for non-intervention. There were sound diplomatic and strategic reasons for doing so. The British were particularly anxious to avoid meddling, and both London and Paris did not want to allow the Spanish conflagration to escalate into a continent-wide war. But another possible explanation for non-intervention speaks explicitly to the impact of a divided French public—fear of civil war in France. Indeed, in a letter to his wife in 1942, Blum himself cited this as an explanation. "Before any foreign war," he insisted, "France would have had civil war, with precious little chance for a victory for the Republic."[96] Conscious of the escalating demands in leftist circles for intervention, Blum addressed a socialist gathering at Luna Park on September 6, telling his audience that he would "do everything to avert war for this country." As Alexander Werth noted, Blum's words had a "curious effect" on his listeners because he had "touched the most vulnerable spot in any Frenchman's heart—the fear of another war."[97]

This fear—perhaps characterized more accurately as an "anxiety"[98]—was amplified in the interwar period by technological advances in warfare (notably in aviation and the use of poison gas) which meant that in a future war all civilians, men, women, and children alike, would be on the front line. What the next war might look like was brought into sharper focus in 1937 when the German Luftwaffe unleashed a brutal aerial assault against the historic Basque city of Guernica. Media coverage—not only words in newspapers but also the striking visual imagery of the aftermath of the raid shown in newsreels and photographs—augmented an apprehension about the "next" war that was already firmly ingrained in the French psyche. It was widely held that the French would suffer greatly should another war come. As Robert Young has noted: "French literature on the subject of an air war rarely used Berlin as a figurative example of an air target. Rather, the French used Tours, or Dijon, or Reims, or, especially Paris."[99] Robert Paxton goes further, noting: "War meant poison gas and the bombing of cities. Paris would be worse than Guernica."[100] France's particular vulnerability to aerial attack also permeated military and diplomatic elites, their fears augmented by an acute awareness of France's own aerial limitations. This was evident at the time of the 1938 Munich Crisis, when Daladier was doubtless swayed considerably to accept the British-led abandonment of Czechoslovakia by appreciations of the aerial balance of power that were "more pessimistic than normal."[101]

But before Czechoslovakia came to dominate the international agenda in the summer of 1938, Hitler executed another diplomatic coup by incorporating into the greater German Reich his homeland of Austria. The Anschluss, though another flagrant violation of the Versailles Treaty, triggered only token protests from the Western democracies. In fact, France was actually without a government when it happened. In his memoirs, the former premier (and former Vichy minister) Pierre-Étienne Flandin, suggests that France's diplomatic impotence at this juncture owed much to the French public. The French people, he suggested, full of "dreams of universal peace [and] illusions of collective security" were simply unwilling to accept the sacrifices that were necessary to "restore civil discipline" and recapture a lost patriotism. "The foreign policy of France," he concluded, "suffered the consequences of the failure of its people."[102] Flandin's memoirs are, of course, flagrantly self-exculpatory, and his apparent frustration at France's inaction over the Anschluss is hypocritical given his own passivity at the time of the Rhineland remilitarization. Still, there can be little doubt that French public opinion accepted the Anschluss as a fait accompli and was unwilling to resist Hitler's latest coup forcibly. Within the press, only *L'Époque* on the right and *L'Humanité* on the left criticized the French government for its meekness.[103]

After the Anschluss, it was clear that Hitler would turn his attention toward the Sudeten areas of Czechoslovakia, positioning himself as the savior of the German-speaking peoples there who were suffering under the oppressive and persecutory policies of their Czech overlords. By the time the Sudeten "crisis" intensified over the summer, internal politics once again took center stage. Édouard Daladier formed a new government in April 1938, but his efforts to distance his administration from its Popular Front predecessors succeeded only in inciting a new wave of widespread industrial unrest that would have diplomatic ramifications. Although Daladier habitually stated over the summer of 1938 that France was resolved to support its Czechoslovakian ally, the country's domestic fragility undermined his assertive posturing. This was undermined further by Britain's determination to resolve the Sudeten crisis through appeasement. After all, as Yvon Lacaze's voluminous study of French public opinion has demonstrated, a divided people could at least agree on one thing: France could do nothing independently of the British.[104]

A further reason for toeing the British line of appeasement was Daladier's choice of foreign minister, Georges Bonnet. Bonnet, like Daladier, was a war veteran, but while Daladier's experiences of the 1914–18 war had left him committed to the cause of French *sécurité*, Bonnet's experiences had instilled in him a visceral pacifism and horror of war.[105] He also exhibited a degree of the "looking glass" mentality by appearing convinced that the majority of his countrymen and women shared his views, and would despair should France be plunged into war over the Sudeten issue. As he told the journalist Geneviève Tabouis: "If war comes, there will be a revolution, and the people will throw me into the river."[106] Bonnet's perceptions were not without merit. As the Sudeten crisis intensified over September, press opinion indicated that there was a far greater appetite for peace than there was for war. Several newspapers (*La République, La Liberté, Le Matin,* and the *Jour-Écho de Paris*) echoed the stance famously articulated in an editorial in the London *Times* on September 7, 1938, advocating that the Sudeten areas be ceded to Germany. Chamberlain's visits to Germany, to speak to Hitler in person in a desperate bid to stave off war, were generally applauded by French opinion. As in Britain, there was a hardening of opinion after Hitler increased his demands during his discussions with Chamberlain at Bad Godesberg on September 22–23, but this proved ephemeral, news of the Munich Conference being welcomed with considerable relief. Even Léon Blum, in the socialist *Le Populaire,* shared this sentiment, describing Munich as "an armful of tinder thrown into the sacred hearth at the very moment the flame had fallen and threatened to go out."[107]

Further indications of the French public's desire to avoid conflict came in the form of petitions and appeals. A notable example was the joint appeal of *La Fédération Postale* and the *Syndicat national des instituteurs,* containing nearly 84,000 signatures collected in just three days, urging Daladier to resolve the crisis peacefully. Such manifestations of public opinion were a further reason to avoid confrontation with Germany, adding to military considerations (not least France's relative aerial weaknesses) and diplomatic isolation (given Britain's steadfast determination to appease). As one minister, Anatole de Monzie, acknowledged, these appeals added to the "expectations and emotions" of the policymakers, coaxing them toward negotiation rather than resistance.[108] This is not to say that the French people were quivering in the face of imminent war. There were, after all, relatively few signs of panic even when war appeared inevitable. A partial mobilization was carried out with minimal disturbance and unrest, and though many people opted to leave Paris, it was by no means an exodus, and calmness prevailed.[109] But there was certainly no determination to stand by Prague and fight a war in denial of Sudeten self-determination. Daladier thus went to Munich in a glum and somber mood, spoke there of French honor and obligations, but ultimately signed the agreement that amounted to the abandonment of the Czechoslovakians.

The *Président du Conseil* was undoubtedly unhappy, even ashamed, at the Munich outcome. However, he was feted as a hero on his return to Paris. The defining image of his return to the French capital is one of streets brimming with joyous crowds, an instinctive and unfettered emotional response to having been spared the bloody catastrophe of war. Above all, the Parisians were eternally thankful for what Sartre labeled *Le Sursis*. As Fleury notes, "The reaction of the great majority of public opinion in France was one of extreme relief."[110] This thankfulness was echoed in the subsequent Chamber debate and vote, with 515 supporting the Munich accords and just 75 (including 73 communist deputies) dissenting. On October 3, the day after the Chamber debate, the archbishop of Paris, Cardinal Verdier, led a service at Notre Dame giving thanks for the maintenance of peace, in scenes that were echoed in similar masses across France.[111] The popular press appeared to confirm that the overriding sentiment was one of thankfulness. The Radical newspaper *L'Œuvre* reported on October 4, 1938, that it had received 4,555 letters expressing approval for Daladier's Munich policy against just 193 articulating opposition.[112] The *Paris-Soir* launched an (ultimately unsuccessful) campaign to fund the purchase of a "peace house" for Mr. and Mrs. Chamberlain near Biarritz in acknowledgment of their role in averting war; the *Petit Parisien* opened a *livre d'or* and claimed that more than a million people had signed their names to voice approval of the Munich diplomacy.[113] Numerous campaigns were launched to rename streets in honor of Daladier and Chamberlain, and a new dance craze—the *Chamberlaine*— swept through Paris in the immediate aftermath of the reprieve.[114] Even Georges Bonnet was feted, the *Petit Parisien* offering him the *Grand Livre de la Paix* containing more than 350,000 signatures offering tribute on behalf of those "who are eternally grateful for [Bonnet's] tireless efforts in September 1938 to save the Peace."[115]

Despite these indicators, French opinion at the time of Munich was far from uniform. Opinion polls, though in their infancy, paint a more nuanced picture than that gleaned from the press and a one-sided parliamentary debate. The data shows that the French public was divided over Munich, perhaps vindicating the apprehension that Daladier felt on his return from Germany. IFOP polls from October 1938 show a small majority (57 percent) approving the accords, against 37 percent expressing disapproval. These results suggest that the French nation was far more divided over Munich than other indicators would have us believe. These early polls are, however, fraught with problems. As Christel Peyrefitte has noted, we cannot be sure *who* was polled, whether these were people in the Paris region or further afield. We also do not know whether the responses were solicited *before* or *after* the parliamentary vote, or whether the political affiliation or allegiance of the respondents was known and accounted for.[116]

However imperfect the early French opinion polls, other sources confirm what they tell us about the evolution of French public opinion after Munich. A vital lesson of Munich had been that French military weaknesses had contributed to the capitulation. A *redressement* was needed, and this was recognized not only in political circles but also in the press. *L'Intransigeant* and *Paris-Soir* were just two prominent papers that campaigned in October 1938 for the urgent strengthening of the French air force.[117] The sentiment grew that the price paid for the Munich reprieve was too high and, moreover, that it was only an ephemeral reprieve—few shared Chamberlain's confident conviction that "peace for our time" was secured. Although Chamberlain continued to win plaudits in France (demonstrated clearly by the warm reception he received when visiting Paris in late November), there were indications of growing discontent. The Paris police reported demonstrations *against* Chamberlain on the prime minister's arrival at the Gare du Nord resulting in several arrests, while further protestors were arrested for whistling and shouting at Chamberlain's car as it passed through Paris.[118]

At the very least, the autumn of 1938 was marked by a growing disillusionment in France toward the policy of appeasement. An almost unanimous resistance to Italy's ill-considered demands for "Tunis, Corsica, and Nice," coupled with a marked lack of public enthusiasm for the Franco-German Declaration signed on December 6 (a French equivalent of the Anglo-German Agreement that Chamberlain had secured at Munich) indicated that the public was gravitating toward a *politique de fermeté*. Signs that France's internal disorder was being overcome (notably the relative failure of the November 30 general strike) encouraged Daladier to accelerate the reorientation of French diplomatic strategy away from appeasement and toward resistance. At the same time, his government took greater control of the media via a series of decree laws and began to use the media (radio and newsreel in particular) to project a more positive image of French unity and resilience, images designed with both a domestic and international audience in mind.

By the time Hitler made a mockery of the Munich accords by marching into Bohemia and Moravia in mid-March 1939, there was little doubt that French public opinion was determined to avoid further acts of concessionary appeasement. Indeed, the public agitated for the creation of a firmer deterrence, a Churchillian "Grand Alliance" alongside the British and Soviets. For myriad reasons (upon which historians still disagree), such an alliance was not forthcoming, and Germany and the Soviet Union concluded the Molotov–Ribbentrop Pact in August 1939. Despite this, and in spite of the presence in the

French cabinet of several defeatists and waverers, there was little question that France would not honor its obligation to Poland and go to war in September 1939. As in Britain, a minority *would* have favored a negotiated settlement of Hitler's demands on Poland (illustrated by Marcel Déat's infamous "Mourir pour Dantzig?" article in *L'Œuvre* on May 4). But where a sizable majority of public opinion in France had endorsed appeasement in summer 1938, an equally sizable majority was opposed to appeasement in summer 1939.

There was still no consensus—French opinion was never unanimous, whether in response to Abyssinia, the Rhineland remilitarization, the Spanish Civil War, or the Sudeten crisis. Yet, amid the many (and often contrasting) opinions that were expressed, dominant perceptions of opinion often emerged (as was the case at the time of the Rhineland crisis when there were few advocates of war, or in September 1938 when few were willing to countenance war over Czechoslovakia without British support). More importantly, perhaps, when confusion reigned, and a dominant "opinion" was conspicuous by its absence, it was always easier for policymaking elites to choose the path of least resistance, which made passivity and inaction more likely than resistance and assertiveness. For much of the 1930s, French governments were concerned not only that their public was hostile to going to war but also that choosing conflict risked tearing their country apart. By the end of the decade, and especially after Munich, opinion had evolved, in part organically but also as a result of the Daladier government's efforts to control and cultivate it, notably via a more prudent and calculated use of the media. The public did not want war, but it wanted a dishonorable peace even less.

Conclusion

French public opinion in the 1930s was never unitary or homogenous. As this chapter has shown, the French people were divided, often bitterly, along partisan political lines. These divisions certainly affected France's diplomatic prestige. Potential allies and adversaries alike saw a decadent France, its people disillusioned, pacifist, anxious, and demoralized, engrossed in internecine rivalries and entirely ill-prepared to stand united against an existential threat. For potential adversaries like Germany and Italy, this encouraged their pursuit of diplomatic adventurism; for potential allies, notably Great Britain, it eroded confidence in France's strength and vitality and arguably contributed to London's decision to shun collective security and, instead, pursue appeasement. It is easy from this to adhere to the "decadence" thesis, suggesting not only that French public opinion was unwilling to confront the diplomatic threats of the 1930s but also that it was morally conditioned to accept defeat and collaborationism. This conclusion is questionable, failing to account for the unity and resolve exhibited by French public opinion during the final months of peace. Ultimately, France went to war relatively united and with precious little dissent. There was, to be sure, no repetition of the jingoism and enthusiasm of 1914, but there was precious little of this in London either, or even in Berlin.

Charles Taylor's 1940 essay was particularly condemnatory of Daladier's speech to the French Chamber of September 2, 1939, in which, instead of declaring war, the premier deferred "to the opinion of the defeatist minority" by delaying the inevitable for a further twenty-four hours. In so doing, Taylor contends, Daladier missed the chance to rally his people for "a crusade for France and freedom" and, instead, asked them "to support stoically an unavoidable catastrophe."[119] For Taylor, this explained France's lack of dynamism and enthusiasm when war came, a situation that was only exacerbated by the lack of action during the *drôle de guerre* and Daladier's steadfast refusal to heed the public's demands to take more decisive action in favor of Finland during the 1939–40 Winter War. The timidity that had defined France's response to the fascist menace for much of the 1930s was mirrored by a timidity in the early months of the war itself. Furthermore, the passivity of the Phoney War allowed fears of a potential "fifth column," which had been evident in France at least since the Great War, to resurface. Cognizant of Germany's mastery of propaganda, France's own publicity routinely evoked the danger of Nazi spies operating in France. Intended to educate the French public of the need for prudence, it succeeded only in demoralizing an unenthused public even further. As Christian Delporte suggests, "by showing the reality of the Fifth Column, [propaganda] prepared people's minds for the idea of a weakened army, eaten from within."[120]

The arguments of Taylor and Delporte are seductive but ultimately unconvincing. French public opinion *was* divided, and often bitterly, throughout the interwar years and especially the 1930s. It is apparent, too, that the diplomatic tumult of the 1930s affected France profoundly. The emergence of the Nazi threat had coincided with the failure of the Geneva Disarmament Conference and, as the decade progressed, French confidence was shaken further by the fatal weakening of the League of Nations, troubled relations with Italy, uncertainty as to Soviet Russia's reliability, unease at events in Spain, and the persistent inability to work in tandem with Great Britain. The public was also affected by the economic hardships of the depression years, the all-too-frequent ideological skirmishes that sometimes escalated into pitched battles on the streets, and a venal and partisan atmosphere that was stoked by an increasingly politicized and commercially driven press. None of this was helped by a chaotic and unstable political landscape, with a political leadership that often put ideological, party, and personal interests ahead of those of the Republic. Yet, in spite of this, the Third Republic and France's democracy survived the 1930s, even emerging at the end of the decade more resolute and unified than it had been for many years. Public opinion *did* contribute to the trajectory of French diplomacy throughout the 1930s, and must, as a result, shoulder some responsibility for the frequent exhibitions of passivity that weakened France's diplomatic response to the revisionist challenge. But, to adduce from this that public opinion contributed directly to the fall of France is reductionist. France was defeated militarily rather than morally in 1940.

American Public Opinion and the War in Vietnam

Few events of the twentieth century provoke such fierce debate as the Vietnam War. In America in particular, explaining the "lost war" has become a national pastime, each new incursion into the field reigniting long-standing historiographical fault lines. Public interest in Vietnam shows little sign of waning, and the recent documentary produced by Ken Burns and Lynn Novick has ensured that the topic remains prominent not only within America's national consciousness but also globally.[1] The Vietnam War was of considerable public interest from the start, especially after 1965 and the escalation of US involvement in Indochina. It is commonplace to argue that "American public opinion ended the Vietnam War," its role becoming one of the "most pervasive" of the many myths that surround this conflict.[2] The reason for this lies in a revisionist attempt to challenge many orthodox assumptions about the Vietnam War, not least the suggestion that the war was unwinnable from the start. The contention that American public opinion—by turning against the war, undermining the morale of US personnel on the ground, sapping political support for the war on Capitol Hill, providing succor to the North Vietnamese and the Vietcong, and encouraging the growth of a damaging anti-war movement at home—prompted a US defeat suggests, by intimation, that defeat was avoidable.

Thus, a winnable war was lost not on the battlefields of Vietnam but in living rooms the length and breadth of the United States, a rising tide of popular dissent permeating Congress and the White House preventing decision-makers from pursuing the war with the single-minded determination necessary to secure victory. As Melvin Small has suggested, Indochina was not the only battlefield of the Vietnam War; another was on the streets of America where a battle was waged "for the hearts and minds of the American public."[3] Especially after the 1968 Tet Offensive a "credibility gap" emerged. Reportage from Vietnam—including striking images of Vietcong guerrillas entering the grounds of the US embassy in Saigon—flagrantly contradicted the assertions furnished hitherto by the American military and government that victory was in sight. This conviction nourished one of the more enduring arguments regarding America's "lost war": that the crucial loss of public and political support was attributable chiefly to media coverage. Within this argument lies a conviction that public opinion—as manifested by both the American peace movement and the media—prompted a growth in "disillusionment among huge swathes of the American population and necessitated the effective resignation of one president, Lyndon Johnson, and the withdrawal of American forces under his successor, Richard Nixon."[4] Although Andrew Priest considers such an argument "far from accurate," he is right to acknowledge the narrative as being peculiarly pervasive and intoxicating. Priest provides a robust rebuttal, nevertheless, claiming that "the idea that a combination of peaceniks, hippies, Marxists and journalists undermined the American effort and, for the first time in US history, forced the government to rethink its policies and eventually withdraw from a foreign war is outlandish."[5]

With regard to the study of public opinion's influence on foreign policy, the Vietnam conflict was a watershed. As noted in this book's introduction, the Almond–Lippmann consensus prevailed to the 1960s, holding that an emotional and volatile public, poorly informed on issues of diplomacy and lacking sufficient knowledge to impart a valid opinion, needed to be kept at arm's length by those in command of the foreign-policymaking process. Vietnam was *the* event that challenged this consensus. It has been suggested that the public's responses to events in Indochina were rational and informed responses to rising casualty levels and growing elite divisions over the war's prosecution.[6] As a result, a new consensus emerged, contending that the public was a stable and rational foreign policy actor whose opinions deserved to be taken seriously. How politicians interpreted these diverse manifestations of public opinion is not easy to discern. More certain is that political elites took their cues from a plurality of sources. Melvin Small suggests that Presidents Johnson and Nixon "received opinions from the polls, correspondence, friends and acquaintances, Congress, and the media."[7] Given the Vietnam War's reputation as the first "television" war, it is appropriate to start here.

A "Television War?" The Media and the Vietnam War

A famous CBS editorial by America's most respected and trusted anchorman, Walter Cronkite, of February 27, 1968, articulated unambiguously what many Americans already feared—the United States had become embroiled in a quagmire. As Cronkite put it: "To say that we are closer to victory today is to believe, in the face of the evidence, the optimists who have been wrong in the past. To suggest we are on the edge of defeat is to yield to unreasonable pessimism. To say that we are mired in stalemate seems the only realistic, yet unsatisfactory conclusion."[8] The journalist David Halberstam contended years ago that Johnson, on hearing this broadcast, considered it a turning point, "losing" Cronkite being akin to losing "Mr. Average Citizen."[9] In all probability, Johnson never uttered such words, nor did he see Cronkite's broadcast as it aired, but it has become a received wisdom that the editorial affected the president personally and profoundly.[10] The argument is a compelling one. After all, Johnson was highly attentive to media coverage of the war and of himself, as shown by the well-known image of him sitting in the Oval Office watching three television screens—and hence the big three networks, ABC, CBS, and NBC—simultaneously. If unable to watch the broadcasts live, they were often recorded.[11] He also had three television sets in his bedroom at the White House and another "strategically positioned in the bathroom."[12]

Johnson's attentiveness to television coverage tells us a great deal about the relationship between Vietnam and the media: this was the first "television war." Television was certainly a significant game-changer and had come a long way since the end of the Second World War. Nearly two-thirds of American homes obtained a television set between 1948 and 1955, and by 1960 it is estimated that nearly 90 percent of American households owned at least one television, with the average American watching five hours each day.[13] Early evening news programs were particularly popular; surveys suggested that both the CBS Evening News with Walter Cronkite and the NBC Huntley–Brinkley Report reached more than ten million American homes during the early weeks of the Tet Offensive.[14] Furthermore, as Daniel Hallin has noted, numerous surveys suggested that television had become, even by the mid-1960s, Americans' most relied-upon source of foreign news. A 1964 Roper survey indicated that 58 percent "got most of their news" from television, against 56 percent citing newspapers and 26 percent, radio. By 1972, television's preeminence was confirmed, leading newspapers by 64 percent to 50 percent.[15]

For politicians and diplomats, the new televisual landscape took some getting used to. The first presidential election of the television era was the 1952 contest between Adlai Stevenson and Dwight D. Eisenhower, the successful Republicans outspending the Democrats ($2.5 million to $1.2 million) on radio and television campaigning.[16] Thereafter, television's importance only grew; it is estimated that by the 1954 mid-terms, a majority of American voters owned a TV set.[17] By 1960 television was such an established medium that it featured prominently in the presidential election that pitted John F. Kennedy against the Republican candidate Richard Nixon. The now legendary televised debates proved disastrous for Nixon; as the then president of CBS, Frank Stanton, put it after the first debate, "Kennedy was bronzed beautifully . . . Nixon looked like death."[18] The impact of this debate on voter behavior can be questioned, but it contributed to a conviction (and one that continued to grow) that television wielded an unprecedented influence on the public. Arguably the most influential account of the media's role—and one that focused specifically on television—was the notorious article penned by the British-American journalist Robert Elegant, who himself had reported the war for the *Los Angeles Times*. Published in *Encounter* in 1981, Elegant's article was titled, evocatively, "How to Lose a War." He asserted that the "thrusting and simplistic character" of television reportage made it the most "immediate," ensuring that the war in Vietnam "was a presence in homes throughout the world."[19] Elegant claimed further that competition between networks led them to intentionally seek sensationalist stories, often portraying the Americans in a poor light, which in turn eroded popular support for the war in the United States. The veracity of the stories was relatively unimportant; presenting a "great story" was everything.[20] The argument is both straightforward and compelling. "For the first time in modern history," he contended, "the outcome of a war was determined not on the battlefield but on the printed page and, above all, on the television screen." Elegant's assessment was inevitably seized upon by many political and military figures who were adamant that the war had *not* been lost on account of military or strategic failures. It provided a convenient scapegoat, suggesting that the media had robbed the United States of victory. The military war had been won, so the argument went, but "the political pressures built up by the media had made it quite impossible for Washington to maintain even the minimal material and moral support that would have enabled the Saigon regime to continue effective resistance."[21]

General William Westmoreland, Chief of Staff of the US Army, also noted the media's proclivity for sensationalism when reflecting on his efforts in spring 1966 to keep the American people informed of the progress of America's war effort. Addressing a luncheon of the Associated Press (AP) in New York at the Waldorf-Astoria on April 24, and noting on his arrival the anti-war demonstrators gathered outside, Westmoreland declared himself "dismayed" by the "unpatriotic acts" taking place across the United States. As he reflected in his memoirs, this "afterthought" dominated subsequent press coverage of his address, to the detriment of all other content.[22] Television "brought war into the American home," but did so in a "distorted" manner courtesy of its unique need to compress information and be "visually dramatic." Hence controversial and violent coverage, often perpetrated by US personnel, was favored over less spectacular reportage of "pacification, civic action [and] medical assistance."[23] Westmoreland also lamented television's potential ability to undermine public confidence in the war effort. That pressmen seized upon an alleged "credibility gap" did much, in Westmoreland's opinion, to allow the enemy's defeat during Tet to be reconfigured as a "psychological victory" given the images permeating American living rooms of Vietcong guerrillas within the US embassy complex in Saigon.[24] For Westmoreland, all this was compounded by the tendency of the news media, notably television, to lavish "undue attention" on the domestic anti-war movement, affording them a legitimacy and perceived degree of representativeness that was unwarranted.[25] This contention reflects a widely held conviction that television coverage of Vietnam directly affected opinion back home, both political and public. As Hammond suggests, Westmoreland was convinced that negative television coverage (noting Morley Safer's 1965 CBS broadcast from Cam Ne in particular) "could only turn public opinion against the war," inducing Westmoreland to look into ways in which television coverage could be controlled.[26] But did television exert any meaningful influence on the direction and attitudes of American public opinion? This is not easy to answer; as Hammond put it, it is simply "hard to tell."[27] What is easier to tell, however, is that political elites invariably *believed* that television *was* having an effect.

For Richard Nixon, the media's role during the Vietnam War had been deleterious. He lamented in his memoirs how the "American news media had come to dominate domestic opinion," shaping perceptions of American objectives, its military tactics, and the nature of its adversary. The American media, he continued, failed consistently to portray the enemy for who they were—"a particularly ruthless and cruel enemy"—and focused instead on "the failings and frailties" of both the American forces and their South Vietnamese allies. Television, in particular, was singled out, guilty, in Nixon's view, of focusing on "the terrible human suffering and sacrifice of war" and thus fueling a "serious demoralization of the home front."[28] As Small has noted, Nixon shared with Johnson a conviction that television was a significant influence on the principal movers and shakers not only in Washington but across the country. Nixon, however, "approached the problem differently," not least by avoiding reading the newspapers (with the exception of the *Washington Post*) or watching the news broadcasts himself. Anticipating criticism from a hostile and largely liberal media, Nixon simply avoided it.[29] Johnson, however, was preoccupied with his public image. He was anguished, too, by the decisions he had taken at the start of his presidency regarding the war in Vietnam. While many hawkish advisers advocated escalation as the only way of preventing South Vietnam succumbing to communism, Johnson was not unmoved by George Ball's famous counterarguments, prophesying that a long and vicious campaign, accompanied by growing casualties, would prompt an erosion in popular support. Indeed, Johnson was careful to avoid acting too quickly too soon, fearful lest he be perceived as a warmonger.[30] Such concerns would only have intensified as 1965 progressed, as evidence emerged that the media wielded the power to influence opinion in unwelcome ways (at least from a US military and administration perspective). Morley Safer's Cam Ne broadcast (CBS) of August 5 was key. Portraying graphically the kind of operation that Safer described as "Vietnam in miniature," US troops struggled to separate friend from foe and did little to win hearts and minds. Johnson, allegedly, was furious. "Frank, are you trying to *fuck* me?" he asked of CBS president Frank Stanton in a phone call: "Your boys just shat on the American flag."[31]

For Hallin, the Cam Ne incident was illustrative of the peculiar power of television, generating "a major public controversy" even though similar incidents had previously been "reported routinely in the newspapers without any significant reaction."[32] Westmoreland was perturbed by the controversy, asking if anything could be done to control and censor television reporters and other representatives of an expanding media presence. The number of correspondents rocketed in the mid-1960s, from 40 in early 1964 to 282 in January 1966, comprising 110 Americans, 67 South Vietnamese, and the remainder coming from all over the world.[33] Vietnam was a truly global story and the world was watching. Initial restrictions on press coverage were few and far between. In his now legendary *Despatches*, Michael Herr evokes a scene of near anarchic chaos:

> There were people in the military who never forgave General Westmoreland for not imposing restrictions against us when he'd the chance in the early days. There were officers and a lot of seemingly naive troops who believed that if it were not for us, there would be no war now. . . . A lot of the grunts had some of that sly, small-town suspicion of the press, but at least nobody under the rank of captain ever asked me whose side I was on, told me to get with the programme,

jump on the team, come in for the Big Win. Sometimes they were just stupid, sometimes it came about because they had such love for their men, but sooner or later all of us heard one version or another of "My Marines are winning this war, and you people are losing it for us in your papers," often spoken in an almost friendly way, but with the teeth shut tight behind the smiles. It was creepy, being despised in such casual, offhand ways. There were plenty of people who believed, finally, that we were nothing more than glorified war profiteers. And perhaps we were, those of us who didn't get killed or wounded or otherwise fucked up.[34]

Herr recalled how, at the start of the Tet offensive in early 1968 there were some 600–700 correspondents in Vietnam. Most were American, many others were Vietnamese, but a significant number of other nationalities were also there, notably British, French, and Australian. Attaining formal accreditation to cover the war was uncomplicated; journalists simply obtained an accreditation card from the Military Assistance Command, Vietnam (MACV). As Herr notes: "There was nothing exclusive about that card. . . . All they did was admit you to the Vietnam press corps and tell you that you could go out and cover the war if you really wanted to."[35] In short, there was precious little formal control or regulation of *who* was permitted to report on the war, or *what* shape or form their reportage would assume.

That said, the issue of *who* was articulating a viewpoint on the war was important when considering its impact upon wider American opinion. Hence Walter Cronkite's post-Tet intervention was noteworthy. In this context, the debate over whether the media leads or shapes public opinion is unimportant. Whether conveying an existing public unease with the Vietnam War or simply contributing to such uncertainty taking hold and proliferating, the net result was the same. It exacerbated a "credibility gap" that was already emerging, media portrayals of a vibrant and powerful adversary undermining the confident assertions of impending victory emanating from the White House and the Pentagon. This in turn had an impact on the decision-makers, not least President Johnson. His press secretary, George Christian, was convinced that he and Johnson had watched Cronkite's Tet broadcast as it was aired, but even when made aware subsequently that this could not have been possible, he insisted that Johnson was worried "immensely" by Cronkite's apparent dovish turn, "because he saw [that] the impact was going to be tremendous on the country."[36]

Crucially, the Cronkite "editorial" was not the only Tet-era media episode that undermined American confidence in the war effort. Even before this,

Mike Wallace on CBS contended that Tet had "demolished the myth" of South Vietnamese strength and viability, while a *New York Times* editorial simply remarked that the offensive did not appear indicative of "an enemy whose fighting efficiency has 'progressively declined' and whose morale is 'sinking fast,' as United States military officials put it in November."[37] On February 19, AP's Eddie Adams's infamous photo of General Nguyen Ngoc Loan executing a Vietcong prisoner on the streets of Saigon was widely disseminated in American newspapers, including the *New York Times* and the *Washington Post*. Video footage of the killing had already been shown on NBC on Friday, February 2, the day after the execution (NBC broadcast the footage again, in greater detail, on March 10). For David Culbert, this video footage has been underplayed within the wider historiography as it does not tally with the conventional argument that television mirrored elite opinion rather than shaping public opinion and turning it against the war. The Loan footage, suggests Culbert, genuinely *affected* people, hence it proves an exception to the rule. It had an "exceptional impact," suggests Culbert, "because people were looking for a reason to change their views on a matter of policy."[38]

It might also be suggested that the media as a whole deliberately misreported the war, consistently favoring stories that made "better copy," often focusing on more controversial aspects of the war including alleged acts of American brutality. These tendencies were compounded by the lack of local knowledge and expertise on the part of the foreign press corps. As a result, American journalists routinely overlooked the role of the South Vietnamese forces (who, in reality, did the bulk of the fighting) because they were less aware of Vietnamese history, culture and customs; were unable to speak Vietnamese; and were also perhaps culpable of racism, whether unconscious or overt. There were clearly numerous shortcomings in the way the Vietnam War was reported, although the suggestion that the media was "against" the war, which in turn nourished an overwhelmingly "anti-war" representation in the pages of newspapers and magazines and on television screens, has been overstated. The majority of the media coverage was positive, and even when negative representations became more commonplace (as was the case after Tet), it is likely that the media was simply reflecting existing doubts and uncertainties. Although Hallin contends that television's "changing images of the war . . . must surely have affected public opinion, both directly and through their impact on opinion leaders," he concludes, nonetheless, that "television was a follower rather than a leader." "It was not until the collapse of consensus was well under way that television's coverage began to turn around," he writes, "and when it did turn, it only turned so far."[39]

Whatever conclusions one draws it is clear that the media's role in Vietnam assumed near legendary proportions even at the time, feeding into a "Vietnam Syndrome" that would, in future, necessitate a more robust and scrupulous oversight of media coverage of American military interventions. Indeed, the carefully stage-managed press conferences that characterized the Persian Gulf War stood in stark contradistinction to the anarchic nature of Vietnam War reportage. This was intentional. As President George H. W. Bush told the nation on January 16, 1991, "this will not be another Vietnam . . . . [Our troops] will not be asked to fight with one hand tied behind their back."[40] The swift and decisive victory subsequently encouraged Bush to proclaim "a proud day for America," and to assert, "by God, we've kicked the Vietnam syndrome once and for all."[41] In short, the Vietnam experience encouraged political and military elites to think more carefully about their relationship with the media, and the extent to which it could be manipulated successfully. Nixon was certainly alert to this by the time he won the 1968 presidential election. As he recalled in his memoirs, the media could be tamed; the president must simply demonstrate the necessary determination to "master the art of manipulating" it.[42]

For Nixon, such presidential manipulation of the media was not pernicious or morally questionable, but, instead, a necessary step in providing a corrective to a media that was, in his eyes, dominated by liberals and thus not providing a level playing field for Republicans like himself. The media, he averred, "are far more powerful than the President in creating public awareness and shaping public opinion, for the simple reason that the media always have the last word." With this in mind, Nixon's presidency oversaw the creation of a new post, a Director of Communications for the executive branch, filled by Nixon's former press spokesman Herb Klein. Justifying the need for this post in his memoirs, Nixon claimed to be seeking a more holistic and accurate picture of the public mood by avoiding it being "filtered through the *Times*, the *Post*, and the three television networks."[43] In a further attempt to avoid being enslaved by media representations of opinion, Nixon insisted that Johnson's three television set-up in the Oval Office be abandoned, favoring, instead, "a single set put in the small office." He also ordered the removal of the wire service machines that had constantly alerted LBJ to news emanating from the AP, United Press International, and Reuters.[44]

From the outset, Nixon was trying to insulate himself from the noisy representations of public opinion emanating from a media that he distrusted, seeking instead to channel almost vicariously the wishes and demands of the great "silent majority." Nixon's evocation of a great 'silent majority' was not necessarily new. Indeed, James Thompson has noted how many British Conservatives in the late nineteenth century sought to portray public opinion as something akin to the "the good sense of the people, in ways that anticipated later eulogies of the silent majority."[45] In many ways, it reflects a persistent conception of a public opinion that was malleable, vulnerable to manipulation, and able to be shaped and molded by prudent politicians. At the same time, there is, perhaps, a case to be made that Nixon was *right*, that a great "silent majority" *did* exist, and that the more vocal and visible manifestations of anti-war dissent were minority rather than majority opinion. To explore this further, it is necessary to scrutinize more closely what opinion poll data reveals about American public attitudes toward the war in Vietnam.

Opinion Polls

The advent of television was not the only significant development informing the public opinion/policymaking nexus in the postwar years, as this was also the era in which opinion polling came of age. The United States was the home of modern opinion polling, the industry beginning in earnest in the 1930s and growing steadily thereafter. Rudimentary straw polls had been employed haphazardly since the 1820s, but the inaccuracies of these approaches were exposed in 1936 when the "straw vote" undertaken by the *Literary Digest* indicated that the Republican candidate, Alf Landon, would win that year's presidential election. At the same time, early pioneers of new, more scientifically rigorous polling techniques—men like Archibald Crossley, Elmo Roper, and George Gallup— called the result correctly, predicting a victory for the Democrat candidate, Franklin Delano Roosevelt. Crossley, Roper, and Gallup were very much men of their time, reflecting a growing interest in marketing and public relations. It was not only commercial imperatives that prompted an interest in early opinion polls, as organizations like the Rockefeller Foundation and the Social Science Research Council promoted further research in the field. Political interest also developed during the 1930s and 1940s, the Second World War in particular proving an effective catalyst. "By the end of the Second World War," note Amy Fried and Douglas B. Harris, "a network of polling professionals from diverse sectors were building polling offices and generating polling acolytes and clients in administrative agencies, the White House, academia, and business."[46]

Notwithstanding the odd setback (the widespread projection of a Dewey victory in the 1948 presidential election being the most noteworthy), polls were increasingly viewed as reliable and accurate, and their prominence and use continued to grow. Between 1948 and the mid-1960s, the polling industry expanded with organizations like Gallup, Roper, Opinion Research Corporation, and Response Analysis leading the way.[47] Another name also entered the mix, with Louis Harris—who had cut his teeth working under Roper—establishing his own organization in 1956 and, according to one practitioner, carrying the industry "to new, laudable heights."[48] By the time American involvement in Indochina intensified during the 1960s, the polling industry was well established and firmly embedded within the political and cultural fabric of the nation. Although political parties and interest groups *did* commission opinion polls, the real catalyst for the industry's rapid expansion was market research and the media's interest in its findings. Many American newspapers began to commission polls in the 1940s and 1950s, a trend continued in the decades that followed by television networks.[49] The three principal networks—CBS, ABC, and NBC—began commissioning their own opinion polls in the 1970s, evidence of the growing purchase of public opinion on policymakers, a purchase much in evidence in the context of the war in Vietnam.

Nevertheless, as Fried and Harris remind us, not all politicians of the Vietnam era accepted that polling should usurp instinct and other, more abstract and opaque means of discerning the public mood.[50] This helps explain why successive US administrations appeared less attentive to opinion polls than other indicators of the vox populi, be it the press, congressional opinion, rumor and hearsay or, most crucially, the television. This was, perhaps, attributable to the conviction that opinion was both divided and in a constant state of flux, a condition that was arguably better reflected by the media rather than the more "scientific" polls. After all, as Hammond contends, neither the press nor the government proved able to control and shape popular responses to the war: "The American public," he insists, "went its own way."[51] This was particularly worrying given the Johnson administration's obsession with public opinion, an obsession that was evident even prior to escalation in 1965. In fact, early opinion polls reflected how fickle opinion could be, wanting victory in Vietnam but already showing signs of becoming disillusioned. Disillusionment grew after the CIA-orchestrated coup that overthrew South Vietnam's premier Ngo Dinh Diem in November 1963, public approval of the government's handling of the war falling from 57 percent to 43 percent by early 1964.

At the same time, poll data indicates a considerable amount of public apathy, with some 63 percent of Americans paying little or no attention to events in South East Asia.[52] Among those who did, there was considerable unease with how things were going. Despite a comfortable victory in the 1964 presidential race, Johnson struggled to convince the American public that Vietnam was going well, with just 38 percent of Americans giving him high marks for his handling of the war by December.[53] The poll data continued to reflect a deep ambivalence in American public attitudes. A January 1965 Gallup poll suggested that most Americans felt that South Vietnam was losing the war and, moreover, that the prospects of establishing a stable South Vietnam were slim, yet few were prepared to countenance an American withdrawal.[54] Even as an anti-war movement began to emerge, most Americans supported the war effort, fearful lest any loss of nerve on Washington's part lead to the loss of South Vietnam to the Communists. So, in spite of considerable unease, substantial increases to American troop numbers in Indochina were accepted, even welcomed, by an American public seemingly convinced that only robust US intervention could save the region from communism. The State Department's Harlan Cleveland simply commented that "public opinion is already substantially conditioned to expect an increase in our force level . . . the surprise would be if [LBJ] decided not to act."[55]

What had become irrefutably clear by the mid-1960s was that events in Vietnam were shaking Americans out of any residual apathy. According to polls, by May 1965 the war in Vietnam had usurped civil rights as the "most important problem confronting the country." By mid-1966, 55 percent of the public believed that Vietnam was the country's most pressing issue. For a frequently asked question in Gallup polls: "In view of developments since we entered the fighting in Vietnam, do you think the U.S. made a mistake sending troops to fight in Vietnam?," the evolution of those answering "no" to this question is tabulated below:

Support for the War as Measured by "No" Responses to the Mistake Question ("In view of developments since we entered the fighting in Vietnam, do you think the U.S. made a mistake in sending troops to fight in Vietnam," posed by the Gallup organization, 1965–71)

Date	% No
August 1965	61
March 1966	59
May 1966	49
September 1966	48
November 1966	51
February 1967	52
May 1967	50
July 1967	48

(*Continued*)

Date	% No
October 1967	44
December 1967	46
February 1968	42
March 1968	41
April 1968	40
August 1968	35
October 1968	37
February 1969	39
October 1969	32
January 1970	33
April 1970	34
May 1970	36
January 1971	31
May 1971	28

From William L. Lunch and Peter W. Sperlich, "American Public Opinion and the War in Vietnam," *The Western Political Quarterly* 32/1 (1979), p. 25.

This table shows a steady decline in support for the war; at the start (August 1965), a clear majority (61 percent) felt that the United States was right to send combat troops; this declined to just 28 percent by May 1971. Although the public's confidence in the war effort was starting to shift, this rarely translated into a loss of support for the troops. Indeed, it has been suggested that support for the troops remained high throughout, even after Tet and into the period of "Vietnamization."[56] To be sure, in spite of some problematic media coverage and an ever-growing (though still marginal) anti-war movement in the United States, opinion polls indicated that support for the war remained quite high. A Harris poll in early 1966 suggested that a majority (60 percent) would endorse the deployment of half a million US troops if this would shorten the war.[57]

Opinion polls are also helpful in revealing which sections of American society were most and least likely to support escalation, with important insights as regards the role of race and gender. Crude but important conclusions can be extrapolated, not least that women were less inclined to favor escalation than men (though also purported to be less well informed), and that African Americans were significantly less supportive of the war than whites (partly due to the greater likelihood of their being drafted). These demographic variables were detected early; Sidney Verba and his colleagues drew attention to them in summer 1967.[58] The generational dimension of pro- and anti-war positions is also worth considering. The following table traces, over time, responses to the Gallup question as to whether respondents considered it a mistake to send troops into Vietnam, broken down by age group:

Support for the War by Age ("No" Responses to the Mistake Question)

Date	21-29	30-49	50+	Most supportive age group
March 1966	71	63	48	Young
May 1966	62	54	39	Young
September 1966	53	56	39	Middle-aged
November 1966	66	55	41	Young
May 1967	60	53	42	Young
July 1967	62	52	37	Young
October 1967	50	50	35	Young and middle-aged
February 1968	51	44	36	Young
March 1968	50	46	35	Young
April 1968	54	44	31	Young
August 1968	45	39	27	Young
October 1968	52	41	26	Young
February 1969	47	43	31	Young
October 1969	36	37	25	Middle-aged
January 1970	41	37	25	Young
April 1970	43	40	25	Young
May 1970	48	41	26	Young
January 1971	41	38	20	Young
May 1971	34	30	23	Young

From Lunch and Sperlich, "American Public Opinion," p. 33.

It is striking that young Americans, despite being the demographic most closely associated with anti-war dissent, were also most likely to support the war effort.

Nevertheless, irrespective of age, race, or gender, American confidence was declining steadily, and John Mueller has ascribed this to casualty fatigue. Mueller compares the Korean War to Vietnam, and maintains that a "cumulative" buildup of casualties leads directly to an erosion in popular support. Ergo, the limited duration of the conflict in Korea meant a fatal loss of support was avoided. Furthermore, the "cumulative" model ascribes little importance to key events such as the 1968 Tet offensive. As Mueller insists, "support for the war changed so little between the fall of 1967 and the spring of 1968, despite a series of presumably momentous events: the Tet offensive, the replacement of General Westmoreland, President Johnson's decision not to run again."[59] This conviction has not gone unchallenged. Garner and Segura maintain that Mueller's approach "artificially" homogenizes different contexts and thus fails to account for the impact of "pivotal effects and shocks."[60] One such shock was certainly Tet, which, despite being a military "failure" for the North, left America clearly shaken. David Wyatt insists that labeling Tet a failure for the Vietcong not only obscures the "obvious victory it achieved in the realm of public opinion" but also understates the "arresting scale" of how far America's adversaries were prepared to go in pursuit of victory.[61]

Opinion poll data also permits an interrogation of whether Tet—or the "credibility gap" it exacerbated—caused popular support for the war to drop. Two Harris polls are indicative here, one conducted before Tet in July 1967, the other after Tet, in March 1968. The data provided below is a composite of free-form responses to the question: "What two or three things about the war in Vietnam most trouble you personally?"

Troubling Aspects of the Vietnam War—July 1967: Free-Form Responses to Harris Poll 1734, Question 6: "What two or three things about the war in Vietnam most trouble you personally?"

CASUALTY OR CASUALTY-RELATED ASPECTS	% of total responses
1 Loss of young men/casualties/loss of lives/killing	31
2 Family separated/destroyed	7
3 Killing innocent people/women & children	6
4 Sending our boys over there/sending them so young	6
5 Boys not trained well/not well supplied/undergoing needless suffering	5
6 Bombings/terrorism	2
OTHER ASPECTS	
1 Not making any apparent progress/should escalate/taking so long to end	12
2 Don't understand the war/why are we fighting?/it's a senseless war	9
3 Rising cost/mishandling of funds	7
4 Danger of becoming a third world war	5
5 Political war/credibility gap	3
6 People not backing the government	3
7 Vietnamese don't care/understand/want to understand	2
8 Inequality of the draft	1
9 No support from our allies	1

Table from Mark Lorrell and Charles Kelley, Jr. (with the assistance of Deborah Hensler), *Casualties, Public Opinion, and Presidential Policy During the Vietnam War* Santa Monica: The Rand Corporation, 1985), p. 25.

Casualties and casualty-related aspects troubled 31 percent of respondents in 1967; only 3 percent were troubled by the so-called "credibility gap" or by an apparent upsurge in anti-war and anti-government sentiment. Into 1968, not much had changed:

Troubling Aspects of the Vietnam War—March 1968: Free-Form Responses to Harris Poll 1813, Question 12c: "What two or three things about the war in Vietnam most trouble you personally? Anything else?"

CASUALTY OR CASUALTY-RELATED ASPECTS	% of total responses
1 Boys being killed/casualties/too young to die/loss of human life/deaths	44
2 Killing of South Vietnamese women and children/destruction of Vietnam	4
3 Against violence/immoral/don't believe in wars	2
4 More African Americans dying in Vietnam/African Americans being used	1
SUBTOTAL	51

OTHER ASPECTS	
1 Should fight to get it over with/our side is limited/limited type of war it is	2
2 Relatives/friends being drafted/having to go	7
3 High cost of living/higher taxes/higher prices	7
4 We should not be over there/it's not our war/attitude of the Vietnamese people/not willing to fight	6
5 Nothing	3
6 Corruption the war has caused/black market	2
7 Dissension here in the US/draft card burners	1
8 Too much politics/no progress/it's not a declared war/why are we fighting?/and all other responses	10
SUBTOTAL	48

Table from Mark Lorrell and Charles Kelley, Jr. (with the assistance of Deborah Hensler), *Casualties, Public Opinion, and Presidential Policy During the Vietnam War* Santa Monica: The Rand Corporation, 1985), p. 27.

Casualties or casualty-related aspects were most troubling for 51 percent of respondents. Of those concerned by other factors, only 1 percent cited the prevalence of dissent in the United States. What this demonstrates, perhaps, is that the role of the media in Vietnam, and the role of the anti-war movement in the United States in particular, has been exaggerated. What troubled the public is what always troubles the public when their young men and women go off to fight—the growing number of them returning injured or maimed or, worse still, in body bags.

Although greater pessimism permeated the media at the time of Tet, opinion polls suggested no immediate correlation in declining public support for the war. In fact, Gallup polls indicated that hawkish attitudes increased by 4 percent between December and February, while dovish attitudes fell by the same amount. Crucially, however, disapproval of Johnson's handling of the war rose significantly over the same period, from 47 percent to 63 percent. For Hammond, this suggests that the impact of Tet—and the media coverage of Tet as played out in American homes—had a greater impact on the Johnson administration than on American public opinion.[62] Johnson himself was clearly shaken, and there can be little doubt that the events of early 1968 contributed substantially to his decision not to seek reelection. Growing unease with events in Vietnam heightened fears that the social fabric of the nation was disintegrating, and Johnson urged the American people to avoid becoming "lost in suspicion, distrust, selfishness, and politics." Stressing that he would not "permit the Presidency to become involved in the partisan divisions that are developing in this political year," Johnson announced on March 31, 1968, that "I shall not seek, and I will not accept, the nomination of my party for another term as your President."[63]

As elite support for the war increasingly wavered, and media representations of both the war overseas and dissent and unrest at home proliferated, it was always likely that public opinion would follow suit. Debates over the reliability of opinion polls notwithstanding, the data indicates a relatively consistent loss of public support for America's war effort in Vietnam. Gallup polls show support for the sending of US personnel to Vietnam peaking in August 1965 at 61 percent, falling thereafter (though not uniformly) to 42 percent in early 1968, and dipping as low as 32 percent in September 1969 and again in March 1970.[64] Considering the impact of media coverage, opinion poll data suggests that the more coverage a topic is afforded, the greater the level of public interest. As Mueller contends, support for America's intervention in Vietnam spiked immediately after the deployment of US ground troops in 1965, but more crucially, perhaps, fewer people were likely to express "no opinion" when asked about the issue. "As the war began to gather more popular attention," he remarks, "people were led to form an opinion on it." Growing media interest in the war saw the "no opinion" percentage decline further. At the same time, many of the purportedly pivotal moments of media influence seemed to have little direct impact. For Mueller, the Tet offensive, the replacement of General Westmoreland, Johnson's decision not to seek reelection, the partial bombing halt, the opening of preliminary peace talks, and growing discontent at Johnson's policy had only a "limited" impact on dwindling levels of popular support.[65]

The tumultuous events of 1968, domestically and internationally, certainly had an impact on the elites, and not just Johnson. Between his 1968 presidential election victory and entering the Oval Office in 1969, Richard Nixon held many meetings with State Department officials in which, unsurprisingly, the "main subject was Vietnam."[66] At the same time, he remained attentive to public opinion, noting how "the opinion polls showed a significant percentage of the public [favoring] a military victory in Vietnam." How to achieve "victory"—or simply anything that could be spun as a "victory"—was difficult, and Nixon identified two options: first, bombing irrigation dykes in North Vietnam to cause widespread flood and famine (resulting in mass casualties); second, the use of tactical nuclear weapons. As Nixon recalled in his memoirs, either option would have provoked massive "domestic and international uproar." Escalation was also ruled out, not least because it was, at best, a long-term solution: "There was no way I could hold the country together for that period of time in view of the numbers of casualties we would be sustaining."[67] Despite opinion polls indicating that the American people desired a victorious outcome, Nixon knew that he "would have to prepare public opinion for the fact that total military victory was no longer possible."[68] According to the *New York Times*, a Gallup telephone poll in the aftermath of Nixon's November 3, 1968, "silent majority" speech revealed that 77 percent approved of the president's policies.[69] Even after the widening of the war into Cambodia and the controversy of the Kent State and Jackson State shootings in May 1970, Nixon's "great silent majority" was apparently holding firm. A Gallup poll suggested that 58 percent of Americans blamed the students at Kent State for their own deaths rather than the National Guardsmen who had opened fire.[70] Polls also indicated that the public had sympathized with the "hard hat" demonstrators who targeted anti-war protestors on Wall Street on May 8, 1970.[71] Indeed, the popularity and influence of the anti-war movement was always questionable, hence it is to this issue that this chapter will now turn.

The Anti-War Movement

The anti-war movement emanated originally from several existing organizations, notably the American Friends Service Committee (AFSC), the Committee for a Sane Nuclear Policy (SANE), and Women Strike for Peace (WSP). Many of its original members were pacifists, while a small fringe comprised old-school leftists with residual links to the communist and socialist workers parties. As the war progressed, the movement took on a more New Left and, ergo, a more student-oriented persuasion. The "New Left" simultaneously rejected communist dogma *and* railed against the iniquities of the capitalist system. Prominent here was the SDS (Students for a Democratic Society). In April 1965, the president of the SDS, Paul Potter, told a group of protestors:

> I do not believe that the President or Mr. Rusk or Mr. McNamara or even McGeorge Bundy are particularly evil men. If asked to throw napalm on the back of a ten year old child they would shrink in horror—but their decisions have led to mutilation and death of thousands and thousands of people. What kind of system is it that allows good men to make those kinds of decisions?[72]

An anti-war sentiment clearly existed from the start, but it was, at least early on, a peripheral movement at best. It was also rather genteel in its early days, notably the "teach-ins" of spring 1965. Most American people had no direct contact with it, only experiencing it via media coverage of the protests. Nevertheless, the movement was getting better at coordinating its activities and making its presence felt. The National Coordinating Committee to End the War in Vietnam (NCC) was established in 1965 to lend the disparate movement more cohesion. And, indeed, the movement was quite diverse. Although students remained prominent (Small estimates that nearly seven million students were part of the movement by 1968),[73] it also appealed to other interest groups, having clear links with, for example, elements of the civil rights and Black Power movements, existing pacifist organizations, women's groups, emerging groups of anti-war veterans, labor organizations, and the New Left more generally.

There was a significant spike in anti-war agitation during 1967, not least due to Martin Luther King's famous "Beyond Vietnam" speech at the Riverside Church in New York on April 4. King evoked the contradiction whereby young African Americans "who had been crippled by our society" were sent eight thousand miles "to guarantee liberties in Southeast Asia which they had not found in southwest Georgia and East Harlem." King noted further the "cruel irony of watching Negro and white boys on TV screens as they kill and die together for a nation that has been unable to seat them together in the same schools." King's speech initially prompted criticism in the mainstream press (*Life* magazine suggested that his words could have been taken straight from Radio Hanoi), and even censure from other civil rights leaders, such as Roy Wilkins and Whitney Young, who asserted that King did not speak for the movement as a whole. Nonetheless, it was a watershed moment inasmuch as the anti-war and civil rights movements began to dovetail more effectively.[74] Furthermore, the anti-war movement as a whole was becoming more cohesive and better organized, as shown by the "March on the Pentagon" in October, orchestrated by the National Mobilization Committee to End the War in Vietnam (MOBE).

All of this would have been particularly worrying for Johnson. It suggested that the anti-war movement was increasingly taking hold within an uneasy and uncertain public, but there was the additional damage that it might do to his "Great Society" program of domestic reforms. Johnson's domestic agenda relied on the adhesion of the leaders of the civil rights movement, so King's gravitation toward an overt anti-war stance was a worrying development. The Spring Mobe, established in late 1966, organized two massive rallies in San Francisco and New York on April 15, 1967, Coretta Scott King one of the speakers at the former, while her husband, along with Stokely Carmichael, addressed the latter. Yet, despite the prominence of civil rights voices on the platforms, few black Americans participated actively in the protests (just five hundred according to one witness).[75] Even so, as Jeffreys-Jones remarks, this did not mean that African Americans supported the war, rather that their opposition remained latent and unexpressed. A broad seam of discontent was already apparent, not specifically attributable to Vietnam but clearly linked to it, especially as the draft affected African Americans disproportionately. Of considerable concern to the authorities was the already visible discontent expressed by notable personalities—Malcolm X, Muhammed Ali, etc.,—and organizations, most worryingly the Black Panthers, which in October 1966 had proclaimed that "black people should not be forced to fight . . . to defend a racist government." Even before King's intervention, therefore, the Johnson administration was acutely aware of "a potential black revolt."[76]

The anti-war movement was also becoming noticeably more militant and visible. The March on the Pentagon initially attracted nearly 100,000 people to Washington—it was certainly a sizable demonstration of anti-war sentiment. The subsequent attempt at occupation—involving maybe up to 20,000 protestors—turned ugly, leading to some 647 arrests and 47 injuries requiring hospitalization. But was it popular? Did it resonate with the wider American public? Did it reflect the views of middle America? Much of the evidence would suggest not—popular perceptions of the peace movement were often negative, associated mostly with hippies, yippies, lazy students, and social misfits. Many of the actions of the anti-war movement—especially as they embraced "direct action"—served only to further alienate them from moderate American opinion. For example, during the 1967 Pentagon occupation, demonstrators had sex in front of National Guardsmen, urinated against the walls of the Pentagon, placed flowers in the barrels of Guardsmens' rifles; the Beatnik poet Allen Ginsberg even led a crowd of protestors in chants of "Om" intended to "levitate" the Pentagon and exorcize it of its "war demons."[77]

How mainstream American opinion perceived the anti-war protests necessitates an examination of how the movement was portrayed by the American media. After all, accepting that a loss of public support for the war contributed to America's defeat suggests, implicitly or explicitly, that domestic anti-war dissent, or at least *representations* of such dissent, played a part. It has been noted, for example, that television brought into American living rooms not only the fighting in Vietnam but also "the concomitant domestic protests."[78] This is not to say, however, that media coverage of anti-war dissent was favorable. Wyatt, for example, has lamented the "mocking and misrepresenting" press coverage, although he does acknowledge that it conveyed "a sense of appalling domestic disarray." In addition, even if press coverage was often disparaging, it influenced the decision-makers. A 1967 Pentagon memo described the president as having been "obsessed with the protest" throughout October, and Wyatt describes further how LBJ's fixation on dissent even led him to read through a list of protestors (and their alleged communist connections) "while having a haircut." Johnson perused the daily newspapers voraciously, including the *New York Times*, the *Baltimore Sun*, the *Christian Science Monitor*, and the *Wall Street Journal*. He also devoured evening newspapers and watched all three network news programs, while the Oval Office "was equipped with a wire ticker from AP, UPI, and Reuters." Johnson was, concludes Wyatt, a "news junkie" who routinely interpreted the news—and its showcasing of anti-war activism—as "being against him."[79]

Yet, in a series of Harris polls conducted in 1967 and 1968, asking respondents to comment on the most troubling aspects of the Vietnam conflict, the issue of domestic dissent barely features. In July 1967 only 3 percent were concerned about "people not backing the government," while in March 1968, only 1 percent considered "dissension here in the U.S." the most troubling aspect of the war. Unsurprisingly, casualties (or casualty-related aspects) were the chief concern for the majority.[80] Furthermore, as noted in the previous section, opinion polls revealed that younger Americans were the most likely to support the war effort, despite also providing the most visible face of anti-war activism. Of course, class is pivotal here; the campuses of American liberal arts colleges were populated largely by an elite of upper-middle-class white Americans, hardly representative of American youth per se. Race and gender also contributed to attitudes. Certainly, by 1967, with anti-war protests escalating, African Americans and women—who had generally supported the war initially—were more inclined to voice dissent. And policymakers tended to interpret opinion poll results at face value. Simply put, any indication of dwindling support was a source of concern.

As one pollster, Louis Harris, remarked, by 1967 Lyndon Johnson "no longer cited public opinion polls supporting him, for there were simply none to be found."[81] Johnson's sensitivity to indicators of dissent and unrest is understandable. After all, the second half of 1967 was a watershed moment for anti-war activism, as it began morphing rapidly from an isolated, fringe movement into something worryingly widespread.[82] Opinion polls indicated a significant drop in public support for the war during 1967, from 52 percent in February to 44 percent in October. A number of other events that year contributed to the perception that the American people were tiring rapidly of the conflict. Martin Luther King's Riverside Church speech was also a watershed, representing a greater symbiosis between the civil rights and anti-war movements. In this context, the unsettling impact of the Tet offensive simply exacerbated Johnson's conviction that he was losing popular support. Indeed, the anti-war stance embraced by Senator Eugene McCarthy, Johnson's challenger for the Democratic nomination, was gaining traction, winning 42.4 percent of the vote in the New Hampshire Primary, only marginally behind the President. With Robert Kennedy also about to enter the race, and McCarthy seemingly set to win the Wisconsin Primary, Johnson decided not to seek reelection in March 1968.[83]

Few years have resulted in as much spilt ink as 1968. Just days after Johnson informed the nation of his decision not to stand, Martin Luther King was assassinated in Memphis, an event that prompted unprecedented unrest across the country. In June, Robert Kennedy was slain at the Ambassador Hotel in Los Angeles. All the while, the festering sore of Vietnam was dividing Democrats down the middle. As Sandra Scanlon notes, these divisions were showcased "publicly and acrimoniously" at the Democratic National Convention in Chicago in August.[84] This played into Nixon's hands, the Republican challenger positioning himself as a champion of law and order. With polls indicating that fewer than 20 percent of Americans felt that the Chicago police had been heavy-handed in their treatment of the anti-war protestors, it seemed that Nixon's confrontational approach to anti-war dissent was chiming with the public. One survey showed that 75 percent of respondents positioned "Vietnam War Protestors" on the "negative end of a feeling scale, with 33 percent placing them at the far end."[85] On assuming the presidency, Nixon was determined to undercut the effectiveness and allure of the anti-war movement. He purported, in his memoirs, to be appreciative of "their concerns," but could barely hide his contempt and "anger at their excesses," not to mention their apparent failure to see that Nixon was motivated by "a genuine desire for peace."[86]

In essence, Nixon suggested that he and the anti-war movement shared the same ultimate goal—an end to the war—but advocated different means. The protestors wanted an immediate withdrawal; this was something that Nixon, having been elected on the back of patriotic, conservative, and often pro-war sentiment, could not possibly countenance. The difference between Nixon and the anti-war movement transcended tactics and methods—the divergences were profound and deep-rooted. As Nixon himself later acknowledged, his overriding perceptions of the movement, and the broader "counterculture" that they were part of, were overwhelmingly disparaging:

> I had no patience with the mindless rioters and professional malcontents, and I was appalled by the response of most of the nation's political and academic leaders to them. The political leadership seemed unable to make the distinction between a wrong that needed to be set right and the use of such a wrong as a justification for violating the privileges of democracy. The young demonstrators held firmly to their beliefs, while the adults seemed stricken with ambivalence about their own guilt and doubts about their own values. By proving themselves vulnerable to mob rule, the political and academic leaders encouraged its spread. Contemptuous of most of the professors, encouraged by others on the faculty and in the political arena, and spotlighted by the rapt gaze of television cameras, the demonstrators and their demonstrations continued and grew, and so did the often rationalized or romanticized violence connected with them.[87]

In his memoirs, Nixon quoted his words at a press conference on September 26, 1969, ahead of the October 15 Moratorium. Responding to a question about this and other anti-war protests, Nixon replied that he was aware "that there has been and continues to be opposition to the war in Vietnam on the campuses, and also in the nation." "As far as this kind of activity is concerned," he continued, "we expect it. However, under no circumstances will I be affected whatever by it." This affected disinterest in the protests was just for show. Nixon later acknowledged that they troubled him, hence his concern that "these highly publicized efforts aimed at forcing me to end the war were seriously undermining my behind-the-scenes attempts to do just that." If his memoirs are to be believed, the Moratorium convinced Nixon that he needed to be more proactive and robust in responding to dissent. It compelled him to tackle "a basic and important question about the nature of leadership in a democracy: should the President or Congress or any responsible elected official let public demonstrations influence his decisions?"[88]

Opting to tackle the problem "head on," Nixon focused on a letter received from a Georgetown University student criticizing his comments in the aforementioned press conference and asserting that a president must acknowledge the "will of the people." In his response, Nixon averred that permitting a noisy but marginal protest movement to dictate policy would mean abdicating decision-making "not to the majority, and not to those with the strongest arguments, but to those with the loudest voices."[89] The contours of his famous "silent majority" speech of November 3, 1969, were already in place. In this speech, Nixon warned that if "a vocal minority, however fervent its cause, prevails over reason and the will of the majority, this nation has no future as a free society." Hence he appealed to "the great silent majority of my fellow Americans" for support in his plan to bring about a satisfactory end to the war. "Let us be united for peace," he continued, "let us also be united against defeat. Because let us understand: North Vietnam cannot defeat or humiliate the United States. Only Americans can do that."[90] The next day, Nixon took great pleasure in demonstrating how his appeal had resonated with the American people, and that the "silent majority" were now making their voices heard. Evoking the bundles of laudatory telegrams he had received in support of his speech, Nixon was convinced that the "great silent majority" endorsed his Vietnam policy. As the *New York Times* noted, the President "summoned reporters and photographers to his office late this morning [November 4] to display a desk piled high with telegrams numbering, he said, in the 'high thousands.'"[91] There were certainly indications that Nixon's response to the 1969 Moratorium corresponded with the public mood. After Nixon rejected the option of an immediate withdrawal from Vietnam, the White House received more than 50,000 telegrams of support in a 48-hour period. Although this was due in part to a coordinated Republican Party operation, it demonstrated, nevertheless, that a growing disillusionment with the war did not automatically translate into a desire to extricate the United States instantaneously. It also suggested further to Nixon that public opinion was not instinctively adversarial. Indeed, he was delighted that the public appeared to endorse his stance, considering it confirmation that the anti-war movement reflected only marginal (if vocal) interests. "We've got those liberal bastards on the run now," he remarked, "and we're going to keep them on the run."[92] As Simon Hall notes, Nixon's ebullience was premature. Within days, the protestors reasserted themselves, with some 46,000 participating in the "March against Death," a symbolic, largely silent, and candlelit march from Arlington Cemetery to the Capitol. Two days later, a massive new protest organized by the New Mobe to End the War in Vietnam resulted in up to half a million people marching on Washington DC.[93]

Nevertheless, Nixon claimed in his memoirs that his November 3 speech had influenced the "course of history," suggesting that the plethora of congratulatory telegrams received in its aftermath rendered it more than a "rhetorical appeal." For him, this was evidence that "the critics and the commentators were unrepresentative of public opinion," with few critical voices to be found within the 50,000 telegrams and 30,000 letters that "poured in" to the White House. He noted, too, the 77 percent approval reported by Gallup, and also the overall approval rating he enjoyed in Gallup polls in the following weeks. All of this, Nixon affirmed, helped undermine the anti-war agitation, the speech resulting in "an element of desperation [entering] the planning of the November Vietnam Moratorium, known as the New Mobe."[94] Although anti-war protests diminished after 1969, they did not disappear entirely, even if, as Simon Hall notes, the movement became increasingly "divided and despondent."[95] The tragic events at Kent State and Jackson State Universities did bring anti-war activism (and the treatment of the protestors) back into the media spotlight. Prompted by Nixon's decision to escalate the war into Cambodia, anger at the deaths of the six students evolved into a new wave of campus protests across the nation.

Despite widespread sympathy for the victims of the campus shootings, Nixon could always point to evidence that this did not translate into a broader critique of his Vietnam policy. He noted how public opinion "seemed to rally" in the weeks after Kent State, especially once the military benefits of the Cambodian operation became visible. He also noted the "hard hat" demonstrations, a clear and emphatic expression of conservative support for his policies and impatience with the protestors. Indeed, the 1970 "hard hat" demonstrations, in which crowds of construction workers targeted anti-war protestors and proclaimed their support for the war effort, were a very visible and vocal articulation of a pro-war stance. The flag-waving of the construction workers, not to mention their chants—"All the way, USA!" and "Love it or leave it!"—exhibited their national pride while portraying the anti-war protestors as unpatriotic.[96] Indeed, an image of the "hard hats" in the popular imagination as hypermasculine, flag-waving patriots was established from the start.[97] These demonstrations (in addition to New York, protests took place in Buffalo and St. Louis) were also notable for what they revealed about class. On the one side were the working-class construction workers; on the other was a largely middle-class anti-war movement, led by unruly students—as one detractor labeled them, "spoiled, gutless middle-class college kids."[98]

These attacks on the protestors also assumed gendered connotations, designed to juxtapose the effeminate protestors with the hypermasculinity of the construction workers. One anti-war protestor recalled being dismissed as "faggots or queers as often as commies or cowards."[99] However, the suggestion that the middle classes opposed the war while the working classes supported it does not hold water—all sections of opinion, whether pro-war, anti-war, or simply uneasy and perplexed, cut across class lines. As Penny Lewis has concluded: "Class and cultural divides did exist in the antiwar movement of the Vietnam era, but the spectre of that divide was always larger than its reality."[100] A similar argument could be made of the anti-war movement in its totality. Historians simply cannot agree as to the impact of the movement on the outcome of the Vietnam War. Tom Wells considers it the "most successful anti-war movement in history," contributing directly to its denouement. Adam Garfinkle, by contrast, suggests that the anti-war movement *prolonged* American engagement in Vietnam, its unpopularity discrediting more reasonable and moderate anti-war voices that might otherwise have led to an earlier disengagement.[101] Hall tends to side with Garfinkle, contending that "the peace movement was one of the few things in the United States that was consistently more unpopular than the war," although he acknowledges that the movement *did* have an impact on policymaking elites.[102] Less controversial is the fact that the anti-war movement was an unusually vocal, visible, and impactful manifestation of public opinion that had *an* impact—however indeterminable—on American diplomacy.

Conclusion

If one accepts that Vietnam was the first "television war," a word or two is necessary about the impact of this particular medium on public opinion. It is prudent here to return to Robert Elegant, who was convinced that television's impact was exacerbated by the fact that, more than any other media, it shifted the emphasis "from fact to emotion."[103] This might be the case, but does it necessarily validate arguments that the loss of public and political support for the war in Vietnam was prompted by television coverage? Was it this, more than any military consideration, that explains how the world's largest and most advanced military power could suffer such a humiliating defeat? The argument is undoubtedly intoxicating. As Daniel Hallin has put it: "On the surface, then, Vietnam seems to confirm the thesis of a shift in American journalism toward an oppositional stance: news content became substantially more critical as the war went on, and the pattern of change cannot be explained away as a simple reflection of the course of events."[104] Hallin goes on to argue that, on closer examination, the "oppositional media" thesis "begins to unravel"—the media did not actively seek negative stories; Morley Safer's 1965 report from Cam Ne was *not* a fabrication. Similarly, the later revulsion caused by news of the massacre at My Lai took several months to surface (being broken initially by a fringe publication rather than the mainstream press), just as media hostility to American actions in Cambodia in 1970 only emerged *after* it had become the focus of a Congressional investigation. In short, there is little evidence that the press actively and consistently *sought* negative headlines with the intention of undermining public confidence in the war effort.

What was happening, suggests Hallin, is that popular support began to fade (perhaps attributable in no small part to general war fatigue and the body-bag syndrome) and the media coverage of this declining support (and in the case of the anti-war movement, outright opposition) inevitably and understandably increased. "The change seems best explained," he argues, "as a reflection of and a response to a collapse of consensus—especially of elite consensus—on foreign policy."[105] Melvin Small concurs, emphasizing an erosion of elite consensus: "The *New York Times'* slow editorial shift against Johnson's policies through 1966 and 1967 was itself affected by the growth of dovish sentiment in the Senate and the alienation of eastern intellectuals and college students and professors at elite colleges. The *Times'* dovish positions in turn encouraged others in the media to question administration policy."[106] A similar appraisal has been furnished by Gary Hess, who is adamant that the "media did not 'lose' the war." Instead, the media's coverage of the conflict "mirrored more than it changed public opinion," and that a more conventional (though less sensational) story of war-weariness best explains America's defeat. Furthermore, contends Hess, the media has been used as "a 'scapegoat' for the shortcomings of the policies of the nation's civilian and military leaders."[107]

Opinion polls support the argument that the media reflected rather than shaped public attitudes, as support for the war fell slowly and steadily over the duration of the conflict, seemingly unaffected by pivotal events or episodes like Cam Ne, Tet, or the Kent State controversy. It is also possible to argue that the "scapegoating" of the media extended to accusations that it both exaggerated and legitimized anti-war activism. A closer reading of the sources shows that anti-war dissent was usually portrayed pejoratively and rarely aroused widespread public sympathy (it more commonly provoked disdain). Still, although exaggerated, the media *did* perform an important role in mirroring and amplifying the doubts and uncertainties that increasingly afflicted American opinion—both political and public—as the Vietnam story unfolded. It was also a new kind of mirror, the impact of television reflecting these uncertainties and doubts with an unprecedented vividness and clarity. The role of public opinion was not decisive, nor did the public speak with a single voice. In fact, it spoke with too many voices, representative of schisms and divisions that nourished fears in elite circles of more widespread social dislocation, fears compounded by the broader social and cultural climate of the mid- to late 1960s. It was not just a fear of unrest should the war continue—in fact, the fear of public anger at "losing" South Vietnam to communism was a key driver of the initial decision to escalate. Public opinion had been inconsistent from the start, and this ambiguity fed into decision-making at every stage, from intervention, through escalation, and ultimately to withdrawal. Public opinion was not responsible for "losing" the war in Vietnam. For policymakers who were answerable to the public, however, it was, by virtue of its visibility and inconsistency, a persistent handicap.

Global Public Opinion and the Demise
of Apartheid

To ascribe the end of apartheid wholly to the influence of public opinion—specifically the influence of public opinion in the West—would be unfounded. Apartheid's demise came about for many, chiefly domestic, reasons. Nevertheless, the anti-apartheid movement, operating on a global scale, *was* significant in mobilizing substantial seams of global public opinion against the apartheid regime. This public opinion worked against apartheid in two ways, first by encouraging and assisting in the economic, sporting, and cultural boycott of South Africa, and second by compelling their respective governments to adopt more overtly anti-apartheid policies. As Enuga S. Reddy, Secretary of the United Nations Committee Against Apartheid recalled, it was only because "of the development of public opinion [that] governments changed their attitudes and co-operated in international action."[1] The global anti-apartheid movement was certainly a prominent example of international solidarity in action, a movement of people transcending national borders that had a profound impact on international affairs. Gregory Houston acclaims the movement's effectiveness, asserting that "there can be no doubt that international solidarity contributed substantially to the ending of apartheid."[2] Like other instances of international solidarity, the movement against apartheid was also a movement of public opinion, or at least a concerted effort to galvanize public opinion in support of a cause.

This was not a new phenomenon. International peace campaigners in the late nineteenth and early twentieth centuries sought to mobilize an international public opinion while also claiming to speak on its behalf. The Anti-Apartheid Movement (AAM) drew particular inspiration from the nineteenth-century abolitionist movement. Audie Klotz highlights this "striking" synergy, how, in both movements, "diffuse groups of people mobilized across national boundaries" despite the two centuries separating them.[3] As Klotz insists, this is a necessary reminder that transnational activism is not a contemporary phenomenon. Another movement predicated on an international solidarity with public opinion at its heart had even more direct links to the anti-apartheid movement. The Pan-African Congress, established in 1900, had its roots in an 1898 initiative undertaken by the Trinidadian, Henry Sylvester-Williams. He issued a statement calling for a conference "in order to take steps to influence public opinion on existing proceedings and conditions affecting the welfare of the natives in the various parts of the Empire, viz., South Africa, West Africa and the British West Indies."[4] The movement against apartheid would embrace similar tactics, emphasizing the need for external pressures to effect internal change in South Africa. Håkan Thörn suggests that the collapse of apartheid involved both an "internal" and an "external" struggle, "the 'struggle' inside South Africa . . . constantly influenced by the 'outside' just as the struggle 'outside' was influenced by, and dependent on, the struggle 'inside.'"[5] This chapter explores how far anti-apartheid citizen activists, operating on a transnational scale, succeeded in galvanizing public opinion in support of their agenda, and thus how far, in turn, manifestations of public opinion affected diplomatic responses to the apartheid regime in South Africa.

The Origins of the International Anti-Apartheid Movement

The early AAM emerged (at least organizationally) in the late 1950s, and its immediate origins can be traced to a meeting between some African activists and their British supporters at Holborn Hall, London, on June 26, 1959. Julius Nyerere, president of the Tanganyika African National Union was the main speaker, accompanied by Kanyama Chiume of the Nyasaland African National Congress and Tennyson Makiwane and Vella Pillay from the African and Indian Congresses of South Africa. The prominent British attendees were Michael Scott, an Anglican priest and longtime critic of the apartheid regime, and Trevor Huddleston, an Anglican bishop whose disdain for apartheid materialized during his fifteen years of working in South Africa.[6] This meeting, held under the banner of the Committee of African Organizations (CAO), drew inspiration from Gandhi's use of boycotts to challenge British colonial rule in India, and advocated similar tactics in the struggle against apartheid, notably the boycott of fruit, cigarettes, and other goods imported from South Africa. Huddleston had, even prior to this meeting and while still living in South Africa, sought to raise the British public's consciousness of the situation there. "For God's sake, wake up!" screamed the headline of a letter he wrote to *The Observer* in August 1953, chastising the "apathy and indifference to-day of the vast majority of Europeans" and asserting that "we, in South Africa, cannot now fight this evil alone."[7] In April 1956, Huddleston advocated a cultural and sporting boycott of South Africa, with a view to exercising "economic pressure against the South African government."[8] Sanctions were also, from the start, considered an appropriate strategy, most early AAM members endorsing the call for sanctions given in 1958 by the president of the African National Congress (ANC), Albert Luthuli.[9]

The early AAM closely echoed its abolitionist antecedent, using similar tactics—demonstrations, petitions, consumer boycotts, etc.—but also drawing on similar constituents of support, notably "religious, rights and labor groups." But this also brought to the surface a weakness, as the AAM, like its abolitionist forebear, was often troubled by "tensions along class and gender lines."[10] Given these echoes of earlier activism, it is unsurprising that the AAM has been described as "the most highly transnationally integrated social movement during the postwar era." Furthermore, Thörn contends that this resulted in the emergence of a "global public sphere" inclusive of historical actors that Habermas's model neglects, not least "publics formed on the basis of . . . workers,' women's and church movements, as well as the alternative political cultures of new social movements emerging during the post-war era."[11] In this sense, the AAM was both part of a broader tradition and also something distinct. As Rob Skinner argues, it was less "part of a golden thread of activism that stretched from the campaign against slavery" and more a phenomenon that "illustrates the transition from imperial networks to global civil society."[12] Althought a global movement, it was particularly prominent in Europe. Although the British AAM was central, numerous analogous organizations existed, including the Irish Anti-Apartheid Movement (IAAM), the Anti-Apartheids Beweging Nederland (AABN), and Komitee Zuidelijk Afrika in the Netherlands, the Comité Contre le Colonialisme et l'Apartheid (CCCA) and Aktiekomitee Zuidelijk Afrika (AKZA) in Belgium, and the Swedish group Isolara Sydafrika Kommitén.[13]

The formative years of anti-apartheid activism established a template for the organizational core of the movement in the decades that followed. First, it was transnational from the start, a fusion of South African émigrés arriving in London in the 1950s, various groups of sympathetic Britons (usually on the left and/or religiously motivated), and existing African advocacy groups such as the CAO. The AAM's leftist proclivities were also an impediment in the stridently anti-Communist ideological climate of the early Cold War. Indeed, anti-communism was prominent in moderate trade union and Labour circles in

Britain, weakening the initial support base of the early AAM. Liberal politicians were also divided; some were early backers of the movement, including David Steele and Jeremy Thorpe (later to become a vice-president of the AAM), but others, including party leader Jo Grimond and former leader Clement Davies, were hesitant. Barbara Castle was one of many prominent Labour figures to back the movement, but support for the AAM in Conservative circles was harder to find, with only Lord Altrincham—by his own admission a somewhat "semi-detached member of the Party"—openly involved.[14]

The AAM attempted from the outset to reach out to public opinion. Christabel Gurney, a prominent AAM activist (and editor of *Anti-Apartheid News*) reminds us how, even in its earliest guise, the AAM's advocacy of a boycott in the late 1950s "tapped a rich vein in British public opinion," appealing almost instinctively to a liberal humanist tradition, the Liberal Party, the trade union and Labour movements, and "a minority of church people." There was also a certain synergy between the anti-apartheid struggle and the Marxist perception of a wider anti-colonial and anti-capitalist crusade. The broad base of support for the AAM's "boycott month" was apparent when it began with a march and rally in Trafalgar Square on February 28, 1960. Up to 15,000 people listened to speeches from the Labour politician Hugh Gaitskell, Jeremy Thorpe (Liberal), Lord Altrincham (Conservative), Rita Smythe of the Co-Operative Women's Guild, and Tennyson Makiwane of the ANC, all presided over by Huddleston. Press coverage of the campaign was substantial, and a Gallup poll in mid-March revealed that the number of people likely to boycott South African goods had risen significantly as a result.[15]

A consistent tactic of the AAM was to cultivate good relations with sympathetic journalists, but it also developed its own weekly publication, *Anti-Apartheid News* in 1965. The widespread production and distribution of posters and leaflets was also a familiar strategy in the 1960s, used to good effect when publicizing the various sporting boycotts in that decade and beyond. The AAM's annual report for 1969–70 noted how more than 200,000 leaflets had been circulated, along with thousands of posters, stickers, and other items of paraphernalia.[16] The IAAM also sought to build public support for its cause, viewing itself as "the instrument through which the voice of the Irish people was heard."[17] There were, however, important differences between the IAAM and its British counterpart. The IAAM viewed the struggle of nonwhite South Africans as analogous to their own struggle for freedom and independence from British colonial rule, while the Irish government, unlike the various Westminster administrations, consistently adopted an anti-apartheid stance at the UN. Ireland was joined by other smaller

European states in doing so, notably Sweden and the Nordic countries.[18] In fact, these countries were arguably more consistent in opposing apartheid than Ireland, as growing economic interests with South Africa led the Dublin government during the 1960s to eschew a confrontational position vis-à-vis Pretoria. In addition, the Irish public's interest began to wane, attention increasingly focused, instead, on Ireland's efforts to join the European Community.[19]

The first decade of the AAM had a limited impact politically, but it was successful in keeping South African apartheid in the global spotlight. It was also beginning to demonstrate the potential of public opinion to become a political actor capable of exerting an influence beyond official political and diplomatic channels. In so doing, the movement was speaking a language that chimed with the new international norms emerging in a postwar era of decolonization, human rights, and self-determination. The international community *was* occasionally speaking the same language, but it was sporadic and inconsistent, with attitudes and policies toward South Africa dictated by Cold War realpolitik rather than moral principles. Even into the 1960s, as Skinner notes, "international opposition to apartheid was restricted to a network of groups and individuals outside of official politics." Nonetheless, he also contends that these networks "began to exert influence in a number of important ways."[20] Particularly significant here are the issues of sanctions, divestment, and boycotts (in multiple forms), all of which demonstrated the ability of citizen activism, on a global scale and rooted in conceptualizations of public opinion, to wield a gradual but decisive influence on politics and diplomacy.

Enforcing Isolation: Sanctions and Divestment

Apartheid South Africa did face early censure from the fledgling United Nations. From the late 1940s, and instigated by the Indian government, the UN made a special case of South Africa, condemning officially its segregationist policies and demanding that white minority rule be replaced by a system respecting the self-determination of all South Africans.[21] The UN's role was important in positioning South Africa as a pariah state but was undermined from the start by Cold War diplomacy. For UN sanctions to be effective, all states must apply them, but certain countries—notably Great Britain, the United States, and West Germany—were consistently reluctant. Indeed, when the UN first debated the possibility of sanctions in 1960, both the United Kingdom and the United States vetoed their use. This was despite 1960 being "Africa Year" at the UN, and in spite of the negative international headlines prompted by the Sharpeville massacre on March 21 (in which an anti-government protest was met with police bullets, resulting in sixty-nine fatalities and many more wounded). It was also despite British support for South Africa recently being called into question by Prime Minister Harold Macmillan's famous "Wind of Change" speech. Addressing the South African parliament in Cape Town, Macmillan admitted that "there are some aspects of your policies which make it impossible for us to [support South Africa] without being false to our deep convictions about the political destinies of free men, to which in our own territories we are trying to give effect." While making it clear that he deprecated "attempts which are being made in Britain to-day to organize a consumer boycott of South African goods," there was little in the prime minister's speech to reassure his audience given the intertwined relationship between the two countries.[22]

Indeed, British financial interests in South Africa were deeply embedded (due in no small part to its colonial history), accounting for roughly 40 percent of all foreign investment in the country by 1978. Alongside other nations with substantial economic interests in South Africa (notably the United States and Japan), Britain's refusal to participate in sanctions meant that the South African economy was relatively untroubled; Macmillan's speech and the broader international condemnation provoked by Sharpeville had briefly shaken confidence, but the recovery was swift.[23] The United States also had considerable economic interests in South Africa, but what animated Washington chiefly was a desire to keep that country out of the clutches of communism.[24] America's position did fluctuate during the Cold War—and criticism of Pretoria was certainly more vocal under Jimmy Carter's presidency—but consistently stopped short of offering anything more robust than rhetorical condemnations of Pretoria. British government attitudes toward South Africa also fluctuated according to the political leanings of the Westminster government, but all administrations, whether Conservative or Labour, vetoed UN sanctions. Moreover, British attention on Africa from 1965–80 focused on Rhodesia and the aftermath of Ian Smith's Unilateral Declaration of Independence. In conjunction with the Cold War climate and the depth of British financial interests in the country, there were too many reasons to avoid rocking the South African boat.

This did not mean that sanctions were not contemplated. Indeed, a potential boycott of South Africa had been politicized in Britain in 1960. Following its unanticipated defeat in the 1959 general election, a divided Labour Party sought an issue around which to coalesce and identified in the fledgling AAM a suitable candidate. Party secretary Morgan Phillips had already suggested making 1960 an "African Year," providing a moral cause around which his fragmented party could unite. The AAM's existing advocacy of boycotts provided a ready-made campaign.[25] The Labour Party formally advocated a boycott of South African goods to last from February 20 to March 19, 1960. The Trades Union Congress followed suit, urging the British public to "express by a consumers' boycott of South African goods their personal revulsion against the racial policies being pursued by the government of South Africa." This was an early example of the AAM using a single moral issue to mobilize public opinion in the hope that the will of the people might inform more far-reaching political changes. As a February 1960 AAM Press Statement remarked, the boycott campaign is "a truly national movement" where the British people could "forget their domestic political wrangles in order to devote themselves to a great cause."[26]

This national boycott was a precursor of the genuinely international movements that would emerge during the 1970s and particularly the 1980s. Publicity was, from the start, considered essential, a means of educating and energizing public opinion. *Boycott News*, a dedicated newspaper to accompany the campaign, was selling over 100,000 copies by February 1960. Hundreds of thousands of explanatory leaflets were distributed, and the mass rally at Trafalgar Square heightened further the campaign's visibility. Despite a well-publicized counterdemonstration orchestrated by Oswald Mosley, and the fact that its political impact was marginal, the campaign ensured that the apartheid issue remained on the public agenda. This became still more pronounced after the events at Sharpeville. More than ever, it seemed that apartheid could only be reversed from without rather than within. Thereafter, as Gurney remarks, the Anti-Apartheid Co-Ordinating Committee (as the Boycott Movement Committee rebranded itself in March 1960) began calling for "an international campaign of international sanctions with the aim of crippling the apartheid economy."[27] Educating public opinion was a clearly defined operational tactic. As Enuga Reddy noted, "without public opinion" it was simply impossible to generate the diplomatic pressure necessary; hence, activists must continue "to inform and educate the public opinion, mobilise the public opinion, so that you can have sanctions."[28]

This "public opinion" also needed to be visible on a global scale. Klotz reminds us that anti-apartheid activism was not confined to the West, with Tanzania and Zambia both influential hubs.[29] There was also a burgeoning movement in the United States, with inevitable links to the civil rights movement in that country. The American Committee on Africa (ACOA) was founded in 1953 and was the most prominent American anti-apartheid group through the 1950s and 1960s, starting educational and propaganda initiatives while also lobbying politicians, organizing demonstrations, and undertaking relief projects in South Africa itself. Into the 1970s, public interest in South Africa grew further. African American employees at Polaroid's headquarters in Cambridge, Massachusetts, created the Polaroid Revolutionary Workers' Movement (PRWM) in 1970, protesting Polaroid's provision of film being used for South Africa's discriminatory passport system. In 1972, a cross section of officials within the Congressional Black Caucus and members of local-level African American activist organizations established the National African Liberation Support Committee. This proved to be short-lived, however, and, as Culverson comments, "failed to create a more substantial Afro-American grassroots base within the larger anti-apartheid movement."[30] TransAfrica, formed in 1977, was more successful, becoming a consistent and vocal critic of apartheid as the global campaign intensified into the 1980s. There were also greater European efforts to internationalize the protests, whether to ensure compliance with the arms embargo or to put further pressure on large multinationals like Shell to divest; as Wouter Goudertier notes, "the Dutch AKZA published posters in multiple languages to increase international visibility and effectiveness."[31]

In Britain, too, there were signs that public opinion wanted a more robust approach to apartheid. As will be discussed in the next section, a great deal of the impetus for this came from the sporting boycott, but it also played out in a demand for economic sanctions and divestment. This was in spite of the British government remaining resolutely hostile. In a move that, according to Gurney, "misjudged public opinion," Edward Heath decided, shortly after winning the 1970 general election, to resume arms sales to South Africa. This prompted a sizable demonstration in October 1970 in Trafalgar Square, while an AAM-organized declaration in support of maintaining the arms embargo gathered 100,000 signatures in just six weeks. This public pressure paid dividends; although the Conservative government never publicly reversed its position, actual arms sales to South Africa were practically negligible.[32] The Irish movement also demanded sanctions. Their "No collaboration with apartheid" campaign was effective, imports of South African oranges falling by 50 percent in 1969–70. Buoyed by this apparent progress, the IAAM sought to gain greater publicity via their monthly newsletter, *Amandla*, and focused heavily on educational initiatives by providing materials and speakers for schools across the country. Membership of the IAAM increased to 2,000 by 1974, augmented by the fact that the movement, like its British counterpart, could claim to represent many more people via affiliations. This allowed the IAAM to build a "broad-based public consensus on opposition to apartheid."[33]

Divestment also became more prominent during the 1970s, notably the sustained campaign against Barclays Bank. It was a long time coming, but in 1986 Barclays announced that it was pulling out of South Africa. Barclays was not alone, being joined by other major British companies like Standard Chartered, Vickers, Norwich Union, and Legal and General. In total, fifty-five British companies disposed of their South African subsidiaries in the period 1986–88, with a further nineteen reducing their holdings.[34] The international community was applying greater pressure on Pretoria. Despite the continued opposition of Britain, France, and West Germany, the European Community decided in 1986 to impose tighter sanctions on South Africa although various loopholes and exemptions greatly limited their effectiveness. Nonetheless, it was a response to a growing public demand, as the AAM had, in August 1985, delivered a formal appeal for tougher sanctions to the Luxembourg presidency of the European Commission. Of course, not all of these developments can be attributed to popular activism, and there were certainly financial imperatives for companies to rethink their South African ventures. A stagnant economy and domestic unrest had made South Africa an unattractive place to invest. Even so, as Gurney insists, "concern about public image was also part of the equation; retrenchment, rather than disinvestment, would have been a more normal response to South Africa's economic difficulties."[35]

AAM activism may have played a small part in encouraging divestment, but it had less success in persuading the British government to back sanctions. The Thatcher administration argued consistently that sanctions would hurt black South Africans disproportionately and would thus be self-defeating. At the same time, the Reagan administration adopted a policy of "constructive engagement" with South Africa, simultaneously encouraging the Pretoria government to embrace change while also severing liaison with anti-apartheid groups like the ANC.[36] Although citizen activism was seemingly unable to effect policy change, the legacy of protest during the 1960s and 1970s was significant. As Culverson notes, on both a national and an international level, it "rendered established institutions more receptive to grassroots activism, while affording citizens greater resources and opportunities for launching meaningful challenges."[37] Opinion polls indicated that the American public was receptive to the message. A 1977 Harris survey suggested that 46 percent of Americans wanted Western governments to pressurize Pretoria into giving black South Africans greater political rights and freedom, while a 1985 Gallup poll showed 47 percent of respondents wanting more pressure applied on South Africa, rising to 55 percent the following year.[38] There was clearly a growing (if not yet overwhelming) popular demand to see more done to end apartheid. This demand would put particular emphasis on divestment, pressuring both government and private corporations to withdraw their investments in South Africa in the hope that the economic repercussions would force the Pretoria government to yield.

By the end of 1986, some twenty-one US states, sixty-eight cities, and ten of America's largest counties had adopted divestment policies, due in no small part to a perceived public pressure. In addition, American colleges and universities embraced divestment and, crucially, so did many sizable corporations. American investments in South Africa stood at $2.8 billion in 1983, falling to just $1.3 billion in 1985; of the estimated 350 American companies operating in South Africa in 1984, 80 had pulled out by 1987, including General Motors, IBM, Coca Cola, Xerox, Eastman Kodak, and Exxon.[39] During this process, *The Guardian* newspaper in Britain was under no illusions as to the cause of the trend. "Most of these decisions are based on commercial rather than moral considerations," it acknowledged, "but the underlying factors, like the result, are the same: US public opinion and the deteriorating business climate in South Africa. Each in turn derives from apartheid." In so doing, *The Guardian* was attacking "the absence of the political will in Britain," suggesting that henceforth the "main impetus against apartheid will come from America."[40] In Britain itself, the AAM was keen to use public opinion as an influencer, the "people's sanctions" campaign asking individuals to boycott South African goods and thus, in an election year, influence the incoming government. Their 1987 *Manifesto for Sanctions* asserted, "People's Sanctions will help to create a climate in which a future British government will be obliged to embrace comprehensive mandatory sanctions."[41]

This form of consumer boycott had already proven effective. A June 1986 opinion poll in *The Observer* suggested that 27 percent of people *had* boycotted South African goods and, in total, South African fruit and vegetable imports fell by 8.5 percent and textile imports by 35 percent. For Stuart Hall, this form of protest was also important for its psychological impact in Britain, as seemingly mundane household conversations about the provenance of oranges and bananas assumed a political hue. Via these everyday domestic encounters (which "especially involved women"), the apartheid issue permeated "everyday life." For Hall this amounted to "one of the most enormous transformations which took place in terms of political consciousness."[42] Victoria Brittain, however, has questioned Hall's verdict, claiming that "society in the 1980s was complacent about apartheid," few caring that "the UN had pronounced apartheid to be a crime against humanity."[43] Writing in 1986, Denis Herbstein drew a similar conclusion, noting how it was "a herculean task to shift British public opinion," and although the boycott campaign had mobilized vast swathes of the population, its ultimate impact was minimal. "The Anglican church, the campuses, most trade unions, the opposition political parties, even housewives in the supermarket," he wrote, "possibly a majority of the citizenry . . . want sanctions, though when questioned in detail, even the easy options like air links or fruit and vegetables are too tough for them."[44]

Gurney, however, celebrates the political impact of the AAM's sanctions campaign, contending that "the strength of public opinion meant that [Thatcher] was unable to renege on the arms embargo [and] was forced to concede the principle of sanctions."[45] It is difficult to dispute that the global demand for sanctions and divestment was growing. Numerous city and municipal authorities in the United States joined the many universities in doing so. Meg Voorhes argues that the divestment movement in the United States went through three waves: the initial spike in the late 1960s; another surge in the late 1970s (especially after the Soweto Rebellion); and finally, the more substantial movement of the mid-1980s.[46] The first wave, spearheaded by the Students for a Democratic Society, cultivated a wider student movement that prompted colleges and universities to rethink their financial relationships with companies invested in South Africa. The second wave called more explicitly for divestment, with some educational institutions (Antioch, Hampshire, Howard, Michigan State, the University of Massachusetts, Ohio University, and the University of Wisconsin) adopting policies of total divestment. "The third and most intensive wave," suggests Voorhes, was a response to growing domestic unrest in South Africa in 1984–85, Pretoria's "state of emergency" response being widely covered by the international media.

To be sure, the sanctions and divestment movement became more powerful and global into the 1980s. Neta Crawford notes the movements' links with other transnational groups like European Nuclear Disarmament, Solidarity, Charter 77, Democracy in China, support for the Sandinistas, and the Nuclear Freeze, helping them "reach broader audiences and allow[ing] them to increase education and mobilization for further sanctions against South Africa." Nonetheless, Crawford acknowledges that sanctions were poorly imposed and often ineffective; although several countries prohibited the import of South African coal, for example, overall imports to the European Economic Community (EEC) increased, to the extent that South Africa had become the major supplier of coal to the EEC by 1986. This was not the only example of economic sanctions being imposed haphazardly and with questionable effect. Although South Africa's trade with several important partners had decreased substantially by the 1980s (trade with Britain falling by 15 percent in 1986, trade with Germany falling by 25 percent, and trade with the United States falling by 40 percent in 1987), trade with other countries actually increased (for example, increasing by 20 percent with Japan in 1987).[47]

Despite these shortcomings, the global escalation of the anti-apartheid campaign induced optimism that widespread activism would "educate the broader public about apartheid and galvanize a larger sanctions movement."[48] As will be seen, the anti-apartheid movement reached its zenith in the 1980s, and the conviction grew that the public *could* influence foreign affairs. In Europe, various national movements tried to tap into this in February 1988 by establishing the "Liaison Group," charged with lobbying the European Community with a view to securing "a fundamental change in EC policy with the confidence that in doing so they reflect public opinion within the EC." As Goudertier asserts, they were attempting to "create a transnational public of European citizens to effect a change in EC policy."[49] During the 1980s, Herbstein was skeptical about its ability to effect meaningful change. Not only were Britain, West Germany, and Portugal opposed to sanctions "of any sort," but others, too, including France, Belgium, and even Ireland, appeared somewhat ambivalent. "But the biggest loophole," he concluded, "lies right in Europe's heartland, in Switzerland, gold importer and unashamed banker to apartheid and to other regimes, good and ugly." As a result, he suggested that P. W. Botha was maybe right "to be quietly confident that when it comes to sanctions, Europe will never get its act together."[50] Despite this, public activism was increasingly difficult to ignore, a fact made all the more visible by the parallel campaigns for sporting and cultural boycotts.

Beyond Economics: The Sporting and Cultural Boycott

The decision not to select Basil d'Oliveira for England's 1968 cricket tour to South Africa was controversial from the start. As he was South African–born and of Cape Coloured descent, d'Oliveira's exclusion was seen as a concession to South Africa's policy of racial segregation in sport. Peter Hain, the South African–born activist who would spearhead the Stop the Seventy Tour (STST) Campaign in Britain (and would later become a Labour MP), noted how d'Oliveira's exclusion enraged British opinion. When injury caused another England player, Tom

Cartwright, to pull out of the tour, d'Oliveira was called up to replace him, rendering the touring party unacceptable to the South African cricketing authorities. South Africa's efforts to influence the make-up of England's touring team led the Marylebone Cricket Club (MCC) to cancel the tour on September 24 and, as Hain remarks, the "reverberations from the cancellation seemed endless." "Under the full glare of world publicity," he continued, "the white South Africans had attempted to pick, according to the doctrine of their white exclusiveness, not only their own teams, but a visiting team as well."[51] The d'Oliveira affair was a catalyst, unleashing a wave of discussion of boycotts around cricket and rugby tours for the next twenty years. But this was not the first time that the issues of sport and apartheid politics intersected. Sport had, since the mid-1950s, been used to protest apartheid. Non-racial South African sporting organizations had already sought formal recognition from the global governing bodies of both table tennis and soccer. These early campaigns, however, were sporadic and isolated, and any fears that they might precipitate the near-total sporting isolation of South Africa were, as Keech and Houlihan note, "more alarmist than prescient."[52] That said, it was a precursor of bigger things to come. As Malcolm Maclean contends, the sporting boycott would become "one of the principal tools that the anti-apartheid movement had in its toolkit to dismantle the white South African government's systematic racial classification and oppression."[53]

Even in its early days, the AAM had suggested protesting tours of Britain by all-white South African sporting teams, and their campaign for winter 1962/3 identified sport, along with culture, films, and education, as "subsidiary fronts in the propaganda war, which can have very far-reaching psychological effects."[54] Prior to this, sport was used as an issue within South Africa itself. The non-racial South African Sports Association (SASA) was formed in 1958, developing by October 1962 into the South African Non-Racial Olympic Committee (SANROC). The pressure on South African sporting authorities to embrace multiracial sport was not just domestic. Indeed, South Africa was excluded from the 1964 Tokyo Olympic Games because the South African Olympic and National Games Association (SAONGA) rejected a demand to abandon segregation. Although SAONGA made *some* concessions by 1968, the threat of a wider boycott from International Olympic Committee (IOC) members saw South Africa excluded from the Mexico City games. Though the Olympic ban was damaging for South Africa, the reality was that many individual sports (notably golf and tennis) and the team sports that white South Africans were most attached to (rugby union and cricket) were relatively unaffected.[55] As Maurice Llewellyn contends, the failure to target white South Africa's "national pastimes" essentially meant that "IOC sanctions failed to inspire any meaningful policy changes from Pretoria."[56]

Rugby was particularly symbolic, the embodiment of the "national dynamism and power [that was] essential to the integrity of Afrikaner masculinity."[57] The failure to target effectively individual sports was also problematic; golf, especially, was seemingly unaffected, Gary Player being a regular fixture in global golfing tournaments.[58] Demonstrations against touring South African teams in the 1960s demonstrated how impactful they could be. In 1965, the South African cricket team faced protests at every match, and the Queen, following governmental advice, did not attend the Lords Test Match (as she would usually have done).[59] In Ireland, the IAAM protested the 1965 visit of the South African rugby team. Student activists at Trinity College forced the Springboks to find a new training base, while sizable protests outside Lansdowne Road were disruptive. Indeed, neither the Taoiseach, Eamon de Valera, nor any cabinet member attended the test match, as would ordinarily have been customary.[60] There was also opposition to South Africa's exclusion of Maoris from touring New Zealand teams during the 1950s and early 1960s, but protests were limited to New Zealand, and even there to Maoris themselves and members of the church. It was only in the late 1960s that the sporting boycott would gather considerable momentum.

By 1967, notes Peter Hain, "it had become obvious that public opinion in New Zealand, coupled with the growing Maori national consciousness, would not allow another all-white team to tour South Africa." After an intervention in the New Zealand Parliament by Prime Minister Keith Holyoake, declaring New Zealand "one nation," it was clear that the tour would be canceled.[61] South Africa's immediate response was to declare that, henceforth, Maoris would be given "honorary white status" and allowed to play. Although this led to a subsequent tour to South Africa being planned for 1970, a domestic campaign in New Zealand resulted in the creation in July 1969 of an ad hoc organization called the Halt All Racist Tours (HART) demanding that the tour be canceled. Although HART failed to stop this tour, an emergent strand of citizen activism, targeting sport, was making itself felt. In Australia, the Campaign Against Racialism in Sport (CARIS) was formed in 1969, which used direct action to protest South African involvement in swimming championships, throwing black dye into the water. In Europe, protestors had, back in 1965, occupied the court during a Davis Cup tennis tie in Norway, and there were further protests at a Davis Cup match in Sweden in 1968. Elsewhere, stink bombs and smoke bombs disrupted badminton championships in Denmark and the Netherlands in 1969 and 1970.[62]

With an established template for more concerted and coordinated action developing during the late 1960s and into the 1970s, the targeting of white South Africa's favorite sports would provide the most effective battleground. The potential of targeting rugby and cricket was recognized overseas, intentionally designed to have maximum impact. Writing in *The Guardian* in November 1969, Peter Jenkins addressed criticism that a sporting boycott would be less effective than a trade embargo:

> Public opinion in western countries, as the number of their black citizens grows, may develop in favour of ostracizing South Africa and suffering the material consequences of a trade embargo. Alternatively, public opinion may condone racialism in South Africa which will be the first stage of condoning and applying it here. If that is what is at stake I argue that the rugby and cricket grounds are as good a place as any to start combating the poison.[63]

The need for more rigorous efforts to target sports was accentuated by the fact that, despite the d'Oliveira affair leading to the cancellation of England's 1968 tour and prompting considerable negative publicity for South Africa, the MCC announced in January 1969 that a South African tour to England in 1970 *would* go ahead as planned. Despite this setback, the d'Oliveira affair did raise the public's consciousness of apartheid issues, something that Peter Hain felt was crucial to the subsequent success of the STST. As he put it: "It was against this background of public interest, coupled with the groundwork done over the years by organizations such as the AAM and the SANROC, that the campaign emerged—a campaign which was to dominate public attention for nine months and which ultimately was to triumph."[64]

Public activism was a key driver of efforts to politicize South African sport. It provided, as Hain suggested, a unique opportunity for a wider global public to "prove their abhorrence of apartheid, and so actually influence developments inside South Africa."[65] From the late 1960s, visiting South African sports teams prompted widespread protest, as demonstrated by the reception afforded the visiting Springboks on their 1969–70 tour to Britain and Ireland. The racial segregation of South African sport was becoming more unpalatable to the global public. The STST's campaign during the 1969 rugby tour demonstrated this further, distributing posters and leaflets to sympathetic groups in every town where the Springboks were scheduled to play. The arriving South Africans encountered dissent from the start, welcomed at Heathrow with cries of "Don't scrum with a Racist Bum." The more direct action of the STST—which later involved attempts to hijack the South African team coach and to undertake pitch invasions—often caused tension with an AAM leadership that largely eschewed such tactics. But the campaign *was* effective, Gurney suggesting that it marked the "AAM's biggest victory since its formation" and tapped into "a deep—and unexpected—vein of public support." Combined with unprecedented media coverage and Britain's own domestic debates on race relations, the STST campaign gave the apartheid issue a prominence that it would not enjoy again until the mid-1980s.[66]

The STST movement flagrantly mixed sports and politics, a fact acknowledged and applauded by the president of the AAM, the Right Reverend Ambrose Reeves in a letter to *The Guardian*. "Throughout the summer," he wrote, "the Anti-Apartheid Movement . . . will be conducting an intensive campaign against racialist sport and, in particular, to stop the South African cricket tour." The world of sport was utilized to showcase the AAM's wider political objectives, "to secure the release of political prisoners in South Africa, to provide a platform for Southern African liberation organizations and generally win public opinion in support of a British policy of non-racialism and democracy for the peoples of Southern Africa."[67] Indeed, the work of the AAM and the STST was intertwined, the AAM deciding in summer 1969 to create the "Stop the Seventy Tour" Committee in the first place (despite the opposition of some members). The STST was launched at a press conference on September 10, 1969, and featured a range of participants reflective of its broad support base, comprising AAM members, International Socialists, Students Union representatives, SANROC, United Nations Youth, the Young Liberal Movement, and many others.[68]

Given its emphasis on winning public support, media portrayals of the STST were crucial. Hain noted how *The Guardian* and the *Morning Star* gave the movement "prominent and analytical coverage" while *The Times* and the *Daily Express* "carried a few paragraphs." "The other national dailies," Hain acknowledged, "ignored us," and these same papers were invariably those that would later portray the STST's activities pejoratively.[69] Press interest grew as direct action was used more widely. Using the current Springbok rugby tour as a trial run, they engaged in disruptive activities that went beyond the usual demonstrations and pickets. Weed killer was used to inscribe the words "Oxford Rejects Apartheid" onto the pitch ahead of the tour match against Oxford University, while protestors occupied the pitch ahead of test matches in Cardiff, Edinburgh, London, and Dublin. Although the games all went ahead (though often before greatly diminished crowds), the aims of the protestors were achieved. "We could never really lose," recalled Hain, as their principal objective was keeping apartheid in the public spotlight. The direct action tactics solicited unprecedented press coverage, and though not always positive, it was still publicity.[70]

In terms of impact, there was a sign of progress when the South African Cricket Association announced on December 16, 1969, that their touring team would be selected on merit rather than color. Not only was this a clear acknowledgment that previous teams had *not* been selected on merit alone but it was also held up as a key victory for the STST's public campaign. John Arlott wrote in *The Guardian* that it "must now seem that the demonstrators, by their action against the Springbok rugby tour, have in a few months achieved more than the cricket officials have done by 15 years of polite acquiescence."[71] The STST took this momentum into 1970, with coordinated protests at fourteen county cricket grounds on January 19, daubing them with painted slogans, digging up the turf, or attacking the pitches with weed killer. Hain emphasized the "psychological" aspect of the protests, instilling in the minds of the cricketing authorities the very real prospect that the cricketing tour, were it to go ahead, would be subjected to unparalleled levels of disruption.[72]

As the sporting boycott gathered pace in the early 1970s, its potential impact was increasingly recognized. In May 1970 the *New York Times* remarked how ironic it would be "if a tennis racket or a rugby ball achieved more change from within than the moral assaults upon the Pretoria government . . . . Apartheid, on and off the field, in the long run will have become a losing game."[73] Peter Hain welcomed how "newsworthy" the protest movement had become, suggesting that it intentionally sought to provide "strong visual images for the new television age." The movement was a product of its time, he observed, drawing inspiration from the "era of student sit-ins, Vietnam demos, the 1968 Paris revolt, and the American anti-war movement."[74] The idea of using sport to showcase the iniquities of apartheid was taking hold, and was by no means confined to Europe. American attention was alerted to South Africa's racialist sporting policies when South Africa banned the African American tennis player, Arthur Ashe, from participating in the 1970 South African tennis championships in Johannesburg. This maladroit decision, suggests Hain, "did much to increase support for the anti-cricket-tour campaign in Britain and the general world campaign against apartheid in sport."[75] A temporary ban from the Davis Cup compelled the South Africans to reconsider, allowing Ashe to play in South Africa in future and even inviting him for a symbolic visit to the country during which he met many government ministers, visited the Soweto township, and spoke to vast crowds of black youths.[76]

Protests also disrupted the Springboks' tour of Australia in 1971, prompting the decision to cancel a South African cricket tour scheduled for later that year.[77] *The Guardian* interpreted the cancellation of the Australia tour as a "body blow" for Pretoria, and the simultaneous cancellation of the New Zealand tour meant that "the isolation of South Africa in the world of sport has become almost total." Noting that rugby union was the only sport still open to South African participation, it concluded, nonetheless, that given the "controversial Springbok tour of Australia earlier this year . . . even this link may shortly snap." The success of the anti-apartheid movement owed much to the efforts of those like Peter Hain who had, in *The Guardian's* estimation, "succeeded in convincing the public (and many sportsmen) that it is the South African authorities who are really responsible for mixing sport with political and racial dogma." Applauding the ability of the non-violent protests in Britain and Australia to "have an effect on public opinion," the paper concluded that the demonstrators had "shown what a force moral pressure can prove when effectively mobilised."[78]

The sporting boycott, however, was applied inconsistently. The IOC allowed the New Zealand team to participate in the 1976 Montreal Olympics despite the decision of the New Zealand government not to cancel the visit of the Springboks to New Zealand that year. To be sure, the New Zealand Rugby Football Union was, as Maclean has noted, "the most important recalcitrant" when it came to the failure to impose consistently a sporting boycott.[79] It was here that anti-apartheid activism became more global and political, as twenty-nine African nations, along with Guyana and Iraq, boycotted the Montreal Games to protest the inclusion of the New Zealand team and the IOC's refusal to condemn the tour.[80] Public anger at the failure to apply sporting sanctions effectively was also becoming more prominent. As Eric Morgan has noted, South African participation in the 1977 Davis Cup "drew the ire of anti-apartheid activists across the United States, who saw South Africa's presence as a legitimization of not only segregated sport, but also larger apartheid society."[81] Indeed, the American Coordinating Committee for Equality in Sport (ACCESS, formed in 1976) undertook more consistent protests thereafter, and their campaigns against South Africa's Davis Cup participation contributed to that country being banned in 1979, not to be readmitted until 1992.

The sporting isolation of South Africa had increased substantially by the end of the 1970s. In 1977, the Gleneagles Agreement stated that its signatories (and this was a Commonwealth initiative) would "vigorously . . . combat the evil of apartheid by withholding any form of support for, and by taking every practical step to discourage contact or competition by their nationals with sporting organisations, teams of sportsmen from South Africa or any other country where sports are organized on the basis of race, colour or ethnic origin."[82] The Gleneagles Agreement was, however, immediately undermined by the reluctance of certain countries (Great Britain and New Zealand in particular) to adhere to it rigidly. Indeed, the decision of the New Zealand rugby authorities to go ahead with the Springbok's tour of New Zealand in 1981 was an immediate indicator of the agreement's fallibility. In light of this, African members of the Commonwealth threatened to boycott the Brisbane Commonwealth Games unless New Zealand was barred. This spurred the Commonwealth Games Federation into action, with the unveiling of a "code of conduct" intended to better police the Gleneagles Agreement. This more robust enforcement was seen at the time as contributing to the decision to stop the planned 1985 tour of South Africa by the British and Irish Lions rugby team, the British wary that this might lead to their competitors being barred from the 1986 Commonwealth Games in Edinburgh.[83]

Although never complete, the sporting isolation of South Africa had become substantial by the 1980s. So-called "rebel" tours undermined this isolation, but the controversy they provoked ensured that apartheid remained in the public and media spotlight. As Llewellyn notes, the various "rebel" initiatives from Australia, New Zealand, and England were rendered "increasingly more difficult, expensive and politically explosive."[84] Furthermore, as Bruce Kidd wrote in 1988, most participants in these "rebel" tours "are well past their prime."[85] That the sporting protests were both visible and popularly supported is also indisputable. Kidd noted how, even in "rugby-mad New Zealand," campaigns against tours with South Africa "mobilized thousands of demonstrators." He notes also the relentless campaign in Britain against the "passport of convenience" given to the South African–born athlete Zola Budd.[86] Llewellyn also emphasizes the interconnectedness of the sporting campaign and that focused on economic sanctions and divestment. Indeed, he suggests that the campaign to ensure South Africa's exclusion from the 1984 Los Angeles Olympics lent impetus to an American anti-apartheid movement that "would later force President Reagan into a stunning foreign policy U-turn, which culminated in the 1986 passage of the comprehensive Anti-Apartheid Act."[87]

However, it might even be argued that the sporting boycott was little more than a release valve for anti-apartheid sentiment that avoided the need to undertake the kind of economic sanctions that would have been more effectual. As Keech and Houlihan have suggested, "sports sanctions were, up until the mid-1980s, a convenient resource for the major trading partners of South

Africa who could attempt to combine moral condemnation of apartheid with a continuation of trading links." Even if they lacked a decisive impact, sporting boycotts and sanctions *did* play an important role as a consciousness raiser. As Keech and Houlihan acknowledge, they "created and sustained an awareness of one of the most flagrant abuses of human rights in the 20th century," an awareness that had, by the mid-1980s, made it "much more difficult for the international community to ignore the calls for the application of trade and financial sanctions."[88] Conversely, Kidd claimed in 1988 that the sports boycott was "significantly more effective than any of the other international campaigns to quarantine the apartheid state." Compared to the piecemeal effectiveness of trade, tourism, cultural, and academic boycotts, "exchanges in the major sports have been virtually eliminated."[89] Reflecting in 1996 on his role in the STST, Peter Hain recalled the comments made to him by Ali Bacher, the cricketer set to captain the South Africa team in 1970. "There's no doubt the cancellation forced us to change," Bacher acknowledged: "We wouldn't have done so otherwise. It was the turning-point. There was no way back for us. You were right—we were wrong."[90] At the very least, a sporting boycott provided an effective mechanism for bypassing uncooperative governments. As Enuga Reddy noted, "certain things can be done by the public—we don't need the government for a sports boycott."[91]

Another unofficial channel for articulating opposition to apartheid (and another channel that was public and visible) was a broader cultural boycott of South Africa. The British Musicians Union adopted, as early as 1961, a policy whereby its members refused to perform in South Africa while apartheid was in force. Another aspect of a cultural boycott came courtesy of forty-five prominent British playwrights (including Arthur Miller and Harold Pinter) signing a declaration in 1963 announcing that they would deny any theater "where discrimination is made among audiences on grounds of colour" performing rights of their works. A total of twenty-eight Irish playwrights (including Samuel Beckett and Eugene McCabe) followed suit in 1964, and the following year saw many of Britain's foremost actors (including Vanessa Redgrave) signing an Equity pledge not to work in South Africa. The boycott also seeped into academia, with 496 professors and lecturers from 34 British universities signing a declaration protesting apartheid and violations of academic freedom, and pledging not to apply for academic posts in South Africa.[92] Music was impacted, too, with the Rolling Stones cancelling negotiations for a proposed tour to South Africa and the Beatles announcing publicly their opposition to apartheid.[93] The AAM's 1987 *Manifesto for Sanctions* also underscored the need for these to be more than simply economic in nature. Alongside the boycott of South African goods, they called for the severing of "all financial, political, cultural and sporting links with South Africa," as well as making mandatory the government's voluntary ban on "the promotion of tourism to South Africa." They also urged churches and educational institutions to sever all ties and called on people more generally to avoid trips to "Sun City" and to support Artists Against Apartheid.[94]

The 1980s: The AAM's Zenith and Apartheid's Endgame

For Gregory Houston, the "most significant impact" of the AAM was "the way in which it shaped public opinion, particularly in the West, leading to a broad international consensus in the second half of the 1980s on the need, and the steps to be taken, to bring an end to apartheid."[95] The mobilization of public opinion was necessary because the altered diplomatic climate at the dawn of the 1980s threatened to overshadow the progress made thus far. In the United States, the more concerted divestment campaign that had emerged in the 1970s was impeded by Ronald Reagan's 1980 electoral success, his administration intent on upping the Cold War ante, part of which meant avoiding antagonizing an amenable, anti-communist South Africa. This led anti-apartheid activists to move away from targeting the executive branch (as had been done with some success during Carter's presidency) and focusing, instead, on influencing public opinion.[96] Indeed, political apathy toward apartheid compelled activists to weaponize public opinion. During the 1980s, however, this weaponization would assume an unparalleled international impetus and reach.

The potential of a genuinely global protest movement had been showcased during the late 1960s. The demonstrators outside the 1968 Democratic Presidential Convention, notes Thörn, chanted "The Whole World is Watching," reflecting a growing attentiveness to the global visibility of protest.[97] A growing internationalism would play out even more visibly in the 1980s, with stage-managed initiatives such as the 1988 "Nelson Mandela 70th Birthday Tribute" concert in London, a carefully cultivated piece of performative activism with an enormous global audience. This resulted from the AAM's deliberate attempts "to create an independent platform, an alternative public sphere that would make it possible to address publics directly," circumventing existing global media industries.[98] To do so, it was necessary for anti-apartheid activism to become more organized and professional. In Britain, the AAM did just that, moving beyond the ramshackle structures of the 1970s (when it consisted of just five paid staff operating out of three rooms in central London). More spacious offices were acquired by the 1980s, and staff also benefited from computers and photocopiers (leaflets had previously been reproduced by hand).[99] The movement also got better at targeting broader constituencies of opinion, not least students, trade unions, church groups, women's organizations, disabled groups, and some professional associations (e.g., architects and health workers). Although its core membership in 1979 of 2,500 was small, these affiliations greatly enhanced its overall reach and influence.[100]

The apparent resolve of Thatcher and Reagan to avoid confrontation with Pretoria actually energized the AAM. As Gurney notes, "a new determination to isolate South Africa in every field" emerged, the movement's strategy predicated on creating "a groundswell of public opinion which would force the Thatcher government to disengage."[101] The largest anti-apartheid demonstration in Britain to date took place in 1982, as 15,000 people marched through central London at the culmination of the AAM's "Southern Africa—the Time to Choose" conference. The 50,000 people attending a June 1984 rally to protest the visit of South Africa's president, P. W. Botha, soon usurped this figure. The 1980s also saw the Irish movement grow in influence and visibility, the continued cultural and consumer boycott winning more publicity, especially after the 1984 "Dunnes strike."[102] The Dunnes strike emanated from the actions of one Dublin shop worker, Mary Manning, who refused to handle South African fruit on July 17, 1984, leading to her being suspended indefinitely from her job at the Dunnes store. The Irish Distributive and Administrative Trade Union (IDATU) backed Manning and, for the following eighteen months, eleven workers (ten women and one man) established a permanent picket line. Although they were originally received with public hostility (spat at and called "nigger lovers"), their crusade soon won more sympathy, providing a catalyst for a more far-ranging boycott of South African goods in Ireland, the success of which reverberated internationally, especially in Britain.[103]

Anti-apartheid activism had become an increasingly visible and noisy political force by the mid-1980s. It had, commented Gurney, "transformed into Britain's biggest ever international solidarity movement," mobilizing hundreds of thousands of people and creating a movement that "cut across class and social boundaries."[104] Public opinion, it seemed, *could* impact directly upon the course of diplomacy. Individuals at the heart of the struggle recognized this reality. As Oliver Tambo wrote to Nelson Mandela:

> Look, there is only one problem: don't manoeuvre yourself into a situation where we have to abandon sanctions. That's the key problem. We are very concerned that we should not get stripped of our weapon of struggle, and the

most important of these is sanctions. That is the trump card with which we can mobilise international opinion and pull governments over to our side.[105]

Although most nonwhite South Africans supported sanctions and divestment (despite the deleterious impact on their own lives), it was not universal. The Inkatha Freedom Party was hostile, Chief Mangosuthu Buthelezi lamenting the "grinding poverty and degradation" of black South Africans: "Divestment will not help the struggle for liberation; it will hinder it." [106]

The AAM looked to rally popular opinion in the West in support of sanctions and boycotts intended to isolate South Africa diplomatically. As Klotz notes of the United States, it was only because of "a groundswell of public sentiment across partisan political lines" that Congress came to enact anti-apartheid sanctions in the 1980s despite the Reagan administration's opposition.[107] To be sure, the American government had proven consistently reluctant to act against Pretoria, and abstained from voting on a UN Security Council resolution in October 1984 condemning apartheid. Yet, as Culverson reminds us, "less than two years later the anti-apartheid movement emerged as a leading force for mobilizing domestic opposition to U.S. policy toward South Africa." This was due, in no small part, to "grassroots activism," through which American public opinion could persuade local-level politicians, college and university authorities, and big business corporations to "reassess their ties to the apartheid state." This, in turn, affected Congress, and in November 1986 it overcame President Reagan's veto and approved the imposition of limited sanctions against South Africa.[108]

Local-level activism—even sanctions undertaken on an individual level— had an effect, even if it took until the mid-1980s for this to be felt. As Guelke remarks: "The climate of opinion was sufficiently hostile to apartheid as to affect the sale and availability of products such as wine in most Western countries."[109] Local-level initiatives soon snowballed, and large American companies themselves began to pull out of South Africa. Financial behemoths like Chase Manhattan Bank began pulling loans to South Africa, precipitating a financial crisis that would rock the white minority government. Public pressure was clearly demanding a shift in governmental policy. In 1985, as Lindsay Michie Eades reminds us, "American public opinion was strong enough to put pressure on Congress to take more direct action against South Africa."[110] Reagan sought to preempt this by passing a very limited sanctions bill, but his reticence aroused considerable public hostility. In July 1986 he publicly urged Pretoria to reform apartheid but argued against sanctions, considering them a "historic act of folly." As Eades notes, Reagan's words triggered "bipartisan criticism for the lack of significant initiative."[111]

Anti-apartheid activism was gaining traction and Reagan appeared powerless to stop it. If the president was dogmatically unresponsive to the public mood, Congress seemed to be more in tune, passing the Comprehensive Anti-Apartheid Act (CAAA) in September 1986 despite Reagan's veto. As Eades concludes, the CAAA, in combination with examples of divestment and other expressions of anti-apartheid citizen activism "reflected the real expression of American public opinion against the apartheid regime." Although the CAAA was poorly implemented, and beset with too many loopholes and exemptions to be properly effective, it demonstrated an unprecedented political determination to take a tougher line. Divestment also gathered momentum; an estimated 200 American companies pulled out of South Africa in the period 1984–89.[112] This amounted to more than one-third of the total number of American companies involved in South Africa in 1984, and these were joined by more than 150 companies from other countries (49 from Britain).[113] The anti-apartheid movement in the United States grew "larger and louder," with some 6,000 Americans being arrested between 1984 and 1986 for picketing the South African embassy and consulate.[114] The reticence of Western governments to take apartheid seriously was a catalyst for the greater transnational cohesiveness that shaped the movement in the 1980s, enabling it, as Guelke suggests, to "bypass governments and be heard regardless."[115]

For Klotz, these global social movements cultivated "epistemic communities," well-informed and educated clusters of individuals who sought actively to use their expertise to exert pressure on policymakers and thus effect change. But Klotz cautions against viewing *all* social movements as merely "epistemic communities," as some benefit enormously from a broader framing that encompasses (and sometimes even prioritizes) the advocacy of public concerns over the articulation of expertise. Klotz reminds us that the exploitation of black South Africans had long been a source of international concern, debated by the UN as early as 1946, but "concerted international opposition . . . only coalesced in the mid-1980s" as organized advocacy networks dovetailed with wider social movements and the participation of influential individuals to lend the movement greater impetus.[116] In short, it required a fusion of many different types of activism for a powerful and potent movement to emerge. In so doing, the AAM became more than a narrow interest group. It transcended a core epistemic community of experts, morphing into a more holistic, all-encompassing movement of multifarious national and transnational networks. Its ambition also grew, seeking to disrupt existing international norms. As Klotz puts it, the AAM offered a form of "moral entrepreneurship" that sought to replace the regressive normative values of the past with a new framework of norms steeped in morality and global conscience. The movement was simultaneously shaping and reflecting a more enlightened and progressive conception of public opinion, more representative of the values of the second half of the twentieth century. In Thörn's analysis, the AAM constituted a "counter-public" that used public communications effectively and imaginatively to challenge the "established media dominating the global public sphere." The challenge, therefore, was to inform public opinion on a *global* scale.[117] Although the 1980s would see this happen on an unprecedented scale, the British AAM would remain a pivotal hub.

Within Britain, the political and social climate of the 1980s provided fertile ground in which a reenergized anti-apartheid movement could flourish. The movement certainly benefited from appealing to the broad church of British opinion that united in opposition to the Thatcher government. "The paradox of the mass support for the AAM in the 1980s," notes Gurney, "was that it was stimulated by Thatcher's hostility."[118] The political hostility was, however, obdurate, making it difficult for the AAM to influence policy. To overcome this impediment, the AAM increasingly sought more imaginative and ambitious ways to mobilize public support. A recognizable public image of the anti-apartheid campaign had been evident from the outset, activists wearing a visible AAM badge, but the merchandising aspect of the movement really took hold in the 1980s. It began at a local level, the Barnet group producing T-shirts and sweaters emblazoned with the AAM logo, but became more coordinated with the establishment of AAM Enterprises in 1985. Thereafter, the visual iconography of the movement began to adorn all sorts of paraphernalia, including mugs, badges, jewelry, and calendars.[119]

In Britain, its leftist credentials played well as an alternative means of attacking Thatcherite policies, while the burgeoning consumerism of the 1980s provided the AAM with myriad ways of accessing and influencing the wider public. The movement as a whole, notes Thörn, "developed new skills in Public Relations, improving its media strategies, and getting involved in merchandise on a scale different from earlier periods."[120] One British member of the AAM, Margaret Ling, recalled the importance of merchandise, considering it "extremely important in conveying a message, in creating and sustaining a sense of identity of the movement." This identity was crucial, the wearing of T-shirts and displaying of posters affording people a sense of inclusiveness and membership, the conviction that they were participating in something meaningful and important. It also, noted Ling, chimed with the sensibilities of the 1980s, a period in which "merchandise was very important for political activism."[121] As Hilary Sapire has noted, the "adroit use of the media would be critical to the successful 'branding' of the ANC and the AAM."[122]

The 1980s was also a decade of technological change, the world becoming ever smaller, and a genuinely global media—facilitated by satellite technology—began to take shape. The AAM harnessed the opportunities provided, the Sun City and Free Nelson Mandela campaigns allowing them to articulate an agenda on an international scale. Danny Schechter's "Artists United Against Apartheid" initiative, resulting in the 1985 album *Sun City*, was just one attempt by the AAM to take ownership of the media, being more proactive in eschewing mainstream channels, and targeting the public directly and unmediated. This was also the impetus behind *GlobalVision*, the television channel that Schechter founded in 1988 with Rory O'Connor. In conjunction with the astute use of merchandise, the AAM became a fashionable brand, a "minor industry," according to Thörn, in which "books, films, photographs, posters, leaflets and T-shirts were produced and distributed."[123] The movement evolved into something that progressives the world over sought to buy into. In this sense, Thörn is justified in emphasizing how the ramifications of globalization should not be viewed only pejoratively through the lens of rampant commodification, but also acknowledged as offering opportunities to showcase "global solidarity" in support of progressive causes.[124] By using a global media advantageously, the AAM could reach a global audience. As one ANC public relations officer recalled, AAM T-shirts were "being worn from New York, to Vancouver, to Moscow, to Sweden, to South Africa."[125]

The global dimension of the anti-apartheid movement, and the ways in which the AAM itself became more adept at maximizing publicity, had an impact. As Welsh and Spence argue, "media coverage [linked] black opposition at home with a global constituency to which it could appeal for redress of grievances."[126] In this sense, rather than taking attention away from local-level resistance in South Africa and apportioning responsibility (and thus agency) exclusively to activists in the West, the two aspects were corollaries. At the very least, the efforts of citizen activists, on a global scale, ensured that the outside world took domestic South African struggles seriously. By the 1980s, this dovetailed with other factors—the end of the Cold War and the severe financial difficulties confronting the white minority government—to accelerate South Africa's transition to representative democracy. In this sense, Welsh and Spence are correct to conclude that "this combination of private sanctions and public pressure from the anti-apartheid movement and its NGO allies . . . provoked the crisis of the mid-1980s and weakened the capacity of the South African state to hold on indefinitely."[127] At the very least, it all had a profound moral and psychological bearing on the endgame of apartheid.

Anti-apartheid activism, doubtless a product of the consumer climate of the 1980s, successfully turned the AAM into a brand. This "branding" featured prominently at the 1988 Nelson Mandela birthday concert, featuring images of woodcuts by the Namibian artist John Muafangejo.[128] The iconography of Nelson Mandela was a huge part of the AAM's success in the 1980s, winning the hearts and minds of people across the globe. The campaign to free Mandela had its roots in the UN, driven by Enuga Reddy, the secretary of the UN Special Committee. After Mandela was awarded the Freedom of the City of Glasgow in August 1982, the city's Lord Provost launched the "Declaration of Mayors," gathering the signatures of 2,200 mayors in 56 countries, calling for Mandela's immediate and unconditional release.[129] The campaign soon transcended politics, becoming a staple of popular activism and culture. The Specials' "Free Nelson Mandela," released in 1984, provided an anthem, while the Specials' Jerry Dammers worked with Jim Kerr of Simple Minds to organize the 1988 Wembley Stadium concert. The initial idea for a concert soon gathered momentum, the BBC agreeing to broadcast it (and to distribute the broadcast rights internationally, resulting in a potential global audience in excess of one billion), and many global stars including Whitney Houston, Sting, Peter Gabriel, and Stevie Wonder agreed to perform.

On June 11, 1988, more than 70,000 people attended the concert, which, unlike the 1985 Live Aid extravaganza, was intended not to raise money but simply raise awareness. The next day saw a protest march depart Glasgow headed for London, a march that would eventually see over 250,000 people assemble at Hyde Park for a rally where the Archbishop Desmond Tutu demanded Mandela's release. The visibility of the Mandela campaign also saw a spike in support for the AAM, its membership rising from 3,500 in 1984 to just shy of 20,000 by March 1989.[130] While this was still relatively small, the movement's various affiliations meant it had a far wider appeal and reach, both in Britain and beyond. Above all, the Wembley concert was an unprecedented consciousness raiser. As Dammers recalled: "The important thing for me was the effect that it had and hopefully it helped coagulate public opinion. And I think it definitely . . . had an effect."[131]

Victoria Brittain described the AAM's relationship with the government as being "tense" for most of the period, even characterized as "hatred" from the point of view of the Thatcher government who considered the movement an embarrassment. For Brittain, it was only "around 1987" that things began to change and all the hard work of the AAM "began to pay off."[132] The change was relatively swift. President F. W. de Klerk announced on February 2, 1990, that his government had "taken a firm decision to release Mr. Mandela unconditionally."[133] Nine days later Mandela left Victor Verster Prison a free man and Wembley hosted another huge concert in celebration two months later. The parlous state of South Africa's economy, the changed diplomatic landscape with the end of the Cold War, and de Klerk's recognition that white minority rule was no longer sustainable, had dovetailed with an enormous amount of global public pressure to ensure that apartheid's days were numbered. With the staging of free elections in April 1994, South Africa's long road to democracy was complete.

Conclusion

Most analyses of the end of apartheid at least touch upon the role of the anti-apartheid movement overseas and, within this, the role of domestic public opinions in encouraging their respective governments to adopt a more robustly anti-apartheid stance. As Guelke has remarked: "Governments could not afford to ignore the strength of public condemnation of apartheid altogether," and a combination of "domestic public opinion" and "pressure from Third World states to take action over apartheid" created a challenging environment for Western governments and diplomacy.[134] Crawford contends that a consensus emerged outside of South Africa, contending "that apartheid was wrong and ought to be eliminated." This contributed to a growth in "the global awareness of apartheid and reinforced the pressures for greater sanctions."[135] Houston's confident assertion that the AAM "contributed substantially" to the end of apartheid is difficult to dispute, especially when the various manifestations of the movement are acknowledged. As Houston notes, economic sanctions and divestment, coupled with the sporting and cultural boycotts, did much to consolidate South Africa's position as a pariah state.[136] Gurney, too, is adamant that the AAM played a crucial role in giving anti-apartheid activism "an international platform" especially in the movement's "difficult wilderness years" when it struggled to resonate both politically and publicly. More than that, however, it was a major actor in the 1980s, its Mandela campaign ensuring that "millions of ordinary citizens in Britain and all over the world came to understand that it was only the people themselves, led by their liberation movement, who could bring genuine democracy to South Africa."[137]

Politicians and diplomats, it seemed, *could* be swayed from their intransigence, and a groundswell of public opinion, mobilized on a global scale, could effect this change. Although numerous other factors led to the abandonment of apartheid, public opinion's role merits recognition. The direct action undertaken by private citizens in Ireland, for example, their "time, money, patience and commitment to march, picket, petition, and generally bring pressure to bear where it was needed," provided a "powerful accompaniment" to more institutional anti-apartheid initiatives.[138] There are, to be sure, other explanations for apartheid's demise. Robert Price emphasizes a "trialectic" of factors comprising growing domestic opposition to apartheid, the increasingly desperate efforts of the government to maintain white minority rule, and growing international pressure being exerted on Pretoria. These factors combined within a broader context of industrialization to engulf South Africa in a political and economic crisis that rendered the end of apartheid unavoidable.[139] Herman Giliomee emphasizes the role of demographics, pointing to a relative decline in the white population, falling from 20 percent of South Africa's total population in 1960 to 15 percent in 1985. The resultant drop in white manpower saw more jobs being filled by nonwhites, in turn intensifying their politicization.[140] Timothy Sisk puts more emphasis on the anti-apartheid movement, asserting that it contributed to a stalemate situation that encouraged moderates in both the regime and the opposition to seek a compromise solution.[141] Voorhes offers a similarly upbeat appraisal of the contribution of the global divestment movement. From its grassroots origins, the movement in the United States grew to such an extent that its impact on major US corporations was substantial. In tandem with similar pressures in Europe, the divestment campaign "supplemented the power of anti-apartheid mobilization" by harnessing a public demand for action. "As the anti-apartheid movement understood early on," wrote Voorhes, "the global public wanted to do something about South Africa; divestment offered a highly visible and low-cost method."[142]

All of this demonstrated, as Danny Schechter put it, "that people can make history, that people can bring about change, and that sometimes very diverse groups of people can unite across borders and boundaries, racial lines and national lines."[143] In conjunction with the cultural and sporting boycotts, the growing isolation of South Africa *did* contribute to the end of apartheid. It was certainly not the only factor, nor should it be considered the most significant. Broader geopolitical changes, not least the end of the Cold War, were pivotal. Pretoria's staunchest Cold War allies, notably Britain and the United States, were no longer prepared to overlook South Africa's racialist policies for reasons of Cold War expediency. That said, the public campaign *had* kept the apartheid issue under the international spotlight, compelling the international community to take the issue seriously. In this sense, an international public played an important performative role in the final act of the apartheid story. For Enuga Reddy, that "public opinion in so much of the world joined the anti-apartheid movement" was evidence that "human beings are basically good."[144] Even solitary acts of activism made a contribution, as noted in 1999 by the then president of South Africa Thabo Mbeki, who applauded "each British housewife, student, parent, who refused to buy South African oranges in supermarkets." These small acts were part of something far greater. "Ordinary people," continued Mbeki, "united in a vision of peace and a future of human beings working together to build a better world, have shown that we can make a difference to the quality of lives of millions."[145]

Public Opinion and European Integration

On January 23, 2013, British prime minister David Cameron began a speech by saying that he wanted to "talk about the future of Europe." He outlined the European Union's contribution to peace since 1945, reiterated Britain's contribution to European history from the Roman era to the present day, and sketched out some of the most pressing contemporary challenges. All of this was merely a prelude to Cameron's vision of a "flexible" union fit for the twenty-first century. Central to this vision was "democratic accountability," a union affording a "bigger and more significant role" to national parliaments. After all, Cameron insisted, "there is not, in my view, a single European demos." Noting that British public disillusionment with the European Union (EU) was at "an all-time high," the prime minister asserted that the British people must now have their say. "It is time," he asserted, "to settle this European question in British politics."[1] Cameron's pledge that, should his Conservative Party win the 2015 general election, there would be a simple "In/Out" referendum concerning Britain's continued membership of the EU was presented as a victory for the Eurosceptics. Nigel Farage, leader of the United Kingdom Independence Party (UKIP) declared the announcement to be his party's "greatest achievement to date," but poured scorn on Cameron's conviction that Europe would compromise sufficiently for a satisfactory deal to be struck. For Farage, UKIP's work was just beginning, the task being to ensure Britain's clear and decisive divorce from the EU.[2]

Cameron's speech set in motion events that would dominate the politics of the EU for years. After a comfortable victory in the 2015 general election, Cameron's government set the date of June 23, 2016, for the referendum that would give the British public the opportunity to have their say on continued EU membership. Opinion polls were clear that victory for either side would be marginal but suggested consistently that the "remain" campaign would prevail. But, as is well known, 51.89 percent of the British electorate voted to leave—

"Brexit" had become a reality, and with it the very future of the EU was put in jeopardy. It was not only in Britain that Eurosceptic voices were heard. Across the Union, including those traditionally pro-European countries at the very center of the project (France, Germany, the Netherlands), doubts were also cast about the future of European integration, and populist anti-European movements have often made considerable electoral ground. The seam of Euroscepticism that led to the Brexit vote threatened to emerge with equally divisive repercussions elsewhere. The popular voice was making itself felt, or so it appeared. In the aftermath of the 2016 referendum, any suggestion of overlooking the vote by remaining in the EU is condemned as treason. British MPs seeking to ensure a parliamentary vote on the final Brexit terms were denounced for their "snake-like" treachery and warned that politicians must not "thwart the will of the British people."[3]

Discussions currently abound about a potential second referendum (a "people's vote"), with arguments on both sides claiming that the sovereignty of "the people" is at stake. Whatever the eventual outcome, there is little doubt that recent debates about European integration have foregrounded the role of the public to an unprecedented extent. At the very least, the Brexit saga stands as a reminder that public opinion can, if allowed, exert a real and significant impact on the course of diplomacy. Notwithstanding the broader debates about *why* the referendum was actually called (Cameron's hubris, internal party politics, a response to the electoral threat of UKIP, etc.), it illustrated clearly that future European integration required the acquiescence, if not the wholehearted support of the people. This need for popular support was not new. Indeed, the Brexit referendum was by no means the first example of the EU's future hinging on a popular vote, and it is unlikely to be the last. Since the 1970s at least, there has been a tacit acknowledgment at the political level that public opinion was a force to be reckoned with, especially after the 1991–92 Maastricht Treaty deliberations prompted a spike in public interest. As one scholar noted early in the twenty-first century: "The era in which relatively insulated elites bargained grand treaties in the shadow of an uninterested and generally approving public has come to an end."[4] This chapter traces the growing awareness of and attentiveness to the vicissitudes of the popular mood in the context of postwar European integration, in so doing, demonstrating the complexity of promoting transnational initiatives in a world where the nation-state still prevails. Despite efforts to cultivate a European "identity" or a "European public sphere," and despite the aforementioned examples of an "international" public opinion being articulated, the European case study demonstrates very clearly that "public opinion" as a concept remains stubbornly nationalistic and continues to be shaped and reflected by media interests that continue to operate within largely national frameworks.

A "Permissive Consensus"?

It was not always the case that the European project heeded the whims and wishes of the people. Within the voluminous literature surrounding the history of European integration it is widely agreed that there existed, certainly until the 1970s, a "permissive consensus" whereby the political elites could drive the European project with little regard for popular opinion. Simply put, the public—at least within the original six member states of the European Economic Community (EEC—or simply European Community (EC) as it will be referred to hereafter) —willingly allowed their elected leaders to press ahead with integration. After all, the process promised exactly the kind of economic, social, political, and strategic advantages that a continent weary of conflict desperately wanted and craved. It has been suggested that this "permissive consensus" persisted even after the first three enlargements of the EC in 1973, 1981, and 1986, and was only challenged when negotiations for the Maastricht Treaty (which founded the EU, paved the way for further integration, and laid the groundwork for a single European currency) commenced. As Catherine de Vries has suggested, European integration had been, at least to this point, "largely uncontested in the eyes of the general public."[5] After Maastricht, however, the illusion of a pliant and acquiescent public was exposed. As Christopher J. Anderson insists, the referenda of the 1990s demonstrated how "European mass publics have the ability and willingness to constrain and possibly forestall further progress toward a united public."[6]

To be sure, European publics had demonstrated an ability to undercut European unification prior to the 1990s debates about Maastricht, not least the Norwegian public's rejection (53.5 percent) of EC membership in 1972. If the "permissive consensus" interpretation was challenged in the 1970s, it was not undermined fatally. Nevertheless, that decade did usher in an unparalleled degree of public debate about European integration. The Norwegian vote was one of several referenda prompted by the first enlargement process, beginning with a French vote that saw 68.3 percent of the public vote in favor of allowing the EC to embrace new member states. Subsequent referenda saw majorities in Ireland (83.1 percent) and Denmark (63.3 percent) vote in favor of joining the

Community, votes which, alongside those in Norway and France, have been seen as marking "the public's first direct participation in Community affairs."[7] The UK joined without holding a referendum, but the opposition Labour Party made an in/out vote a central pledge of their 1974 election campaign. Once elected, Harold Wilson's government held a vote concerning Britain's continued membership (after a renegotiation). This 1975 referendum saw 67.2 percent vote in favor of remaining.

This initial flurry of public interventions was a game-changer. European integration had been, hitherto, an elite-driven process, and it had been this way from the outset. As Robert Shepherd noted in the mid-1970s, the founding fathers of European unification—Jean Monnet, Robert Schuman, Alcide De Gasperi, and Konrad Adenauer—"created the European Community with no direct consultation of the people."[8] Leon Lindberg and Stuart Scheingold agreed, remarking how the entire "scheme was devised and elaborated by technical elites and presented to the public only after compromises had been worked out among political leaders."[9] This is not to say that the elites intentionally *ignored* public opinion, rather that there was an assumed acquiescence. This was not an entirely misplaced assumption, as early opinion polls and surveys suggested that some form of European unification was popular. Surveys undertaken by the United States Information Agency (USIA) across the original six member states (and one non-member, the UK) revealed that 78 percent of West Germans favored the idea of creating a European government to which their own government would abdicate powers. Even in the least supportive countries (Britain and France), there was still a majority in favor, at 55 percent and 56 percent, respectively.[10] Even before European institutions were afforded a more direct democratic legitimacy with the holding of elections to the European Parliament (first held in 1979), it would be misleading to contend that the process was simply imposed on a reluctant public.

Indeed, the public appeared willing to let the elites get on with the job. In so doing, politicians and diplomats could press ahead with European integration with only occasional recourse to the people, an assumed "permissive consensus" giving them the necessary latitude to do so. This is not to say that the public was ignorant, rather that European issues lacked the daily relevance needed to pique its interest. As one mid-1990s study maintained, "public opinion on Europe was favourable towards European integration but did not see the issue as salient."[11] As long as this was the case, the theory of a "permissive consensus"— as outlined in 1970 by Lindberg and Scheingold—would hold.[12] The public's ambivalence, perhaps even apathy, vis-à-vis European integration is compatible with a functionalist interpretation in which the political elites were the principal drivers of the European project with the public little more than passive passengers whose opinions (if they held any) were of negligible import.[13] Such an approach, often associated with Ernst Haas, was the product of its time. It emerged before de Gaulle's 1963 veto of Britain's application for membership of the EC, and hence before that organization confronted its first genuine crisis. To that point, as Shepherd has noted, there was an assumption that the European Coal and Steel Community (the forerunner of the EC) would "inevitably transition . . . to a full economic union, and ultimately to a full political union," a process that appealed to "the optimists in the European movement."[14]

The functionalist approach did not go unchallenged. In 1966 Stanley Hoffmann dismissed as premature predictions that an integrated Europe would eclipse the primacy of the nation-state, suggesting, instead, that a Rousseauian "general will" exists at the national rather than the European level, hence European integration remained contingent on public opinion.[15] As Richard Sinnott notes, this challenge brought forth a new consensus by the early 1970s that included revised neo-functionalist interpretations from scholars like Haas and Philippe C. Schmitter, ascribing a more prominent role to the people.[16] The timing of this transition is notable, emerging as America's experiences in Vietnam saw the Almond–Lippmann conception of an ignorant and volatile public usurped by a more positive conception where public opinion was ostensibly prudent and rational. Indeed, Lindberg and Scheingold always warned that the "permissive consensus" might unravel should the EC "broaden its scope or increase its institutional capacities markedly."[17] The growing scope and ambition of the European project challenged this consensus, a challenge that grew as the integration process gathered pace in the 1990s. Policymakers were no longer insulated from the perceived demands and wishes of their publics. As Sinnott has remarked, the tendency to equate "permissive consensus" with a relatively passive public that simply accepts elite cues is too simplistic, as the consensus evoked is always conditional and public opinion had always been one of the most important conditioning tools.[18] It has been contended elsewhere, however, that this "permissive consensus" (perhaps better articulated as a "soft consensus" on account of the lack of strident public enthusiasm), though predicated on collective public support, affords considerable power and maneuverability to policymaking elites.[19] Nevertheless, the lingering conception of an elite-driven process has contributed to an increasingly problematic perception of a "democratic deficit," the integration process being engineered by aloof and out-of-touch elites and imposed subsequently on a marginalized public.

But this alleged "democratic deficit" can be overstated. For Moravscik, the allegation holds water only if "European elections were the only form of democratic accountability," which is simply not the case. Policymaking powers have always resided largely with national parliamentarians, as demonstrated recently by the ability of the British Parliament to embark along the Brexit path. Moravscik goes further, claiming that the specter of a "European superstate" governed by a Brussels-based "bureaucratic despotism" has been fabricated by "British tabloid articles, often fuelled by an ignorance of what the EU actually does."[20] There remains, nonetheless, an overarching impression that EU decision-making has taken place without sufficient public oversight. As Dimiter Toshkov contends: "Scholars have mostly *assumed* that there has been no link between European public opinion and day-to-day policy-making in Brussels," contributing to a perceived wisdom that, at least until the late 1970s, a "permissive consensus" allowed policymakers to press ahead with the European project with little or no concern for public accountability.[21] Toshkov, however, queries this, identifying a correlation between public support for the EU and policymaking activity. He suggests that policymakers *are* constrained by public opinion, only able to press ahead with further integration when public support (or at least acquiescence) is apparent. Despite the "absence of institutional mechanisms linking mass preferences and policy change directly, the political system of the EU has been more attentive and more responsive to public sentiment than previously assumed."[22]

A more quiescent public sentiment was likelier when the European project was a chiefly economic enterprise, but this began to change by the 1970s. Prior to this, a degree of public ambivalence (or even support) for integration was assured because the public benefited economically from the process. As Shepherd noted, popular support for European integration rested on the people applying a utilitarian cost-benefits analysis to its outcomes.[23] Indeed, Ronald Inglehart noted in 1970 that there "is evidence that the publics of the EC countries *have*, in fact, generally attributed beneficial economic effects to the EC over the past ten years."[24] Into the 1970s, however, the European project assumed a more political and cultural hue that rendered such utilitarian support insufficient. A greater degree of political and cultural unification required more emotional, affective support mechanisms.[25] According to Shepherd's reading of the available survey data, there did exist (at least across the original six member states) "a clear demonstration of the extent of affective support for European unification" but this fell well short of support for anything approximating federalism. Even within the "pro-European Six," the public was "wary of policies which may require some form of personal sacrifice in the common 'European' good."[26] Already, it seems, the public was articulating an unease with unification that threatened to derail or at least obstruct the process.

The flurry of referenda in the 1970s is evidence of this, including the 1975 vote on Britain's EC membership. If the 2016 referendum was intended to resolve fissures regarding Europe within the Conservative Party, the 1975 referendum was largely conducted to resolve the Labour Party's internal divisions. Like David Cameron in 2016, Harold Wilson supported continued British membership of the EC, and much effort (not to mention money) was spent on a government-led campaign to convince the British people to support this stance. Nonetheless, British public opinion proved "resistant" to government propaganda, remaining largely apathetic throughout the referendum campaign.[27] The efforts made to ensure pro-Community coverage in the printed press and on television demonstrated the government's concerns about how a volatile public might vote, and the extent to which public attitudes might be swayed by an irresponsible media. Wilson was fortunate that the public's apathy in the mid-1970s approximated something more akin to a sanguine "permissive consensus" rather than the febrile and partisan atmosphere that characterized the 2016 vote. The 1975 referendum took place in an unusually favorable climate; thereafter, anti-Europe forces would become more potent and influential. Today, European governments still, as they did in the 1970s, back the European project, and can thus throw their considerable weight behind pro-European campaigns, but anti-European forces now have more resources (financial, business, press, social media etc.) at their disposal, making it far less certain that a government-backed pro-European campaign would prevail.[28]

What the series of referenda in the 1970s *did* show was a new commitment on the part of the EC to become more accountable to public opinion. This commitment was enhanced further by the introduction in 1979 of direct elections to the European Parliament. For the first time, a proportion of the decision-making elites within the EC would be elected by, and answerable to, the electorate. The community clearly understood that more efforts to inform the public about European affairs were required. Indeed, the Eurobarometer surveys (which have been conducted since 1973) were more than simply appraisals of opinion poll data, revealing also the concerns held at the highest levels of Europe as regards the potentially deleterious ramifications of an ill-educated public. Most of the early surveys in the 1970s indicated that the public in all countries felt that not enough information was available about Europe, either in newspapers, television or via radio. This was an issue that the EC recognized and sought to address. "It is clearly of the utmost importance," it was observed in 1978, "that the public should be well-informed about Community problems, especially with the first direct elections to the European Parliament only a few months away."[29] The following year, the public's previous lack of information was starting to change, with two-thirds of respondents having read or heard something about the European elections in April 1979 (two months prior to polling day). This was attributed to the EC's "multimedia campaign" (targeting television, newspapers and radio in particular) launched in January 1979, which had three objectives: "To make as many citizens as possible aware of the election, to encourage them to turn out on polling day and to provide the public with unbiased information on Parliament and the Community."[30]

Efforts to increase public awareness of European issues continued into the 1980s. A 1980 Eurobarometer report acknowledged the widespread conviction that the European project had been, to date, an "elitist phenomenon" that was quite divorced from a public opinion that remained "largely indifferent" to the process or, at best, afforded only a "permissive" consensus.[31] This emergent sense of a democratic deficit was attributed principally to the lack of information about European affairs.[32] Nonetheless, attempts to imbue Europe's political institutions with greater democratic legitimacy struggled to gain traction. A worsening (and worrying) "democratic deficit" was noted in 1994, Eurobarometer observing the steady decline in voter turnout at European elections from 63 percent across the community in 1979, to 61 percent in 1984, 58.5 percent in 1989, and 56.5 percent in the most recent 1994 polls.[33] As the 1990s dawned, the end of the Cold War, German reunification, emergent troubles in the Balkans, and the greater impetus lent to European integration by the Maastricht Treaty all posed challenges for an expanding international organization in a rapidly evolving international context. The greater prominence afforded the political and cultural aspects of unification meant that the utilitarian, economic calculations, upon which much of the "permissive consensus" was constructed, were no longer sufficient to guarantee popular legitimation.

As Dalton and Eichenberg contend, public endorsement of the European project now depended not only on perceived economic benefits but also on "political campaigns, elite actions, and the international environment." The changed international climate, coupled with an unanticipated rise in public disenchantment with the European project in the late 1980s and early 1990s, led to a reorientation of the public opinion–policymaking nexus. In particular, the Danish public's rejection of Maastricht in a June 1992 referendum (rejected by 50.7 percent) and the very narrow endorsement (51 percent) of Maastricht in a French referendum in September revealed the public's unease with the pace and extent of European integration. Europe's leaders now had to heed public opinion, renegotiating "the terms of Danish adherence to the Maastricht bargain in an explicit attempt to gain the future approval of Danish voters."[34] The authors of a 1995 Eurobarometer survey recognized this new and more prominent role for public opinion. "We see public opinion and attitudes as co-determining the speed of European integration," it was noted, "and as *contributing* to defining the nature and form of political union."[35] The Maastricht debates clearly left their mark, and the majority of the literature on European integration agrees that it was a turning point as regards the relationship between the unification process and European public opinion.[36] As one 1994 study noted, the 1992 referenda in Denmark and France revealed a "greater opposition to the ongoing European project than previous polls had generally indicated."[37]

The EC's own Eurobarometer surveys did, however, detect this dwindling popular support, even noting how the decline had started in the late 1980s as concerns about the Single European Market emerged. These initial cracks in the "permissive consensus" were massively "accelerated as soon as 'Maastricht' had taken place."[38] The real crisis of popular support arose in the early 1990s, as further steps toward expanding the union and ushering in a single currency prompted a greater degree of circumspection. As Toshkov notes, the accession of Austria, Finland, and Sweden in 1995, coming so soon after Maastricht, exacerbated concerns that Europe was moving too far and too quickly.[39] As Gabel and Palmer wrote at the time, it had only recently become apparent "that the public is neither as supportive of European integration nor as deferential to elites on EC issues as previously assumed."[40] In short, as a 1993 Eurobarometer survey commented, the "chances for a simple return to the 'permissive consensus' of the past are slim."[41]

Tracing Public Opinion

It is surely no coincidence that the "permissive consensus" model points to the 1970s as the decade in which things changed. It was also in the 1970s—and 1973 in particular—that a dedicated mechanism for gauging public attitudes toward European issues emerged, via the Eurobarometer surveys, initially conducted under the direction of Jacques-René Rabier. Since its inception, Eurobarometer has asked respondents twice yearly whether they consider their country's membership of the community to be "a good thing." The fundamental results are familiar, showing higher levels of support through the 1970s and 1980s, dropping in the 1990s, before recovering slightly by the turn of the century (though never returning to pre-1990 levels).[42] Of course, the public had an opinion on European integration before Eurobarometer polls commenced. There are problems, too, with relying exclusively on poll data, especially given the convenience of the Eurobarometer surveys. As Anderson and Hecht warn, although the data has become "an indispensable resource for students of European public opinion and political behaviour," there has been an unintended consequence, whereby the data are "often 'retrofitted' to suit the analysis."[43]

The potential risk of "retrofitting" poll data to serve an analytical model or argument does not apply only to Eurobarometer results, but also to the opinion polls covering the earlier years of the European project. Nonetheless, the data itself is revealing, and tends to confirm that something approximating a "permissive consensus" was in evidence, at least until the 1970s. Take France for example, one of the original "Six" but whose public frequently projected mixed messages about Europe. Christine Manigand suggests that while French support for the European project was initially quite high, a degree of Euroscepticism emerged by the end of the twentieth century as the more rapid and substantial enlargement of the EU provoked unease.[44] Prior to this, however, the French were a willing if passive advocate of European integration. Indeed, from 1947 to the late 1950s, six in ten people in France were in favor, rising to seven in ten during the 1970s. By 1979, some 75 percent of French citizens claimed to be very favorable to the European project, the figure rising to 81 percent in 1984, and a high of 86 percent in 1989. It soon dipped below 80 percent where it remained thereafter.[45] In short, French support for European integration was always ambivalent; a passive consensus, largely mirroring elite leadership and cues, persisted until the late 1980s, after which a greater degree of skepticism began to take hold.

In another of the original "Six," West Germany, early support for European integration was consistently high, not falling below 60 percent in the period from 1950 to the early 1970s. Surveys in 1970 and 1971 even revealed that over 80 percent of West Germans would embrace the evolution of the Common Market into something approximating a "United States of Europe," figures only surpassed in this period by the Italians and Luxembourgers.[46] Indeed, across the original "Six," there was substantial support for European integration in these early years, especially once a latent mistrust of Germany (particularly in France) was overcome. There was also support for European unification in the UK, albeit of a less pronounced and more conditional variety. A 1954 survey conducted by the USIA showed that 78 percent of British respondents were inclined to favor efforts toward uniting Western Europe, not too far behind the 82 percent figure for West Germany.[47]

It is clear that British support for European integration was relatively high in the early years (the 1950s). One possible explanation for the British public's more lukewarm attitude thereafter is the legacy of twice being rejected for membership in the 1960s. As Inglehart postulated in 1970, the British public's "current reserve toward European integration could be seen, then, as a psychological defence against further disappointment."[48] It is certainly a truism that Britain's relationship with Europe has always been ambivalent. One Dutch study simply describes the relationship as "turbulent," drawing attention to Britain's close ties with the United States, its role within the Commonwealth, and a reluctance to accept the demise of its Empire as reasons for its tentative approach to the European project.[49] Despite this, one must be circumspect when assessing the poll data. After all, results from the 1950s until the end of the 1980s—whether Gallup surveys or those conducted by Eurobarometer—show that even when the British public was most hostile to British membership of the community, more Britons favored European integration than opposed it.[50]

This apparent enthusiasm for the European project is ascribed to utilitarian economic calculations, not least the desire to create a mutually beneficial European open market. But this enthusiasm for closer economic integration was never mirrored by an equivalent appetite for closer social and political ties. Indeed, the various concessions negotiated by John Major's government at Maastricht—the opt-out from the Social Charter, being shielded from a single currency, as well as various clauses ensuring the primacy of governmental rather than supranational decision-making in regard to foreign and home affairs, defense matters, and justice—was emblematic of Britain's instinctive resistance to the dreaded "F"-word: federalism.[51] This fear of federalism is not a uniquely British trait. As noted, French public support for Europe waned into the 1990s, a phenomenon that was actually common across the union. Eurobarometer data shows clearly that the pace of European integration in the late 1980s and early 1990s prompted a backlash in all member states.

During the final three decades of the twentieth century, the Eurobarometer surveys consistently posed four questions concerning attitudes toward the EC. These are as follows:

(1) "In general, are you for or against efforts being made to unify Western Europe? If for, are you very much for this, or only to some extent? If against, are you only to some extent against this or very much against?"

(2)   "Generally speaking, do you think that (your country's) membership in the Common Market is a good thing, a bad thing, or neither good nor bad?"

(3)   "If you were told tomorrow that the European Community (the Common Market) had been scrapped, would you be very sorry about it, indifferent, or relieved?"

(4)   "Taking everything into consideration, would you say that (your country) has on balance benefited or not from being a member of the European Community?"

Oskar Niedermayer has labeled these four questions the (1) "unification" indicator, (2) the "membership" indicator, (3) the "dissolution" indicator, and (4) the "benefit" indicator. By grouping responses to the four questions into three categories—positive, indifferent, and negative—Niedermayer attempted to identify trends that were suggestive of either the "Europeanization" of public opinion (where positive responses are increasing over time) or a "nationalization" of public opinion (where negative responses are increasing). His findings indicate a move toward the "nationalization" of public opinion at the end of the 1970s, followed by a move to "Europeanization" in the 1980s, and then a return to a "nationalization process" around 1991–92 (the Maastricht era).[52]

Though these wider trends applied to all member states, the pattern was never uniform and varied according to country. Support for the European project was consistently high in the six original member states, but notably lower in Denmark and the UK. Support in the other 1973 newcomer, the Republic of Ireland, was also high, and Britain's lack of enthusiasm also found no echo in those states (Greece, Portugal, and, especially, Spain) that joined in the 1980s. In fact, as Niedermayer acknowledges, the "Europeanization" of public opinion in the 1980s was attributable chiefly to the inclusion of these new member states, where the publics were generally supportive of the process.[53] Overall, Niedermayer points out that support for the European project had, by the end of the 1980s, "reached the highest level ever measured" based on the four consistent questions posed in the Eurobarometer surveys. However, the June 1992 Danish referendum on Maastricht reflected a period when a "nationalization" of public opinion was once more in evidence, although Niedermayer is keen to stress that the Danish vote was a symptom rather than a cause. He contends that a more latent public discontent with the Single Market, coupled with a growing uncertainty as to the EC's role in the post–Cold War world, prompted a greater degree of disillusionment across the continent, manifested in largely pejorative media commentary about a potential single currency.[54]

A greater disillusionment might have been continent-wide, but it is clear that Britain and Denmark led the way when it came to Euroscepticism. If British apprehensions can be explained by that country's place in the Commonwealth, its relationship with the United States, and the struggle to reconcile itself with the end of Empire, how can one explain the hostility of the Danes? Well, Niedermayer contends that the Danes consider themselves closer to the Nordic nations than the rest of Europe, but, perhaps more importantly, feared being dominated by larger continental powers (notably Germany). In short, anything that might amount to "a flight from the country's historical inheritance" is significant in conditioning the public's receptiveness to the European project.[55] A potential loss of cherished Danish independence was particularly apparent on the political left. Unease with the European project might be strange for a leftist tradition keen to stress its adherence to internationalism, but from the days of the Rome Treaty skeptical Danish voices warned of an imperialist initiative led by the larger member states. For the Danish left, suggests Sebastian Lang-Jensen, international cooperation must be predicated on "an international peace-keeping pillar represented by the UN and a regional pillar represented by the Nordic countries." Given this tradition and focus, a Europe-wide perspective struggled to resonate with sizable sections of Danish political and public opinion.[56]

Like Denmark, Austria had a particular historical legacy to navigate. Its past *might* have preconditioned Austrians to supporting the project of European unity, the prospect of a united entity free of borders, visas, and passports, and based on an educated European citizenry evoking positive parallels with the Austro–Hungarian Empire.[57] Indeed, Jürgen Elvert contends that how far a national public buys into and embraces a concept of "European-ness" is contingent on each country's "particular historical heritage." Consequently, of the various states joining during the 1970s, 1980s, and 1990s, Austria was the most enthusiastic, ahead of Spain and Greece, with the others (the UK, Ireland, Portugal, and the Nordic countries) lagging behind.[58] Still, popular enthusiasm was by no means unanimous. To be sure, the 1994 referendum *did* facilitate Austria's adhesion, and during the campaign the majority of the political and media class in Austria campaigned in favor of joining the EU, helping to secure a 66.6 percent "yes" vote on June 12. However, as Gehler insists, a considerable seam of Austrian opinion remained indifferent or even hostile to the European project, fearful lest this new direction result in Austria losing the cherished neutrality enjoyed during the Cold War, but concerned, too, that Austria's distinctiveness and independence might be jeopardized by too close an alignment with their "big

German brother."[59] Like the Danes, therefore, a kernel of reticence was never far from the surface.

For various reasons, and to different degrees, popular support for the EU dipped in the final decade of the twentieth century. Data from Eurobarometer polls indicates this trend clearly:

Percentage Support, by Country, for the European Union, 1990–2002—Eurobarometer

Country	Autumn 1990	Autumn 1991	Autumn 1993	Autumn 1997	Autumn 1998	Autumn 2001	Autumn 2002
Ireland	76	78	73	83	79	81	74
Luxembourg	76	79	72	71	77	81	83
Netherlands	82	86	80	76	75	74	69
Italy	77	78	68	69	68	64	62
Greece	75	73	77	60	67	68	62
Portugal	69	77	59	56	58	63	56
Denmark	58	61	58	53	56	62	61
Spain	69	73	54	53	63	57	68
France	66	63	55	48	52	50	52
Germany	73	69	53	38	48	55	59
Belgium	73	71	59	42	47	58	60
Finland	-	-	-	39	45	37	41
Austria	-	-	-	31	38	44	46
UK	53	57	43	36	37	33	31
Sweden	-	-	-	31	35	43	43
Average	69	69	57	49	54	54	55

Anne Dulphy and Christine Manigand, "Introduction," in Anne Dulphy and Christine Manigand (eds), *Les opinions publiques face à l'Europe communautaire: Entre cultures nationales et horizon européen* (Brussels: Peter Lang, 2004), p. 13.

An October 2000 Eurobarometer report noted how public support waned in the 1990s, from "the all-time high of 72% recorded in the spring of 1991" to a low of 46 percent by spring 1997. Support for the EU hovered around the 50 percent mark for the remainder of the century. Eurobarometer explained this dip in support by citing the impact of the Gulf War, the economic crisis (and concomitant rise in unemployment), debates over Maastricht, the war in Yugoslavia, the 1995 extension of the EU to include "three relatively euro-sceptic nations" (Sweden, Finland, and Austria), and the Bovine spongiform encephalopathy (BSE) crisis (especially the controversy arising from Europe's decision to impose a worldwide ban on British beef exports).[60]

Yet, despite the decline in overt support for the EU, there was no equivalent rise in outright dissent. It was reported in 2000 that 43 percent of European citizens "have a positive image of the European Union" with only 18 percent asserting that "the EU conjures up a negative image, of which 5% feel very negative."[61] Had the EU weathered the Maastricht storm? Writing in the context of Brexit, the obvious response to this question is "no," but this was less obvious at the time. Perhaps the relative recovery from the early 1990s slump in public support owed much to the EU's efforts to address accusations of elitism and an alleged "democratic deficit" (alongside Europe's economies beginning to recover from recession). In short, the EU responded to disappointing referenda results by making changes and concessions, seeking to show that the Brussels elite could be attentive to the vox populi. Toshkov's reading of Eurobarometer data suggests that this is the case, concluding that "public support for European integration is related to the legislative output of the EU." In Toshkov's analysis, European policymakers "have been much more attentive to movements in public opinion than previously suggested." As had been demonstrated by the ramifications of Maastricht, Europe's policymakers were unable to travel much farther down the integration road than public opinion would allow.[62]

That the elites had to be more alert to the vicissitudes of the public mood owed much to the growing visibility of European issues in the public sphere. The broader issues of European integration and unification were becoming increasingly salient to a public that was far from simply passive and permissive. It was not only the union's growing focus on political and cultural integration that increased this salience but also the growing prominence of European affairs in the news media. It also tied in, of course, with broader technological advances that were already revolutionizing the projection of foreign news across the globe, as demonstrated by coverage of the Vietnam War. This process continued apace during the 1970s and 1980s. It has been noted of Austria, for example, that media interest in international events (especially as played out on television screens) grew rapidly, attributable in no small part to international terrorism, the era of détente in Europe, and the "new" Cold War prompted by the Soviet Union's invasion of Afghanistan. This in turn fed into a growing interest in the European project even before the end of the Cold War paved the way for Austria's eventual accession in 1995.[63]

A 1980 Eurobarometer survey asked specifically for the sources of the public's information about European affairs, the results suggesting that 60 percent saw a television item on Europe at least daily, with 47 percent hearing daily of European affairs via the radio, and 41 percent who encountered a daily newspaper story.[64] Although media coverage of European affairs *was* growing, and in spite of the EC's own efforts to augment publicity, the European public remained ambivalent. A 1982 survey noted that "public awareness of the European Parliament is currently very low, with very little difference from one country to another."[65]

As with most Eurobarometer surveys in the 1970s and 1980s, it was observed that "opinion leaders" were more attentive to European affairs than the wider public, which in turn meant that men were better-informed than women and the young less aware of European affairs than the older generations. Elite "opinion leaders" were becoming more interested and invested in European integration while the majority of the people remained peripheral bystanders. These "opinion leaders," however, defined by Eurobarometer as those respondents who "report that they engage in political discussion 'frequently' *and* that they persuade their friends, relatives or coworkers 'often' or 'from time to time,'" were considered to be pivotal actors capable of shaping wider public moods.[66]

This helps explain why some semblance of a "permissive consensus" endured until the 1990s. An educated group of transnational "opinion leaders" gave the impression to policymaking elites that awareness of and support for the European project was growing steadily. Gender and age may affect attitudes toward European integration, remarked one 1987 survey, but socioeconomic status was the chief determinant. "Those who have enjoyed more formal education," it was noted, "are distinctly 'more European.'"[67] Not for the first time, there was something of an assumption in elite circles that the more informed and educated the masses, the more inclined they will be to support elite-driven progressive projects. There was also confidence that the European public *was* becoming more pro-European. By late 1990 it was claimed that "public support for Community membership has reached an all-time high," with 69 percent of citizens proclaiming their country's membership to be a "good thing."[68] The Maastricht debates shook this confidence, and it was acknowledged that the previous "permissive consensus has eroded." While warning against exaggerating the repercussions (that is, suggesting that a lack of public support would cause the community to crumble), it was accepted that "a significant proportion of the public in several member countries—although still being 'for Europe'—[want] an explicit say in the debate about 'which Europe' and as to 'how much of it.'"[69]

For the authors of the Eurobarometer surveys, the Maastricht legacy marked a fundamental shift in conceptualizations of public opinion. Back in 1987 it was still maintained that "Consensus about 'Europe' and about 'more of it' is more permissive, acceptive [*sic*], benevolent than demanding, challenging, pressing or pushing."[70] By late 1992, the "climate of public opinion towards 'Europe,' towards West European unification and the European Community has changed." Many European citizens look "at 'Brussels' in a different way now," it was remarked, largely due to Maastricht being portrayed in the media as "still much more Europe to come."[71] Seeking to explain this post-Maastricht crisis of public confidence,

Eurobarometer cited "a serious information gap," and started to consider ways of rectifying this (noting that it would not be "an easy task"). More EC-level "orientation" was needed, because elite cues at the national level were inadequate. "At times when the traditional 'permissive consensus' is eroding," it observed, "the building up and consolidation of an 'active positive consensus' depends on efforts to close the information gap as well as the orientation gap."[72] Part of the commission's response was to bring forth a "revolution" in the way that it "communicates with citizens." Noting how the Maastricht debate demonstrated that Europe had become "too remote" from the citizenry, the commission elaborated a new commitment to "openness." This included investing more in making the EU's presence more visible within member states, commissioning more polls to alert officials to the public mood, and formalizing a consideration of public opinion within commission decision-making processes.[73]

At the very least, the Maastricht era brought to the surface an emergent and growing divergence between political elites and mainstream opinion. This "gap" has arguably been a defining characteristic of the European project from day one, and certainly one that has never been sufficiently reconciled. The chickens, perhaps, have come home to roost with the recent upsurge of anti-EU populism. After all, elite opinion has always tended to support European integration more than the broader public. With regard to Britain, for example, it has been noted how, since the mid-1960s, "those well-informed and interested in European integration tended to support British entry to a large extent, whereas the broader British public was more 'ambiguous.'"[74] Such a divergence between elite opinion and the wider public was not (and is not) a uniquely British phenomenon. How might this troublesome "gap" have been reconciled more adequately? One possible solution lies in the cultivation of a European "public sphere," which could constitute the vital prerequisite for a legitimate supranational organization.

A European Public Sphere

Two conceptions of a European public sphere exist: the first is the "ideal image" of a pan-European public sphere that transcends individual nation-states; the second is a public sphere that stems from the "Europeanization of national publics."[75] The former, "ideal" model, appears a non-starter, the absence of either a common language or a Europe-wide media meaning that the "most important preconditions" for such a public sphere simply do not exist.[76] Indeed, Toshkov insists that a key explanatory factor for the link between public opinion and policy being less pronounced in the EU context (compared to domestic situations) is that Europe lacks a "common media and public sphere that can voice and amplify public opinion."[77] The alleged need for a European public sphere rests on the assumption that only this can ensure that "the requirements of democracy beyond the nation state [are] met." As Erik Oddvar Eriksen suggests, "the public sphere is a precondition for the realization of popular sovereignty."[78] The contention that a European public sphere is necessary to legitimize European political institutions is contested. Ignacio Sánchez-Cuenca argues that the political institutions themselves, by demonstrating their effectiveness and value, will *create* a European public sphere rather than needing the latter for its existence. "The point is," he maintains, "that the creation of a European *demos* largely depends on the EU itself, and is not a precondition for a supranational democracy . . . . The much-discussed question of the *demos* is endogenous, rather than exogenous, to the EU institutions."[79]

Much of the debate stems from contested definitions of the term "public sphere." As noted in this book's introduction, the term originates with Jürgen Habermas, especially his evocation of the "public sphere" that emerged around the coffeehouse culture of eighteenth-century Europe. In this emergent "public sphere," a civil society was able to express itself, the voice of the public evolving into a genuine political actor. For Habermas, therefore, a public sphere is not a political actor per se, but, instead, operates as a mechanism through which an "anonymous" public opinion wields a tangential rather than direct impact on the policymaking process.[80] The problem for the EU, given the absence of either a common language or (for the most part) a common, continent-wide media, is that public opinion is not only dispersed but also atomized along national boundaries. This is important when one considers the "Europeanization" of the public sphere—whether such a process is desirable and, if so, how far a stubbornly national rather than pan-European media environment facilitates it. National media outlets remain the key source of citizens' information about EU issues, and this media coverage contributes substantially to public attitudes toward European affairs. Downey and Koenig suggest that, despite the growing prevalence of distinct "European framings" across national media, they remain atomized and rooted in national identities, within a narrative where "representatives of ethnic nations" clash and compete.[81]

There are certainly differences in how the various national media choose to portray European affairs. Barbara Pfetsch suggests that media coverage in some member states—France, Spain, Italy, and Germany in particular—conveys transnational linkages that help foster a greater degree of Europeanization;

in other states (including the Netherlands) such positive coverage was less pronounced but still in evidence. The only outlier was the UK, where the media generally "maintained rather national angles and opposed EU integration."[82] But even in more pro-EU media environments, issues were still conveyed in broadly "national" rather than "transnational" terms, indicative of impediments to the creation of a genuinely Europeanized public sphere. For Pfetsch, however, writing in 2008, these findings did not mean that the European media would reject further EU integration. In fact, she contended that the media in the early 2000s tended to be "rather positive" about this issue, although warned simultaneously that such support might prove ephemeral. As Pfetsch put it, media opinion "is part of the general political culture of a country, and the media resonate with the national political cleavages and the 'ups and downs' of public opinion."[83]

The media is thus simultaneously a driver *and* a mirror of underlying public debates and dialogues. On the one hand, the media encourages Europeanization by emphasizing positively the transnational element of the European project; on the other, it is compelled to convey a more skeptical and even hostile tone if that is perceived to be more attuned to domestic popular opinion. Once established, a Eurosceptic media environment might have profound political ramifications, bolstering support for populist anti-European movements. As Anderson warned in the late 1990s: "When anti-establishment and anti-European parties gain public support by opposing the unification of Europe, even established parties may be tempted to advocate policies critical of European agreements if they promise electoral pay-offs."[84] This was a risk understood clearly by the European Commission. As a 1995 Eurobarometer survey contended, a "permissive consensus" facilitated further integration only "as long as those parts of the elites who are opposed to [it] do not succeed in mobilising significant support." "If and when they do," it prophesied, "this slows down the speed of integration, stops it, or even reverses its direction."[85]

Does the absence of a "Europeanized" media preclude the existence of a European public sphere? After all, we have seen how Eurobarometer surveys frequently evoked important "opinion leaders," and it could be asserted further that these "leaders"—being better educated and no doubt better-travelled than the majority of the public—resided in a transnational public sphere (albeit a somewhat exclusive one). Philip Schlesinger has claimed that something approximating a European public sphere—one consisting chiefly of an *Economist*-reading political and business elite—*had* emerged by the end of the twentieth century. This in turn provided the genesis of a group of people living within the EU who "have begun to think of their citizenship, in part at least, as transcending the level of the member nation-states."[86] This process had been underway for some time, facilitated by some of the aforementioned technological advances that better enabled a continent-wide public sphere to emerge. As Inglehart noted back in 1970, "ownership of television sets and automobiles has spread widely during the [1960s], providing the potential for far broader communication among the various spheres of society."[87] For Inglehart, these advances dovetailed with a growing number of young Europeans attending university, thus providing the cognitive mobilization necessary for the cultivation of a genuinely European identity. Using data gathered by a 1963 Reader's Digest Association survey, he argued that education was "the strongest single predictor of European political mobilization."[88]

Enhanced travel, communication, and access to education would only increase the number of those more favorably inclined to the European project. With regard to education, it has become, as Hakhverdian et al. note, "a well-established fact that the lower educated are more sceptical of European integration than their higher educated counterparts."[89] In addition, their analysis confirmed that those "with low or medium levels of educational attainment were found to be significantly more eurosceptical than highly educated Europeans," a process that became more pronounced over time, especially after Maastricht.[90] Of course, levels of Euroscepticism are not contingent solely on levels of educational attainment. In the early years of European integration, opposition was based chiefly on ideological opposition to the Common Market project; after Maastricht, it became increasingly associated with an opaque notion of defending a national community against a supranational behemoth.[91] As a 1993 Eurobarometer survey remarked, the post-Maastricht malaise was emblematic of a "diffuse fear of 'more Europe,'" the problem being that these fears "nourish the discourse of political elites who are against Europe (or against more of it)." "It is them [sic]," continued the survey, "who constitute the potential that is electorally mobilizable [sic] by such 'anti-European' political leaders."[92] Whatever the motivation for skepticism, it is clear that the inability to fashion a genuinely European "identity" has hindered further European integration and unification.

This was an enormous frustration for European elites given that one of the "basic objectives of the European Community [was] to strengthen the feeling of solidarity between the people of the Member States." Its own Eurobarometer data, analyzing responses to questions about "European solidarity" yielded consistently disappointing results. In 1981, it was observed that the majority across the EC (74 percent) felt that the community should assist a member state encountering difficulties, but fewer were prepared to make personal sacrifices (e.g., paying higher taxes) to do so (just 40 percent across the EC, ranging from a low of just 20 percent in Belgium to a high of 69 percent in Italy).[93] By 1982, the percentage of Europeans willing to make such sacrifices was declining in all countries, including Italy.[94] Indications of "European-ness" can also be derived from responses to the Eurobarometer question asking "Do you ever think of yourself as a citizen of Europe? Often, sometimes, or never?" In 1983, just 16 percent answered "often," 34 percent "sometimes," and 46 percent "never."[95] These figures barely moved for the remainder of the century. In 1996, just 16 percent of respondents considered themselves "above all" a citizen of the EU, against 61 percent who gave primacy to their national identity.[96]

Interestingly, a 1984 Eurobarometer survey reported that 52 percent of Europeans believed a "United States of Europe" to be a good idea, with just 22 percent taking the opposite view. Explaining why support for this was greater than the figure supporting speedier integration (48 percent) the report contended that the "United States of Europe" concept possesses "a rather dreamlike quality . . . appearing as something desirable, but attainable only in the distant future, if at all."[97] It would seem that the idea was supported because it was strictly aspirational; much like support for "world peace" or the elimination of poverty, people like the sound of it but are less willing to undergo the sacrifices necessary to make it a reality. Nevertheless, there *was* reason to believe that the European public sought more integration. A special Eurobarometer report in 1987, commemorating the thirtieth anniversary of the Treaty of Rome, noted simply that "two-thirds of the Europeans are in favour of the European Community doing more than manage butter mountains or wine lakes: they want it to be responsible for defence, foreign affairs, and the economy in general."[98] Still, a European identity struggled to take hold. Eurobarometer acknowledged in 1995 that "there is not a single European *Öffentlichkeit, espace public* or public" because of the absence of a common political culture, language, and Europe-wide media. As a result, "we still deal with national public opinions towards 'Europe.'"[99]

The struggle to overcome distinct national identities was particularly pronounced in the early 1990s as the Maastricht-era debates raged. During this period, identities became less "European" and more polarized, hardly providing the fertile ground in which a genuinely European "demos" could take hold and flourish. Eriksen asks the vital question: "Can there be a public sphere when there is no collective identity?" On the surface, the absence of the latter is a major problem:

> The lack of a collective identity renders the prospect for a viable European public
> sphere rather bleak. There is no agreement on common interests; different
> languages and disparate national cultures make opinion formation and common

action unlikely. The intermediate structures of civil society in the shape of a
Europeanized party system, European organizations, social movements
and European media are lacking as well as a common language making a
transnational binding debate. . . . A common public debate—which enables the
citizens to take a stand on the same issues, at the same time and under the same
premises—is, thus, not achievable.[100]

Yet, as Habermas has remarked, a post-national identity can provide the basis
of a "public sphere," one rooted less on primordial identification and more on
constructed notions of citizenship and shared identities. As he put it, "collective
identities are made, not found."[101] Thomas Risse concurs, insisting that a
Europe-wide public sphere is not a fixed or tangible entity but rather a fluid
social construct.[102] Jan-Henrik Meyer, meanwhile, contends that a "discursively
constructed European public sphere does not require a common language
nor common European media."[103] Ergo, it need not matter that European
publics continued (and continue still) to receive news and information
from predominantly national medias that are necessarily mediated through
peculiarly national frameworks and lenses. What matters is how national
media can successfully construct and perpetuate a European identity capable
of usurping, matching, or simply existing alongside established national
identities.

Efforts to establish a continent-wide, transnational media could only assist in
this endeavor, and there were, to be sure, some signs of progress in this direction
by the turn of the twenty-first century. Eriksen notes how television, the printed
press, and, particularly, the internet began to facilitate multilingual (with English
the predominant *lingua franca*) transnational news networks (EuroNews, BBC
World, Deutsche Welle, *Le Monde Diplomatique*, etc.) that created "communicative
spaces in Europe." Europe-wide debates about Jörg Haider's "Freedom Party" in
Austria and Joschka Fischer's May 2000 call for federalism demonstrated further
the commonality of debate and newsworthy issues across national boundaries.
Similarly, the widespread protests in 2003 against the US-led invasion of Iraq can
be considered indicative of a European civil society in action, and not for the first
time (this had arguably been apparent during the events of 1968, or the CND-
led antinuclear protests in the early 1980s).[104] For Bølstad, the suggestion that a
European "public sphere" was emerging is not without merit. After all, even in a
climate in which national, rather than a Europe-wide media prevail, they "may
increasingly be reporting on the same issues, using the same communicative
styles and discourses."[105] Indeed, Bølstad concludes that "a pan-European public
opinion" *does* exist, but that the public's attachment to the European project

is variable, with those states joining in 1973 and later proving discernibly less enthusiastic. For him, this has resulted in a two-tier European public opinion, a "core" (comprising the original member states) and a "periphery" (emanating chiefly from states that joined in the 1970s and 1980s).[106]

As regards the influence of this "European public opinion," Bølstad is more circumspect. He notes that policymaking elites *are* concerned by public attitudes, as demonstrated by the multiple Eurobarometer surveys conducted each year. These surveys, he suggests, demonstrate "a keen interest" in the views of the public, to such an extent that "European policy makers might well be responding directly to the results." But this conclusion remains speculative, and he acknowledges that "we cannot confidently conclude that public opinion has a causal influence on integration." Moreover, Bølstad reflects a consistent theme within the literature on public opinion and diplomacy when suggesting that the relationship is two-way. "It is thus quite likely," he writes, "that public opinion is not only *influencing* political elites, but is also *influenced* by these—and that the same elites largely determine integration policy."[107] This feeds into broader discussions about how far public opinion is a "top-down" or "bottom-up" phenomenon. Is the public still, as per the Almond–Lippmann model, a fickle, ill-informed, and unruly mass that necessarily responds to elite cues? Alternatively, does it find expression and influence via a public sphere, becoming an irresistible force that politicians, reliant on popular mandates, must respond to? And, within this relationship, what role does the media play?

Of course, the perennial problem of whether the press leads or reflects public opinion is no less important here. Menno Spiering has challenged the rather reductive argument that "the British are Eurosceptic because many of them read Eurosceptic newspapers," suggesting, instead, that an (albeit passive) Euroscepticism "is clearly manifest in British public opinion."[108] Still, as noted above, there are discrepancies in how distinct national media elect to convey the image of European political institutions, and the British media has been peculiarly and consistently hostile. A good deal of this Euroscepticism stems from an alleged "democratic deficit," the perception that an out-of-touch elite simply presses ahead with unification and imposes its whims on an unwilling public. These arguments resonated in the post-Maastricht environment, the results of the Danish and French referenda leading to the EU being accused of lacking transparency, undermining national sovereignty, and monopolizing decision-making powers.[109]

The upsurge of anti-European sentiment in the British press is noteworthy because it shows how a greater degree of press coverage of European affairs does not automatically cultivate a greater degree of "European-ness" or an augmented sense of a collective European identity. In 1990, the *Sun* newspaper raised the profile (in Britain, at least) of EC president Jacques Delors to an unprecedented degree, first by labeling him "the most boring bureaucrat in Brussels," and then headlining with "Up Yours Delors!" on November 1.[110] Eurosceptic media coverage gained further ground after Maastricht and the events of Black Wednesday (Britain's forced withdrawal from the Exchange Rate Mechanism on September 16, 1992). Thereafter, the press reveled in what Wilkes and Wring have termed "Euromythology" through exaggerated or even fabricated stories of EU meddling in banal trivialities, most notoriously the *Sun*'s 1994 report on the EC's efforts to ban bananas that were "too bendy." Indeed, the foreign office was so alarmed by such reports that they published several pamphlets during the 1990s in an attempt to disabuse people of misperceptions they might hold as a result of "euromyths," "euroscares," and "eurolunacies."[111]

It had not always been this way, and it has been noted previously that the majority of the British press supported adhesion to the EC in 1975, including the *Sun* (the *Daily Express* was the most consistently anti-European newspaper at this time).[112] What changed, according to Oliver Daddow, was the "Murdoch effect." This refers specifically to the role played by the Australian media mogul, Rupert Murdoch, and his growing influence on the British press from the 1970s onward. By steering the British media toward a greater interest in European issues, Murdoch was a pivotal player in guiding the press from a "permissive consensus to destructive dissent."[113] Although partly ideological, the move toward an anti-Europe orientation had commercial motivations. As Spiering has suggested, the cultivation and exploitation of public unease with European integration amounted to a sensationalized Euroscepticism that helped sell newspapers, providing abundant "stories about foreigners trying to lord it over 'us,' or about absurd rulings imposed on the UK by alien institutions."[114]

The role of the press was already recognized, as it had (arguably) performed a decisive role in ensuring a "yes" vote in the 1975 referendum. Thereafter, it started to transition toward a more anti-European slant, especially by the end of the 1980s.[115] As Daddow notes:

> Tabloid coverage of European affairs took on a qualitatively different tone in Britain during the 1980s. It became more bombastic, injected a greater sense of urgency into the debates, by presenting treaty reform as existential threats to British sovereignty and identity, became less deferential to politicians and the "elites," and was deeply critical of "foreign" machinations that threatened supposedly objective British interests.[116]

The overall impact of the "Murdoch effect" was, for Daddow at least, "dramatic." Murdoch's intervention transformed political and popular debates about Europe, creating a prevailing narrative of an existential European threat to British identity and interests. "Tabloid outrage against 'Europe' has become the stock national style of debating European affairs in Britain," remarks Daddow, "and this is unlikely to change in the near or even the distant future."[117] Of course, the British example might be the exception that proves the rule. Indeed, one study has contended that the UK constitutes a "special case," as the British media "report on EU topics and other EU states comparatively rarely." Britain must not be taken as the norm, as the degree to which a "Europeanized" public sphere exists is contingent on how much attention each national media devotes to European affairs, not to mention the tone that this coverage takes. In this context, the public spheres of Denmark, Germany, and the Netherlands are "the most Europeanized," with those of France, Spain, and Austria sitting somewhere in the middle, while the Belgian, Italian, and Irish media lag behind.[118]

In spite of all the indications of a growing Euroscepticism across the entire Union, opinion polls at the turn of the twenty-first century suggested that there remained considerable public backing for further integration (although not necessarily further enlargement). Support remained high for a common defense and security policy (supported by 7 in 10 EU citizens), and a majority (6 in 10) even favored a common foreign policy. Six in ten favored a single currency (32 percent opposed it), but fewer were keen on enlargement, a process welcomed by just 3 in 10 citizens. That said, it did assert rather confidently that the recent "institutional crisis" had not shaken the public's support for further integration, noting how 45 percent of EU citizens wanted to see movement in this direction.[119] Eurobarometer attributed the public's resistance to enlargement to the fact that opinion was yet to crystallize, "with many people still opting for the 'don't know' response when asked about their support."[120] "Enlargement fatigue," as Sara Hobolt has termed it, was clearly apparent before the more rapid expansion of the EU into central and eastern Europe in the early twenty-first century, and certainly before the more recent Eurozone crisis prompted by the 2008 economic crash.[121] Overall, Britain may have been an outlier, but the overriding conclusion is that a "Europeanized" public was struggling to take hold across the community. There *were* early signs of a Europeanized media emerging, but this lagged behind the processes of integration especially as EU expansion accelerated into the new century bringing in a greater plurality of languages, traditions, and national public spheres.[122] Given the public's previous unease with more rapid integration and enlargement (both during the 1970s and again in the early 1990s), the acceleration of these processes into the twenty-first century was always unlikely to win the unquestioning support of European public opinion.

Conclusion

The basic contours of the historiography concerning public opinion's influence on European unification are familiar. From its origins in the immediate aftermath of the Second World War until the first expansion of the community in the early 1970s, there existed a "permissive consensus" whereby public opinion appeared content to allow the elites to press ahead with the project with little recourse to popular opinion. Once the residual postwar distrust of Germany had dissipated, the establishment of an economic union was accepted by the publics of all six original member states, their support based on the utilitarian calculation that membership served their interests financially while also salving the wounds of recent conflict. This consensus began to erode for several, overlapping reasons. New member states were often more hesitant than the original "Six," the British public only narrowly confirming their country's membership while the Norwegian people rejected the opportunity to join. Meanwhile, the process morphed from something strictly economic into a more explicitly political and cultural project that troubled the public in all countries. Reflecting on this in the mid-1970s, Robert Shepherd warned prophetically that "it would be quite erroneous to press for the speedy creation of a United States of Europe in which political institutions at the national level would be rapidly superseded—clearly, this would conflict with popular sentiment."[123]

Even into the 1980s, however, a "permissive consensus" held even as it began to fray around the edges. A further expansion saw the adhesion of Greece, Spain, and Portugal, countries where public opinion was initially more enthusiastic about the European project. By the close of the 1980s, however, things again began to change. The diplomatic landscape altered fundamentally, the collapse of the Iron Curtain and denouement of the Cold War removing many of the diplomatic and strategic imperatives that had initially underpinned Western European integration. In addition, the EC had already begun formulating schemes for ever-tighter integration—including monetary union—that would see the "permissive consensus" evaporate as debates and popular votes over the Maastricht Treaty brought the need for public support into sharper focus. At the same time, sections of the British press, under the influence of Rupert Murdoch, began to exploit successfully a long-standing seam of Euroscepticism.

A 1994 article analyzing the outbreak of anti-European sentiment after Maastricht concluded with words that seem remarkably prescient today. Noting how electorates are instinctively cautious and conservative, it contended that allowing "the democratic genie out of the bottle by calling a referendum does not serve well the purpose of change." The public is rightly cautious, but their hesitancy and fears vis-à-vis Europe are manipulated easily both by the media and political parties for their own ends. "If there is a crisis of legitimacy in Europe today," concluded Franklin, Marsh, and McLaren, "it seems to us that national parties and their leaders are far more responsible than the people of the European Union or the Eurocrats of Brussels."[124] In the contemporary climate of populism and petty nationalisms, this conclusion seems very perceptive. This is not to say that the public is, as per the Almond–Lippmann model, fickle and driven by emotion in its advocacy of myopic and foolhardy policies. Nor does it assume that the public is a passive recipient of elite cues, whether from political parties or the media, and thus manipulated easily by unscrupulous and pernicious interests. Instead, it is an assertion that public opinion *must* have a say in the formulation of foreign policy and diplomacy, but it need not always be expressed directly, and especially via the mechanism of crudely binary referenda. As long as it is considered malleable and vulnerable to manipulation, politicians (and other interest groups) will use and abuse public opinion as a tool for both domestic political and diplomatic ends. To avoid this, public opinion must be permitted to perform—freely and unhindered—its function as a tool of democratic oversight and legitimacy. Only then will its influence on diplomacy be authentic and beneficent.

Conclusion

Public opinion's influence on diplomacy over the course of the twentieth century has been substantial. Charting its influence is no easy task, made all the harder by the proclivity of international historians, perhaps more than others, to fetishize the archive and thus avoid what is harder to "prove." Public opinion itself is an immensely slippery concept. It is so notoriously difficult to ascertain that efforts to do so are comparable to attempts to nail jelly to a wall. Still, as noted in the introduction, the only public that really *matters* as an influence on diplomacy is that which the policymakers themselves believe to exist. As D. G. Boyce put it: "Public opinion is mainly what contemporaries perceived it to be."[1] Identifying "public opinion" becomes, therefore, a little more straightforward (at least in theory). Politicians and diplomats throughout the twentieth century alluded to it frequently, hence visible traces of public opinion do exist in the archival record. Nevertheless, it is rare to find emphatic evidence of this public opinion—whether real or imagined—actually informing policy outcomes in any significant way. It is also difficult to ascertain what the policymaking elites actually perceived public opinion to be, or, indeed, where these perceptions of public opinion emanated from. All too often "public opinion" appears in the archives in opaque and abstract ways, frequently employed to justify policies that have already been chosen, and on occasion presented simply as an inconvenient impediment. Nevertheless, as the previous chapters have shown, public opinion emerges consistently as a constraint on policymakers, just as economic concerns, strategic considerations, military assessments, party politics, and myriad other factors affect diplomatic choices. In short, public opinion is a causal factor that international historians must take as seriously as any other.

It has long been acknowledged that public opinion is an important political actor, but its influence was certainly acknowledged more readily during the modern period. With the Enlightenment came a mounting recognition that public opinion wielded a growing degree of political power, especially as a news-hungry and literate public sphere expanded rapidly. Understanding what this emergent public sphere wanted was difficult, and confusion often reigned. For

Sir Robert Peel, public opinion was that "great compound of folly, weakness, prejudice, wrong feeling, right feeling, obstinacy, and newspaper paragraphs."[2] As Peel's final two words suggest, there was, amid the confusion and uncertainty, a shared assumption that the press provided the public's principal mouthpiece. As Benjamin Disraeli put it in his 1844 political novel *Coningsby*, "Opinion now is supreme, and opinion speaks in print."[3] A demonstration of this was William Gladstone's use of the Bulgarian "atrocities" during the 1870s, capitalizing on "a new form of evangelical mass politics" and contributing to the "wave of moral outrage" that swept the country.[4] It is also clear, as Simon Potter has noted, that British diplomats of the Victorian era acknowledged the opportunities that the press provided to "present imperial policy aims and objectives to a wider audience." Press support was cultivated successfully in the early stages of the Second Boer War "to develop wider enthusiasm for British imperial consolidation."[5] At the same time, the processes of internationalization that shaped the late Victorian period (and with it the more rapid dissemination of news) was a troublesome element for politicians and diplomats. The Boer War might have demonstrated how the press could be used to whip the public into a jingoistic and pro-imperial frenzy, but it later provided a platform for Emily Hobhouse and others to reveal the British use of concentration camps, revelations that would, as K. O. Morgan asserts, have a "powerful impact on opinion."[6]

At the start of the twentieth century, two functions of public opinion appeared to cohabit uneasily. On the one hand, opinion was susceptible to governmental control and could be used advantageously in pursuit of specific diplomatic strategies. On the other, it was becoming an increasingly autonomous independent actor, with the ability to undercut a nation's ability to project its will internationally. Public opinion *was* an integral facet of the flag-waving jingoism that shaped responses to war in 1914, but was, as explored in Chapter 1, equally prominent when positioned by Woodrow Wilson and others as the moral cornerstone of a durable and peaceful postwar order. Of course, the much vaunted "moral" force of public opinion was powerless to withstand the challenges of interwar revisionism, shaking substantially the conviction that the public would stand at the vanguard of enlightened global causes. Moreover, the apparent ability of the interwar dictatorships to manipulate opinion via more concerted and targeted propaganda indicated that public opinion was malleable and compliant rather than autonomous and probing. The dictatorships were not alone in demonstrating this; a public relations industry emerged within democratic countries, intent on pioneering publicity efforts for commercial purposes. Politically, however, the European dictatorships proved adept at cultivating an obedient public; by contrast, the democracies seemed unable to control theirs. Chapter 2 explored how this conviction nourished the influential "decadence" thesis that emerged in France. According to this narrative, an unruly and fractured French public opinion contributed substantially to France's diplomatic passivity during the 1930s and ultimately to that country's capitulation in summer 1940. Although this thesis is now widely rejected as overly simplistic and reductionist, its allure, both at the time and since, is instructive. It confirmed that public opinion, if left uncontrolled, might degenerate into a volatile and emotional mass, an unruly crowd that hindered rather than helped the successful prosecution of diplomacy. In the context of 1930s France, the media performed a dual purpose, both exacerbating social unrest and anxiety, and eventually functioning as a tool for fashioning unity and sangfroid. Much was learned during the 1930s, especially as regards the harnessing of new technologies like radio and cinema newsreels, resulting in new approaches that would be further developed and enhanced during the Second World War and beyond.

Another lesson of what Becker considers the "era of public opinion manipulation"[7] was the need to understand better what public opinion as regards foreign affairs actually *was*. Little surprise, therefore, that the fledgling opinion poll industry of the interwar period grew exponentially in the postwar years. This growth was most evident in the United States, yet despite apparently "scientific" polls providing more and more "objective" data this was not enough to prevent public opinion from playing an allegedly decisive role in causing America's defeat in the Vietnam War. The media again was a disruptive element, especially the new and relatively unfamiliar medium of television. As discussed in Chapter 3, it remains unclear whether the media led public opinion or reflected it, or, indeed, whether both the media *and* public opinion simply responded to elite "cues" by echoing a loss of confidence in the war effort that emanated from the policymakers themselves. Whatever happened (and we will probably never know for sure), public opinion was at least *perceived* to be a pivotal player, apparently possessing the power and influence to make or break the diplomatic strategies of even the most powerful nation on earth. Its impact would also linger, informing a subsequent "Vietnam Syndrome" and directly informing how American elites would manage the media in future combat zones. The stage-managed press conferences of the Persian Gulf War, and the ubiquity of "embedded" journalists in the 2003 Iraq war, are just two examples of this. Unlike in Vietnam, American military and political personnel were now able to control the narrative that would (arguably) shape public responses.

The Vietnam War was, of course, not only a newsworthy story in the United States; it was also a global issue, and media coverage of the conflict—and the domestic schisms that it provoked—assumed an international dimension. As the demonstrators outside the 1968 Democratic Party Convention in Chicago remarked, the "whole world is watching."[8] This was not necessarily new: the nineteenth-century anti-slavery movement possessed an undeniably transnational character, as did emergent movements advancing the causes of peace, socialism and women's rights. After 1900, and particularly after the Second World War, advances in technology made international cooperation, and with it the possibility of mobilizing a genuinely global public, still more achievable. As Douglas Foyle suggests, it was only now that people were more inclined to "act as globalized citizens, evidencing in some circumstances more loyalty to broader concepts than to their individual states."[9] Nancy Fraser, however, insists that the earlier processes of globalization must not be overlooked, suggesting that we must remember the "long history" of transnationalism, even while acknowledging that public opinion has only relatively emerged from its "Westphalian frame."[10] The international movement against South African apartheid, as assessed in Chapter 4, showed public opinion operating internationally, often eclipsing the primacy of the nation-state. Citizen activism, on a transnational scale, was able to circumvent unwilling and even hostile governments to isolate South Africa diplomatically, in so doing at least contributing to the endgame of apartheid. The success of this campaign owed much to its visibility (aided particularly by satellite television into the 1980s), but also its salience. Pretoria's segregationist policies appeared woefully out of step with developing international norms, especially in the context of European decolonization and the domestic Civil Rights movement in the United States. South Africa's apartheid policy was rendered more noteworthy and controversial simply because many Western societies were themselves grappling with issues of multiracialism.

Less visible and less salient, at least at first, was the process of European integration. As shown in Chapter 5, this initially resulted in a "permissive consensus" emerging, the European public seemingly content to allow the elites to press ahead with the European project without consulting their people. This was certainly the case as long as the "project" offered sizable economic benefits at the same time as preventing another European war. But, as the processes of integration assumed a distinctly political and cultural hue, with a concomitant challenge to national sovereignty, this consensus began to unravel. Concerns about an alleged "democratic deficit" proliferated, and despite efforts to cultivate a European "public sphere," national identities continued (and continue still) to prevail. Although European elites had at their disposal more abundant evidence of public opinion than ever before—courtesy of the regular and detailed Eurobarometer surveys conducted since 1973—recurrent episodes of Euroscepticism illustrate how public opinion remains fickle, elusive, and worryingly vulnerable to manipulation. This manipulation can emanate from elites seeking to manufacture consent for the European project as well as from other interests seeking to exploit any seeds of discontent for more pernicious and commercial purposes. Notwithstanding the progress made during the twentieth century, the very real fear persists that public opinion succumbs too readily to existential pressures.

As long as public opinion has been recognized as a political actor, and certainly for as long as concerted efforts have been made to gauge it, there has been an analogous seam of critical theory warning that the very concept itself is vulnerable to elite manipulation. A Marxist outlook highlights the ability of the ruling classes to impose hegemonic constructions of public opinion on a society. Antonio Gramsci was one of those advancing such warnings, but he was not alone. As Herbst reminds us, both Max Horkheimer and Theodor Adorno contended that the public was "greatly susceptible to media persuasion and therefore ruling class ideology."[11] Jürgen Habermas was also worried. For him, what had begun as an organic, emancipatory, and free expression of public opinion in the emergent public sphere of the early modern period had become, by the late nineteenth and early twentieth centuries, homogenized and stifled by the increasingly corporate and interest-driven industries of the mass media and survey research.[12] And, famously, Pierre Bourdieu has questioned whether an "authentic" public opinion actually exists at all. He asserts that opinion polling, by its very nature, produces a "simple aggregation" of opinions that reflects the questions being posed rather than a genuine expression of sentiment.[13] This critique questions whether people ordinarily hold firm and crystalized opinions on a given topic, contests the assumption that all opinions carry equal weight and influence, and compels us to interrogate *how* and *why* pollsters choose to ask the questions that they do. In this sense, opinion pollsters *create* a public opinion that is fabricated rather than organic, perhaps contributing to the "hyperreality" that, according to postmodernists like Jean Baudrillard, we live in.[14]

Such a "hyperreality" is, if anything, more intense now than it was when Baudrillard was writing. The advent of the internet and social media has only exacerbated the idea, as articulated by Herbert Blumer back in the 1940s, that public opinion is never static. As Herbst remarks, Blumer would "view our blogs, webpages, and constant chatter as extraordinarily helpful in understanding public opinion, [providing] precisely the sort of textured discourse that is so superior to the aggregation of anonymous individuals gathered in our artificial 'publics' produced by the polls." Herbst went still further, writing how, "at the moment [she was writing in 2011], those who wish to connect with others, spread ideas, and get a sense of public opinion on any issue have a tool like no other."[15] This may be true, but recent experiences demand that we treat the impact of modern technology on public opinion with caution. In many ways, the rise of the internet (and social media in particular) is a double-edged sword. It *is* a great democratizing tool, allowing each of us, as individuals, to express opinions on just about every topic imaginable. But it has made it more difficult than ever to define accurately the "will of the people." The alarmingly febrile and toxic debates surrounding "Brexit" illustrate this all too clearly. Discussions of "fake news," of "echo chambers," the use and misuse of Twitter and other social media platforms (notably the Facebook/Cambridge Analytica scandal) suggest that public opinion, while able to express itself more freely and frequently than ever before, remains alarmingly susceptible to efforts to control it. There is also the challenge posed by the so-called "deep fakes," making it more difficult for individuals to separate fact from fiction within the myriad manifestations of information to which we are all exposed. As one newspaper article noted recently, "the only rational response from the citizen will be extreme cynicism and apathy about the very idea of truth itself. They will conclude that nothing is to be trusted except her own gut instinct and existing political loyalties."[16]

How all of this might influence foreign policymakers today and into the future is unclear, but a better understanding of how public opinion has influenced diplomacy in the past can be enlightening. A central contention throughout this book is that the only public opinion that *matters* as a diplomatic actor is that which is *perceived* to exist by those who formulate policy. This is unlikely to change, so an enhanced appreciation of how policymakers make sense of public opinion (and how far they opt to respond to it) is valuable. Historians must try to locate which specific representations of opinion have successfully pervaded the decision-making milieu, how they have done so (i.e., which sources of opinion are the most important), how contested are the perceptions of opinion that emerge, and how far the resultant conception(s) of public opinion inform policy choices. This is no easy task, especially given how the mechanisms for reflecting and shaping "public opinion" changed dramatically over the course of the twentieth century. The growth of the popular press (in combination with growing literacy rates and an extended franchise) was followed by the emergence of radio, cinema, and television, as well as the development of ever-more-sophisticated opinion polling techniques. At the same time, the ongoing processes of globalization (most of which were facilitated by technological advances, especially satellite television and the internet by the century's end) have seen broader conceptions of public opinion shift, beginning to transcend strictly national parameters and morphing into something more akin to a genuinely "global" or "international" public.

Much work is required if public opinion is to assume its rightful place within broader histories of the foreign-policymaking process. Writing in 2011, Douglas Foyle called for more variation and cross-fertilization in public opinion research, necessary steps if the discipline was to become less US-centric and more attentive to the diversity of opinions based on demographic characteristics. He also called for more "integration and synthesis" when studying the link between public opinion and foreign policy, suggesting that "a fully integrated model of public opinion, the media, and foreign policy remains a challenging, important, and unrealized task."[17] Nearly a decade on, this task remains unrealized, and this book makes no claim to have done so. What it hopes to demonstrate is simply that historians —and international historians in particular—have an important role to play in shaping the "fully integrated model" that Foyle demands. One way of doing this is simply to become more global in outlook. To be sure, the case studies explored in the previous chapters are undeniably Western-centric—even the topic of apartheid-era South Africa focused on a public opinion emanating predominantly from the developed world. Given the existing literature on the topics covered in this volume, such a focus is unavoidable, but the scope for further research is considerable. Future scholars can embrace non-Western case studies, and even explore how non-Western conceptions and definitions of "public opinion" might differ from their Western counterparts.

Yet, even within the more familiar diplomatic histories of the Western world, the role of public opinion is conspicuous by its relative absence. This omission of public opinion, chiefly because it is a troublesome concept to work with, is regrettable. The preceding chapters have demonstrated that "public opinion" (or any of its many synonyms) *has* played a part in diplomatic decision-making, proving to be a pivotal contextual and conditioning influence. To ignore public opinion only solidifies an erroneous impression that foreign policymaking takes place in a vacuum, the policymakers themselves acting in a dispassionate and rational manner, sheltered from the whims and demands of an unruly public. This proclivity originates, to a considerable degree, from debates about public opinion that have raged since the days of ancient Greece, in particular the persistent (and pejorative) view of public opinion as emotional, ill-informed, and fickle, and thus ill-equipped to dictate policy. This conceptualization of public opinion demanded that diplomatic decision-makers either ignore it or seek to mold it in support of predetermined strategies. But public opinion can also be conceptualized in a more positive way, positioning it as a progressive force. Another theme running through this book is how two competing visions of public opinion have been present throughout, the negative conflation of the public with an unruly crowd sitting alongside a positive conception of the public as an enlightened diplomatic actor. Diplomats and politicians during the twentieth century embraced both views of public opinion, sometimes simultaneously. This demonstrates that the elites were *always* attentive to public opinion, and that this opinion *did* have an influence on their diplomatic choices. It is, therefore, incumbent on international historians to pay further attention to it. This might necessitate a more imaginative use of sources, and will almost certainly require them to move further away from the strict empiricism of the Rankean tradition to which the discipline remains so wedded, but the benefits truly outweigh the risks.

Notes

Introduction

1 E. M. Carroll, *French Public Opinion and Foreign Affairs, 1870-1914* (London: The Century Co., 1931), 3–4.

2 See Daniel Hucker, "International History and the Study of Public Opinion: Towards Methodological Clarity," *International History Review* 34:4 (2012), 776–78.

3 For a thoughtful discussion of this, see David Reynolds, "International History, the Cultural Turn and the Diplomatic Twitch," *Cultural and Social History* 3:1 (2006), 75–91.

4 Patrick Finney, "Introduction: What Is International History?" in Patrick Finney (ed.), *Palgrave Advances in International History* (Basingstoke: Palgrave Macmillan, 2005), 1.

5 Daniel Waley, *British Public Opinion and the Abyssinian War, 1935-6* (London: Temple Smith, 1975), 11.

6 Tom Harrisson, "What is Public Opinion?" *The Political Quarterly*, 11:4 (1940), 368–69.

7 V. O. Key, *Public Opinion and American Democracy* (New York: Alfred Knopf, 1963), 14.

8 Adam J. Berinsky, "Introduction," in Adam J. Berinsky (ed.), *New Directions in Public Opinion*, second edition (New York: Routledge, 2016), 2.

9 Harrisson, "What Is Public Opinion?" 374–75.

10 Yvon Lacaze, *L'opinion publique française et la crise de Munich* (Bern: Peter Lang, 1991), 15.

11 Pierre Milza, "Opinion publique et politique étrangère," in École Française de Rome (ed.), *Opinion publique et politique extérieure en Europe, tome I, 1870-1915: Actes du Colloque de Rome, 13-16 février 1980* (Rome: École Française de Rome, 1981), 664.

12 Josiah Ober, *Mass and Elite in Democratic Athens: Rhetoric, Ideology, and the Power of the People* (Princeton: Princeton University Press, 1989), 87–88.

13 Cited in Carroll J. Glynn, Susan Herbst, Mark Lindeman, Garrett J. O'Keefe, and Robert Y. Shapiro, *Public Opinion*, third edition (Boulder: Westview, 2016), 32.

14 John Durham Peters, "Historical Tensions in the Concept of Public Opinion," in Theodore L. Glasser and Charles T. Salmon (eds.), *Public Opinion and the Communication of Dissent* (New York: Guilford Press, 1995), 7–8.

15 Wilhelm Bauer, "Public Opinion," in E. R. A. Seligman (ed.), *Enyclopaedia of the Social Sciences*, vol. XII (New York: Macmillan, 1934), 669–72.

16 David W. Minar, "Public Opinion in the Perspective of Political Theory," *The Western Political Quarterly* 13:1 (1960), 34.

17 See Hans Speier, "Historical Development of Public Opinion," *American Journal of Sociology* 55:4 (1950), 378.

18 Glynn et al., *Public Opinion*, 35.

19 Bauer, "Public Opinion," 669.

20 Speier, "Historical Development of Public Opinion," 378.

21 Ibid., 379–80.

22 James Van Horn Melton, *The Rise of the Public in Enlightenment Europe* (Cambridge: Cambridge University Press, 2001), 2; see also Jürgen Habermas, *The Structural Transformation of the Public Sphere: An Inquiry into a Category of Bourgeois Society* (Cambridge: Polity, 1989).

23 Glynn et al., *Public Opinion*, 37.

24 Speier, "Historical Development of Public Opinion," 382.

25 Glynn et al., *Public Opinion*, 11.

26 Susan Herbst, "The History and Meaning of Public Opinion," in Andrew J. Berinsky (ed.), *New Directions in Public Opinion*, second edition (New York: Routledge, 2016), 26.

27 Paul Corner, "Introduction," in Paul Corner (ed.), *Popular Opinion in Totalitarian Regimes: Fascism, Nazism, Communism* (Oxford: Oxford University Press, 2009), 2.

28 Paul Corner, "Fascist Italy in the 1930s: Popular Opinion in the Provinces," in Paul Corner (ed.), *Popular Opinion in Totalitarian Regimes: Fascism, Nazism, Communism* (Oxford: Oxford University Press, 2009), 141.

29 Ian Kershaw, "Consensus, Coercion and Popular Opinion in the Third Reich: Some Reflections," in Paul Corner (ed.), *Popular Opinion in Totalitarian Regimes: Fascism, Nazism, Communism* (Oxford: Oxford University Press, 2009), 43–44.

30 Bauer, "Public Opinion," 673.

31 Van Horn Melton, *The Rise of the Public*, 29–30. A similar point is made by Jeremy Black in *Debating Foreign Policy in Eighteenth-Century England* (Farnham: Ashgate, 2011), 30.

32 Cited in Van Horn Melton, *The Rise of the Public*, 31.

33 Ibid., 38.

34 Black, *Debating Foreign Policy*, 21.

35 Speier, "Historical Development of Public Opinion," 385.

36 All cited in Harold Nicolson, *Diplomacy* (Washington DC: Institute for the Study of Diplomacy, 1988), 37.

37 Cited in Harold Holzer, *The War for Public Opinion: Lincoln and the Power of the Press* (New York: Simon & Schuster, 2014), xxix.

38 Cited in John G. Nicolay and John Hay (eds.), *Complete Works of Abraham Lincoln*, vol. V (New York: Francis D. Tandy Company, 1905), 331.

39 Cited in Black, *Debating Foreign Policy*, 231.

40 As discussed in Glynn et al., *Public Opinion*, 11–12.

41 Cited in John Carey, *The Intellectuals and the Masses: Pride and Prejudice Among the Literary Intelligentsia, 1880-1939* (Chicago: Academy Chicago, 2002), 27.

42 Cited in Carey, *The Intellectuals and the Masses*, 12.

43 See Ibid., 13–15.

44 See John G. Gunnell, "Democracy and the Concept of Public Opinion," in Robert Y. Shapiro and Lawrence R. Jacobs (eds.), *The Oxford Handbook of American Public Opinion and the Media* (Oxford: Oxford University Press, 2011), 274.

45 James Bryce, *The American Commonwealth, Volume 1: The National Government* (London: Macmillan, 1888), 410.

46 Both cited in in Daniel Hucker, "British Peace Activism and 'New' Diplomacy: Revisiting the 1899 Hague Peace Conference," *Diplomacy & Statecraft* 26:3 (2015), 415.

47 James Thompson, *British Political Culture and the Idea of "Public Opinion," 1867-1914* (Cambridge: Cambridge University Press, 2013), 167.

48 Gunnell, "Democracy and the Concept of Public Opinion," 277–78.

49 Speier, "Historical Development of Public Opinion," 387.

50 Walter Lippmann, *The Phantom Public* (Abingdon: Routledge, 2017 [1927]), 55.

51 Ibid., 60–61.

52 Jean-Jacques Becker, "L'opinion publique: un populisme?" *Vingtième Siècle: Revue d'histoire* 56 (1997), 96.

53 Edward Bernays, "Manipulating Public Opinion: The Why and the How," *American Journal of Sociology* 33:6 (1928), 33.

54 Ferdinand Tönnies cited in Edward Bernays, *Crystallizing Public Opinion* (New York: Liveright Publishing Corporation, 1923), 217.

55 Gabriel Almond, "Public Opinion and National Security Policy," *Public Opinion Quarterly* 20:2 (1956), 376–77. See also Almond's *The American People and Foreign Policy* (New York: Harcourt, Brace and Company, 1950).

56 Lester Markel, "Opinion – A Neglected Instrument," in Lester Markel et al (eds.), *Public Opinion and Foreign Policy* (New York: Harper & Brothers, 1949), 3.

57 Ibid., 5.

58 Ibid., 19 (original emphasis).

59 Douglas C. Foyle, "Public Opinion, Foreign Policy, and the Media: Toward an Integrative Theory," in Robert Y. Shapiro and Lawrence R. Jacobs (eds.), *The Oxford Handbook of American Public Opinion and the Media* (Oxford: Oxford University Press, 2011), 659.

60 Bernard C. Cohen, *The Public's Impact on Foreign Policy* (Boston: Little and Brown, 1973), 62. See also Cohen's "The Relationship between Public Opinion and Foreign Policy Maker," in Melvin Small (ed.), *Public Opinion and Historians: Interdisciplinary Perspectives* (Detroit: Wayne State University Press, 1970), 65–80.

61 Cited in Joshua D. Kertzer and Thomas Zeitzoff, "A Bottom-Up Theory of Public Opinion about Foreign Policy," *American Journal of Political Science* 61:3 (2017), 544.

62 Cited in Thomas Knecht and M. Stephen Weatherford, "Public Opinion and Foreign Policy: The Stages of Presidential Decision Making," *International Studies Quarterly* 50:3 (2006), 707.

63 Kertzer and Zeitzoff, "A Bottom-Up Theory of Public Opinion," 544.

64 See Bruce W. Jentleson, "The Pretty Prudent Public: Post Post-Vietnam American Opinion on the Use of Military Force," *International Studies Quarterly* 36:1 (1992), and (with Rebecca L. Britton), "Still Pretty Prudent: Post-Cold War American Public Opinion on the Use of Military Force," *The Journal of Conflict Resolution* 42:4 (1998). See also Philip J. Powlick and Andrew Z. Katz, "Defining the American Public Opinion/Foreign Policy Nexus," *Mershon International Studies Review* 42:1 (1998), 30; Jon Hurwitz and Mark Peffley, "How are Foreign Policy Attitudes Structured? A Hierarchical Model," *American Political Science Review* 81:4 (1987); Robert Y. Shapiro and Benjamin I. Page, "Foreign Policy and the Rational Public," *The Journal of Conflict Resolution* 32:2 (1988); and Thomas W. Graham, "The Pattern and Importance of Public Knowledge in the Nuclear Age," *The Journal of Conflict Resolution* 32:2 (1988).

65 Ole Holsti, "Public Opinion and Foreign Policy: Challenges to the Almond-Lippmann Consensus," *International Studies Quarterly* 36:4 (1992), 451–52.

66 Kertzer and Zeitzoff, "A Bottom-Up Theory of Public Opinion," 543–44.

67 Ibid., 555.

68 John Mueller, "Public Opinion, the Media, and War," in Robert Y. Shapiro and Lawrence R. Jacobs (eds.), *The Oxford Handbook of American Public Opinion and the Media* (Oxford: Oxford University Press, 2011), 678.

69 Ibid., 683.

70 Tanja R. Müller, "The Long Shadow of Band Aid Humanitarianism: Revisiting the Dynamics between Famine and Celebrity," *Third World Quarterly* 34:3 (2013), 473.

71 Mueller, "Public Opinion, the Media, and War," 684.

72 Jacob Sohlberg, Peter Esaisson, and Johann Martinsson, "The Changing Political Impact of Compassion-Evoking Pictures: The Case of the Drowned Toddler Alan Kurdi," *Journal of Ethnic and Migration Studies* 45:13 (2019).

73 See "Photo of Drowned Migrants Captures Pathos of Those Who Risk It All," *The New York Times*, June 25, 2019: https://www.nytimes.com/2019/06/25/us/father-daughter-border-drowning-picture-mexico.html (accessed July 12, 2019).

74 Susan Herbst, "Critical Perspectives on Public Opinion," in Robert Y. Shapiro and Lawrence R. Jacobs (eds.), *The Oxford Handbook of American Public Opinion and the Media* (Oxford: Oxford University Press, 2011), 310–11.

Chapter 1

1 Bryce, *The American Commonwealth, Volume 1*, 134.
2 James Bryce, *The American Commonwealth, Volume 2: The Party System* (London: Macmillan, 1891), 240.
3 Ibid., 256.
4 This was a point made in 1939 by Francis G. Wilson, reflecting on Bryce's contribution to the study of public opinion. "James Bryce on Public Opinion: Fifty Years Later," *Public Opinion Quarterly* 3:3 (1939), 422.
5 Cited in Keith Robbins, "Lord Bryce and the First World War," *The Historical Journal* 10:2 (1967), 268.
6 Ibid.
7 Sakiko Kaiga, "The Use of Force to Prevent War? The Bryce Group's 'Proposals for the Avoidance of War,' 1914-15," *Journal of British Studies* 57:2 (2018), 312.
8 Cited in Ibid., 328.
9 Wilson address to the Third Plenary Session of the Preliminary Peace Conference, February 14, 1919: Woodrow Wilson Papers, Library of Congress, Washington DC, Reel 448.
10 David Lloyd George, *Memoirs of the Peace Conference*, vol. 1 (New Haven: Yale University Press, 1939), 136.
11 Carl Bouchard, *Le citoyen et l'ordre mondial (1914-1919): Le rêve d'une paix durable au lendemain de la Grande Guerre en France, en Grande-Bretagne et aux Etats-Unis* (Paris: Editions A. Pedone, 2008), 6.
12 J. Michael Hogan, *Woodrow Wilson's Western Tour: Rhetoric, Public Opinion, and the League of Nations* (College Station: Texas A & M University Press, 2006), 22–23.
13 Wilson address at Mount Vernon, July 4, 1918: James Brown Scott Papers, Georgetown University, Box 9, folder 5.
14 Arno J. Mayer, *Political Origins of the New Diplomacy, 1917-1918* (New Haven: Yale University Press, 1959), 54.
15 Ibid., 56.
16 Marc Trachtenberg, "Versailles after Sixty Years," *Journal of Contemporary History* 17:3 (1982), 488.
17 E. H. Carr, "Public Opinion as a Safeguard of Peace," *International Affairs* 15:6 (1936), 854.
18 Bouchard, *Le citoyen et l'ordre mondial*, 88–91.
19 Kaiga, "The Use of Force to Prevent War?" 312.
20 Ruth Henig, "New Diplomacy and Old: A Reassessment of British Conceptions of a League of Nations, 1918-20," in Michael Dockrill and John Fisher (eds.), *The Paris Peace Conference, 1919: Peace Without Victory?* (Basingstoke: Palgrave, 2001), 159–60.

21 Peter Yearwood, *Guarantee of Peace: The League of Nations in British Policy, 1914-1925* (Oxford: Oxford University Press, 2009), 100.

22 Glenda Sluga, *Internationalism in the Age of Nationalism* (Philadelphia: University of Pennsylvania Press), 150.

23 Kaiga, "The Use of Force to Prevent War?" 328.

24 Goldsworthy Lowes Dickinson, cited in Kaiga, "The Use of Force to Prevent War?" 317–18.

25 Jean-Michel Guieu, *Le rameau et le glaive: Les militants français pour la Société des Nations* (Paris: Presses de Sciences Po, 2008), 181.

26 Cited in Guieu, *Le rameau et le glaive*, 181.

27 James Bryce in the 1915 draft proposals, cited in Kaiga, "The Use of Force to Prevent War?" 328.

28 Letter to Wilson from the Carlisle Women Citizen's Association, December 4, 1918: Wilson Papers, Reel 385.

29 Letter from the British Section of the Women's International League to Wilson, December 11, 1918: Wilson Papers, Reel 417.

30 Margaret Macmillan, *Peacemakers: The Paris Conference of 1919 and Its Attempt to End War* (London: John Murray, 2001), 22.

31 Bouchard, *Le citoyen et l'ordre mondial*, 222.

32 Annual Meeting of the Board of Trustees of the Carnegie Endowment for International Peace, April 21, 1916: Papers of the Carnegie Endowment of International Peace, Rare Book and Manuscript Library, Columbia University, New York, Series I, box 13, folder 3.

33 Cited in Michael Graham Fry, *And Fortune Fled: David Lloyd George, the First Democratic Statesman, 1916-1922* (New York: Peter Lang, 2011), 23.

34 Ibid., 75.

35 Ibid., 23–25.

36 Martin Ceadel, *Semi-Detached Idealists: The British Peace Movement and International Relations, 1854-1945* (Oxford: Oxford University Press, 2000), 238.

37 Macmillan, *Peacemakers*, 196, 173, 200 respectively.

38 Fry, *And Fortune Fled*, 179.

39 Cited in ibid., 184–85.

40 Patrick Cohrs, *The Unfinished Peace after World War I: America, Britain and the Stabilisation of Europe, 1919-1932* (Cambridge: Cambridge University Press, 2006), 39.

41 William Mulligan, *The Great War for Peace* (New Haven: Yale University Press, 2014), 268.

42 Macmillan, *Peacemakers*, 200.

43 Zara Steiner, *The Lights That Failed: European International History, 1919-1933* (Oxford: Oxford University Press, 2005), 28.

44 As recalled by Lloyd George in his *Memoirs of the Peace Conference*, vol. 1, 55.

45 American Commission—Great Britain: Weekly Summary, March 2, 1919: Library of Congress, Washington DC: Henry D. White Papers, Box 40.

46 Macmillan, *Peacemakers*, 172.

47 Lippmann, *The Phantom Public*, 139.

48 Paul Rich, "Reinventing Peace: David Davies, Alfred Zimmern and Liberal Internationalism in Interwar Britain," *International Relations* 16:1 (2002), 120.

49 Macmillan, *Peacemakers*, 22–23.

50 Henig, "New Diplomacy and Old," 163–64.

51 Steiner, *The Lights That Failed*, 17.

52 Macmillan, *Peacemakers*, 4.

53 Ibid., 6.

54 Steiner, *The Lights That Failed*, 16.

55 Bouchard, *Le citoyen et l'ordre mondial*, 115–18.

56 Marc Trachtenberg, "Reparation at the Paris Peace Conference," *The Journal of Modern History* 51:1 (1979), 25–26, 37.

57 Macmillan, *Peacemakers*, 95.

58 Cited in Yearwood, *Guarantee of Peace*, 101.

59 The Right Honourable Lord Hurd of Westwell, "The Rise and Fall of Morality in Peace Making," in Michael Dockrill and John Fisher (eds.), *The Paris Peace Conference, 1919: Peace Without Victory?* (Basingstoke: Palgrave, 2001), 8.

60 Henig, "New Diplomacy and Old," 168.

61 Ibid., 168–69.

62 Macmillan, *Peacemakers*, 489.

63 H. W. V. Temperley (ed.), *A History of the Peace Conference of Paris*, vol. 1 (London: Hodder & Stoughton, 1920), 267–68; Steiner, *The Lights That Failed*, 55.

64 American Commission—Great Britain: Weekly Summary, March 30, 1919: White Papers, Box 41.

65 Robert Cecil to Lloyd George, May 27, 1919: Cecil Papers, British Library, Add. MS 51076.

66 Bouchard, *Le citoyen et l'ordre mondial*, 217.

67 Jean-Michel Guieu notes that the Anglo-Saxon League that emerged in 1919 left the French establishment cold, failing, as Léon Bourgeois put it, to impose the only effective sanction, namely a military sanction backed by an international force. *Le rameau et le glaive*, 60.

68 Guieu, *Le rameau et le glaive*, 287.

69 Temperley, *A History of the Peace Conference of Paris*, 278.

70 Harold Nicolson, *Peacemaking, 1919: Being Reminiscences of the Paris Peace Conference* (Boston: Houghton Mifflin Company, 1933), 187.

71 Fry, *And Fortune Fled*, 193.

72 Riddell diary entry, April 9, 1919: Lord Riddell, *Lord Riddell's Intimate Diary of the Peace Conference and After, 1918-1923* (London: Victor Gollancz, 1933), 48–49.

73 Lloyd George, *Memoirs of the Peace Conference*, vol. 1, 136–37.

74 Ibid., 96–97.

75 Geoffrey Best, "Peace Conferences and the Century of Total War: The 1899 Hague Conference and What Came After," *International Affairs* 75:3 (1999), 633; Daniel Hucker, "'Our Expectations Were Perhaps Too High': Disarmament, Citizen Activism, and the 1907 Hague Peace Conference," *Peace & Change* 44:1 (2019), 13.

76 Lloyd George, *Memoirs of the Peace Conference*, vol. 1, 136.

77 Wilson to White, December 17, 1918: Library of Congress, White Papers, Box 38.

78 Secretary's note of a meeting held in M. Pichot's office at the Quai d'Orsay, 3pm, January 17, 1919: Wilson Papers, Reel 448.

79 Ibid.

80 Temperley (ed.), *History of the Peace Conference of Paris*, vol. 1, 254–55.

81 Cecil diary entry, January 11, 1919: Lord Cecil's Diary of the British Delegation, Paris, January 6–June 10, 1919: Cecil Papers, British Library, Add. MS 51131.

82 Cecil diary entry, February 6, 1919: Lord Cecil's Diary of the British Delegation, Paris, January 6–June 10, 1919: Cecil Papers, British Library, Add. MS 51131.

83 Steiner, *The Lights That Failed*, 17.

84 American Commission—Great Britain: Weekly Report, April 6, 1919 and April 14, 1919: White Papers, Box 41.

85 Cecil to Lloyd George, April 4, 1919: Cecil Papers, British Library, Add. MS 51076.

86 Lloyd George speech, April 16, 1919: *Hansard* (114 H.C. Deb, 5s), cols. 2947–50.

87 Ibid., cols. 2951–53.

88 Ibid., cols. 2954–55.

89 *Daily Mail*, editorial, "Mr. Lloyd George Overdoes It," April 17, 1919.

90 *The Times*, editorial, "The Prime Minister's Apologia," April 17, 1919.

91 Fry, *And Fortune Fled*, 28–29.

92 Temperley, *A History of the Peace Conference of Paris*, 277–78.

93 Riddell diary entry, March 24, 1919: *Lord Riddell's Intimate Diary*, 39.

94 Riddell diary entry, March 28, 1919: ibid., 39–40.

95 Riddell diary entry, April 5, 1919: ibid., 46.

96 Henry White to Cabot Lodge, May 29, 1919: Library of Congress, Washington DC: Elihu Root Papers, Box 161.

97 Fry, *And Fortune Fled*, 259.

98 Riddell diary entry, week ending May 3, 1919: *Lord Riddell's Intimate Diary*, 64–65.

99 Riddell diary entry, May 5, 1919: ibid., 70–71.

100 Cited in Macmillan, *Peacemakers*, 469.

101 Cecil diary entry, May 29, 1919: Lord Cecil's Diary of the British Delegation, Paris, January 6–June 10, 1919: Cecil Papers, British Library, Add. MS 51131.

102 Fry, *And Fortune Fled*, 263.

103 Riddell diary entry, June 28, 1919: *Lord Riddell's Intimate Diary*, 100.

104 Steiner, *The Lights That Failed*, 68.

105 Riddell diary entry, August 22, 1919: *Lord Riddell's Intimate Diary*, 111.

106 Lloyd George, *Memoirs of the Peace Conference*, 383–84.

107 Ibid., 371.

108 James Bryce to Elihu Root, June 6, 1919: Root Papers, Box 137.

109 E. H. Carr, *Conditions of Peace* (London: Macmillan, 1942), 239.

110 R. B. McCallum, *Public Opinion and the Last Peace* (London: Oxford University Press, 1944), 86. A similar argument has more recently been articulated by Keith Robbins, in "'The Treaty of Versailles, Never Again' and Appeasement," in Michael Dockrill and John Fisher (eds.), *The Paris Peace Conference, 1919: Peace Without Victory?* (Basingstoke: Palgrave, 2001), 103–14.

111 Henig, "New Diplomacy and Old," 157–58.

112 American Commission—Great Britain: Weekly Review, May 11, 1919: White Papers, Box 42.

113 Carr, "Public Opinion as a Safeguard of Peace," 855–61.

114 Harold Nicolson, "Modern Diplomacy and British Public Opinion," *International Affairs* 14:5 (1935), 603–5.

115 Ibid., 609–10, 607–8.

116 Ibid., 613.

117 Bouchard, *Le citoyen et l'ordre mondial*, 219–20.

Chapter 2

1 Edmond Taylor, "Democracy Demoralized: The French Collapse," *Public Opinion Quarterly* 4:4 (1940), 649.

2 Cecil Melville, *Guilty Frenchmen* (London: Jarrolds, 1940); André Géraud (the notable French journalist, writing under his *non de plume* "Pertinax"), *Les fossoyeurs: défaite militaire de la France*, 2 vols. (New York: Éditions de la Maison française, 1943).

3 Marc Bloch, *L'étrange défaite: Témoignage écrit en 1940* (Paris: Société des Éditions Franc-Tireur, 1946).

4 Maurice Baumont, *La faillite de la paix, 1918-1939* (Paris: Presses universitaires de la France, 1946), 766.

5 Pierre Renouvin, *Histoire des relations internationales* (Paris: Hachette, 1958); Jean-Baptiste Duroselle, *Histoire diplomatique de 1919 à nos jours* (Paris: Dalloz, 1953).

6 Jean-Baptiste Duroselle, *La décadence, 1932-1939* (Paris: Imprimerie Nationale, 1979). This is available in English as *France and the Nazi Threat: The Collapse of French Diplomacy, 1932-1939* (New York: Enigma Books, 2004).

7 Duroselle, *La décadence*, 493.

8   Eugen Weber, *The Hollow Years: France in the 1930s* (London: Sinclair-Stevenson, 1995), 277–78, 7.

9   Taylor, "Democracy Demoralized," 634.

10 Ibid., 636.

11 Ibid., 641.

12 For more on the shifts in the historiography, see Peter Jackson, "Post-war Politics and the Historiography of French Strategy and Diplomacy before the Second World War," *History Compass* 4:5 (2006), 870–905, and Patrick Finney, *Remembering the Road to World War Two: International History, National Identity, Collective Memory* (London: Routledge, 2011), chapter 4.

13 Robert J. Young, *France and the Origins of the Second World War* (Basingstoke: Macmillan, 1996), 58.

14 Philip Nord, *France 1940: Defending the Republic* (New Haven: Yale University Press, 2015), 155.

15 Benjamin Franklin Martin, *Years of Plenty, Years of Want: France and the Legacy of the Great War* (De Kalb: Northern Illinois University Press, 2013), 208.

16 Taylor, "Democracy Demoralized," 649.

17 Nord, *France 1940*, 166.

18 Jean-Louis Crémieux-Brilhac, *Les Français de l'An 40, tome I: La guerre, oui ou non?* (Paris: Gallimard, 1990), 15.

19 Ibid., 620.

20 Charles Micaud, *The French Right and Nazi Germany, 1933-1939* (New York: Octagon Books, 1972 [1942]), 4.

21 For a more detailed discussion of public opinion in totalitarian countries, see Corner (ed.), *Popular Opinion in Totalitarian Regimes.*

22 Cited in Daniel Hucker, *Public Opinion and the End of Appeasement in Britain and France* (Farnham: Ashgate, 2011), 20.

23 Christel Peyrefitte, "Les premiers sondages d'opinion," in René Rémond and Janice Bourdin (eds.), *Édouard Daladier, chef de gouvernement: avril 1938 – septembre 1939* (Paris: Presses de la FNSP, 1977), 265.

24 Raymond Kuhn, *The Media in France* (London: Routledge, 1995), 17–18.

25 Fernand Terrou, "L'évolution du droit de la presse de 1881 à 1940," in Claude Bellanger et al., *Histoire générale de la presse française*, tome III (Paris: Presses Universitaires de France, 1972), 22–23.

26 Vincent Bignon and Marc Flandreau, "The Price of Media Capture and the Debasement of the French Newspaper Industry during the Interwar," *The Journal of Economic History* 74:3 (2014), 803.

27 Cited in Fabrice d'Almeida and Christian Delporte, *Histoire des médias en France de la Grande Guerre à nos jours* (Paris: Flammarion, 2010), 7–8.

28 Kuhn, *Media in France*, 21.

29 Bignon and Flandreau, "The Price of Media Capture," 802. On the comparison with Britain, see Jean K. Chalaby, "Twenty Years of Contrast: The French and British Press during the Inter-war Period," *European Journal of Sociology* 37:1 (1996), 143–59.

30 Kuhn, *Media in France*, 21.

31 D'Almeida and Delporte, *Histoire des médias*, 65–67.

32 Jessica Wardhaugh, "Crowds, Culture and Power: Mass Politics and the Press in Interwar France," *Journalism Studies* 14:5 (2013), 744.

33 Jean-Noël Jeanneney, *Une histoire des médias des origines à nos jours* (Paris: Éditions du Seuil, 2001), 163.

34 Chalaby, "Twenty Years of Contrast," 152.

35 D'Almeida and Delporte, *Histoire des médias*, 55.

36 Simon Dell, *The Image of the Popular Front: The Masses and the Media in Interwar France* (Basingstoke: Palgrave, 2007), 29.

37 Pierre Albert, "La presse française de 1871 à 1940," in Claude Bellanger et al., *Histoire générale de la presse française*, tome III (Paris: Presses Universitaires de France, 1972), 143–45.

38 Bignon and Flandreau, "The Price of Media Capture," 799.

39 Chalaby, "Twenty Years of Contrast," 145; Bignon and Flandreau, "The Price of Media Capture," 802; Albert, "La presse française," 486–90.

40 See Bloch, *L'étrange défaite*, and Jean-Noël Jeanneney, *L'argent caché: Milieux d'affaires et pouvoirs politiques dans la France du XXè siècle* (Paris: Fayard, 1984).

41 Jeanneney, *Une histoire des médias*, 173.

42 Cécile Méadel, *Histoire de la radio des années trente* (Paris: Anthropos/INA, 1994), 198.

43 Kuhn, *Media in France*, 83–84.

44 Méadel, *Histoire de la radio*, 35.

45 Kuhn, *Media in France*, 84.

46 Jeanneney, *Une histoire des médias*, 157.

47 Méadel, *Histoire de la radio*, 49.

48 Jeanneney, *Une histoire des médias*, 157.

49 Crémieux-Brilhac, *La guerre, oui ou non?* 85.

50 Méadel, *Histoire de la radio*, 99.

51 Crémieux-Brilhac, *La guerre, oui ou non?* 297–98.

52 Jean A. Gili, "Un élément constitutif de l'opinion publique: les actualités cinématographiques en France de 1914 à 1918," in École Française de Rome (ed.), *Opinion publique et politique extérieure en Europe, II: 1915-1940: Actes du Colloque de Rome (16 – 20 février 1981)* (Rome: École Française de Rome, 1984), 235–42.

53 Janine Bourdin, "Introduction," in René Rémond and Janine Bourdin (eds.), *La France et les Français en 1938-1939* (Paris: Presses de la FNSP, 1978), 16.

54 Jessica Wardhaugh, *In Pursuit of the People: Political Culture in France, 1934-39* (Basingstoke: Macmillan, 2009), 230.

55 Jean Touchard and Louis Bodin, "L'état de l'opinion au début de l'année 1936," in Pierre Renouvin and René Rémond (eds.), *Léon Blum: Chef de gouvernement, 1936-1937* (Paris: Presses de la FNSP, 1981), 61.

56 Ibid., 66.

57 Colette Audry, *Léon Blum ou la politique de la juste* (Paris, 1955), 126–27.

58 Daniel Hucker, "Public Opinion, Policymakers, and the Munich Crisis: Adding Emotion to Diplomatic History," in Julie V. Gottlieb, Daniel Hucker, and Richard Toye (eds.), *The Munich Crisis, Politics and the People* (Manchester: Manchester University Press, forthcoming).

59 Jessica Wardhaugh, "France in the Blue Light of Munich: Popular Agency, Activity, and the Reframing of History," in Julie V. Gottlieb, Daniel Hucker, and Richard Toye (eds.), *The Munich Crisis, Politics and the People* (Manchester: Manchester University Press, forthcoming).

60 See, for example, J. Coudurier de Chassaigne, "M. Neville Chamberlain à Paris," *L'Illustration*, November 26, 1938.

61 Cited in Daniel Hucker, "The French Media and the Forging of a Franco-British Alliance in the late 1930s," *Media History* 23:3–4 (2017), 337.

62 Jean Zay, *Souvenirs et solitude* (Paris: René Julliard, 1945), 169.

63 Geneviève Tabouis, *They Called Me Cassandra* (New York: Charles Scribner's and Sons, 1942), 378.

64 Talbot Imlay, "Paul Reynaud and France's Response to Nazi Germany, 1938-1940," *French Historical Studies* 26:3 (2003), 505.

65 Pierre Guillen, "Opinion publique et politique extérieure en France, 1914-1940," in École Française de Rome (ed.), *Opinion publique et politique extérieure en Europe II: 1915-1940: Actes du Colloque du Rome (16-20 février 1981)* (Rome: École Française de Rome, 1984), 40.

66 Elizabeth Grottle Strebel, "Political Polarisation and French Cinema, 1934-39," in Nicholas Pronay and D. W. Spring (eds.), *Propaganda, Politics and Film, 1918-45* (London: Macmillan, 1982), 163–66. See also Charles Rearick, *The French in Love and War: Popular Culture in the Era of the World Wars* (New Haven: Yale University Press, 1997), 233–34.

67 Grottle Strebel, "Political Polarisation," 167–68; Rearick, *The French in Love and War*, 235.

68 Hucker, "The French Media and the Forging of a Franco-British Alliance," 337–39.

69 Daniel Hucker, "De 'quantité négligeable' au 'renouveau de la France': représentations de la France en tant qu'alliée militaire à la fin des années 1930," *Revue historique des armées* 264:3 (2011), 57.

70 Peyrefitte, "Les premiers sondages d'opinion," 274.

71 Alexander Werth, preface to the 1935 edition of *France in Ferment, 1933-1935* (London: Jarrolds, 1935), 7.

72 William Shirer, *The Collapse of the Third Republic: An Inquiry Into the Fall of France in 1940* (London: The Literary Guild, 1970), 181.

73 "Projet de mémoire destiné au Conseil Supérieur de la Guerre," August 1, 1933, cited in Peter Jackson, "French Intelligence and Hitler's Rise to Power," *The Historical Journal* 41:3 (1998), 809.

74 Thomas Davies, "France and the World Disarmament Conference of 1932-34," *Diplomacy & Statecraft* 15:4 (2004), 770–71.

75 Alain Fleury, *"La Croix" et l'Allemagne, 1930-1940* (Paris: Les Éditions du Cerf, 1986), 101.

76 Cited in Davies, "France and the World Disarmament Conference," 777.

77 Duroselle, *La décadence*, 87; Micaud, *The French Right*, 24.

78 Robert J. Soucy, "French Press Reactions to Hitler's First Two Years in Power," *Contemporary European History* 7:1 (1998), 36.

79 Ibid., 23.

80 Alexander Werth, *The Twilight of France, 1933-1940* (New York: Howard Fertig, 1966 [1942]), 42.

81 Micaud, *The French Right*, 38.

82 Cited in Élisabeth du Réau, *Édouard Daladier, 1884-1970* (Paris: Fayard, 1993), 159–60.

83 Cited in Micaud, *The French Right*, 41.

84 Duroselle, *La décadence*, 112–20.

85 Cited in Micaud, *The French Right*, 44–45.

86 Richard Davis, *Anglo-French Relations before the Second World War: Appeasement and Crisis* (Basingstoke: Macmillan, 2001), 113.

87 Fleury, *"La Croix" et l'Allemagne*, 186.

88 Davis, *Anglo-French Relations*, 162.

89 Duroselle, *La décadence*, 169.

90 Micaud, *The French Right*, 224.

91 Julian Jackson, *The Fall of France: The Nazi Invasion of 1940* (Oxford: Oxford University Press, 2003), 113.

92 Cited in Lindsey Dodd, "Are We Defended? Conflicting Representations of War in Pre-War France," *University of Sussex Journal of Contemporary History* 12 (2008): http://eprints.hud.ac.uk/id/eprint/14675/ (accessed March 13, 2019).

93 Zay, *Souvenirs et solitude*, 67.

94 Richard Davis, "Le débat sur l'« appeasement » britannique et français dans les années 1930: Les crises d'Éthiope et de Rhénanie," *Revue d'histoire moderne et contemporaine* 45:4 (1998), 835.

95 Jackson, *The Fall of France*, 112.

96 Cited in Audry, *Léon Blum ou la politique de juste*, 126–27.

97 Werth, *Twilight of France*, 119–20.

98 For more on this distinction see Daniel Hucker, "French public attitudes towards the prospect of war in 1938-1939: 'pacifism' or 'war anxiety'?" *French History* 21:4 (2007), 431–49.

99 Robert J. Young, "The Use and Abuse of Fear: France and the Air Menace in the 1930s," *Intelligence and National Security* 2:4 (1987), 103.

100 Robert Paxton, *Vichy France: Old Guard and New Order, 1940-1944* (New York, 1982), 11.

101 Cited in Hucker, *Public Opinion and the End of Appeasement*, 69.

102 Pierre-Étienne Flandin, *Politique Française, 1919-1940* (Paris: Les Éditions Nouvelles, 1947), 246.

103 Fleury, *"La Croix" et l'Allemagne*, 221.

104 Yvon Lacaze, *L'opinion publique française et la crise de Munich*, 168.

105 Jacques Puyaubert, *Georges Bonnet (1889-1973): Les combats d'un pacifiste* (Rennes: Presses universitaires de Rennes, 2007), 163.

106 Cited in Tabouis, *They Called Me Cassandra*, 355.

107 Blum, *Le Populaire*, September 29, 1938.

108 Anatole de Monzie, *Ci-devant* (Paris: Flammarion, 1941), 38.

109 Hucker, "Public Opinion, Policymakers and the Munich Crisis."

110 Fleury, *"La Croix" et l'Allemagne*, 231.

111 Benjamin Martin, *France in 1938* (Baton Rouge, 2005), 183.

112 L'Œuvre, October 4, 1938.

113 Duroselle, *La décadence*, 356.

114 Julie V. Gottlieb, "Neville Chamberlain's Umbrella: 'Object' Lessons in the History of Appeasement," *Twentieth Century British History* 27:3 (2016), 378.

115 Cited in Puyaubert, *Georges Bonnet*, 170.

116 Peyrefitte, "Les premiers sondages d'opinion," 266–67.

117 Hucker, "'Pacifism' or 'War Anxiety'?" 443.

118 Hucker, *The End of Appeasement in Britain and France*, 88.

119 Taylor, "Democracy Demoralized," 641.

120 Christian Delporte, "The Image and Myth of the 'Fifth Column,'" in Valerie Holman and Debra Kelly (eds.), *France at War in the Twentieth Century: Propaganda, Myth and Metaphor* (New York: Berghahn Books, 2000), 61–63.

Chapter 3

1 *The Vietnam War* (2017), [TV program] Dirs. Ken Burns and Lynn Novick, PBS, September 2017.

2 Andrew Priest, "Power to the People? American Public Opinion and the Vietnam War," in Andrew Johnstone and Helen Laville (eds.), *The US Public and American Foreign Policy* (London: Routledge, 2011), 41.

3 Melvin Small, *Covering Dissent: The Media and the Anti-Vietnam War Movement* (New Brunswick: Rutgers University Press, 1994), 161.

4 Priest, "Power to the People?" 41.

5 Ibid., 42.

6 For a brief analysis of this shift, see Powlick and Katz, "Defining the American Public Opinion/Foreign Policy Nexus", 30.

7 Melvin Small, "Influencing the Decision Makers: The Vietnam Experience," *Journal of Peace Research* 24:2 (1987), 187.

8 Cited in Daniel Hallin, *The "Uncensored War": The Media and Vietnam* (Oxford: Oxford University Press, 1986), 170.

9 David Halberstam, *The Powers That Be* (New York, 1979), 514.

10 See David Culbert, "Television's Visual Impact on Decision-Making in the USA, 1968: The Tet Offensive and Chicago's Democratic Convention," *Journal of Contemporary History* 33:3 (1998), 419–49.

11 Small, *Covering Dissent,* 26.

12 William C. Westmoreland, *A Soldier Reports* (New York: Doubleday & Company, 1976), 232.

13 Lynn Spigel, *Make Room for TV: Television and the Family Ideal in Postwar America* (Chicago: The University of Chicago Press, 1992), 1.

14 Don Oberdorfer, *Tet! The Turning Point in the Vietnam War* (Baltimore: Johns Hopkins University Press, 2001), 159–60.

15 Hallin, *The "Uncensored War,"* 106.

16 Mary Ann Watson, "Television and the Presidency: Eisenhower and Kennedy," in Gary R. Edgerton (ed.), *The Columbia History of American Television* (New York: Columbia University Press, 2010), 210.

17 Ibid., 214.

18 Cited in James N. Druckman, "The Power of Television Images: The First Kennedy-Nixon Debate Revisited," *The Journal of Politics* 65:2 (2003), 563.

19 Robert Elegant, "How to Lose a War: Reflections of a Foreign Correspondent," *Encounter* LVII/2 (August 1981), 77.

20 Ibid., 80.

21 Ibid., 73.

22 Westmoreland, *A Soldier Reports*, 225–26.

23 Ibid., 420.

24 Ibid., 325.

25 Ibid., 364–66.

26 William H. Hammond, *Reporting Vietnam: Media & Military at War* (Lawrence: University Press of Kansas, 1998), 61.

27 Ibid., 159.

28 Richard Nixon, *The Memoirs of Richard Nixon* (New York: Grosset & Dunlap, 1978), 350.

29 Small, *Covering Dissent*, 29–30.

30 Hammond, *Reporting Vietnam*, 57.

31 Cited in Rodger Streitmatter, *Mightier Than the Sword: How the News Media Have Shaped American History*, fourth edition (Boulder: Westview, 2016), 166.

32 Hallin, *The "Uncensored War,"* 123.

33 Hammond, *Reporting Vietnam*, 63.

34 Michael Herr, *Dispatches* (London: Pan Books, 1980), 183–84.

35 Ibid., 177.

36 Cited in Culbert, "Television's Visual Impact," 432.

37 Both cited in Hammond, *Reporting Vietnam*, 111–12.

38 Culbert, "Television's Visual Impact," 437.

39 Hallin, *The "Uncensored War,"* 163.

40 George H. W. Bush's address to the nation, January 16, 1991, cited in David L. Anderson, *The Columbia Guide to the Vietnam War* (New York: Columbia University Press, 2002), 283.

41 George H. W. Bush's remarks to the American Legislative Exchange Council, March 1, 1991, cited in Anderson, *The Columbia Guide to the Vietnam War*, 283.

42 Nixon, *The Memoirs of Richard Nixon*, 354.

43 Ibid., 355.

44 Ibid., 368.

45 Thompson, *British Political Culture and the Idea of "Public Opinion,"* 89–90.

46 Amy Fried and Douglas B. Harris, "Governing with the Polls," *The Historian* 72:2 (2010), 338.

47 Barbara A. Bardes and Robert W. Oldendick, *Public Opinion: Measuring the American Mind*, fourth edition (Lanham: Rowman & Littlefield, 2012), 26.

48 Kenneth F. Warren, *In Defense of Public Opinion Polling* (Boulder: Westview Press, 2001), 93.

49 Mervin D. Field, "Political Opinion Polling in the United States of America," in Robert M. Worcester (ed.), *Political Opinion Polling: An International Review* (London: Macmillan, 1983), 202–3.

50 Fried and Harris, "Governing with the Polls," 344.

51 Culbert, "Television's Visual Impact," 295.

52 Poll data taken from Hammond, *Reporting Vietnam*, 19.

53 Ibid., 30.

54 Ibid., 35, 56.

55 Cited in Hammond, *Reporting Vietnam*, 56.

56 Bardes and Oldendick, *Public Opinion*, 215.

57 Hammond, *Reporting Vietnam*, 71.

58 Sidney Verba et al., "Public Opinion and the War in Vietnam," *The American Political Science Review* 61:2 (1967), 331.

59 John Mueller, *War, Presidents, and Public Opinion* (London: Wiley, 1973), 57.

60 Scott Sigmund Garner and Gary M. Segura, "War, Casualties, and Public Opinion," *The Journal of Conflict Resolution* 42:3 (1998), 279.

61 David Wyatt, *When America Turned: Reckoning with 1968* (Amherst: University of Massachusetts Press, 2014), 13.

62 Hammond, *Reporting Vietnam*, 121–22.

63 Cited in Anderson, *The Columbia Guide to the Vietnam War*, 277.

64 Gallup figures cited in John E. Mueller, "Trends in Popular Support for the Wars in Korea and Vietnam," *The American Political Science Review* 65:2 (1971), 363.

65 Ibid., 364–65.

66 Nixon, *The Memoirs of Richard Nixon*, 336.

67 Ibid., 347.

68 Ibid., 349.

69 "Nixon declares 'silent majority' backs his speech," *New York Times*, November 4, 1969.

70 Simon Hall, *Rethinking the American Anti-War Movement* (New York: Routledge, 2012), 47.

71 Joshua B. Freeman, "Hardhats: Construction Workers, Manliness, and the 1970 Pro-War Demonstrations," *Journal of Social History* 26:4 (1993), 725.

72 Paul Potter speech to the April 17, 1965, march on Washington, cited in Irwin Unger and Debi Unger (eds.), *The Times were a Changin': The Sixties Reader* (New York: Three Rivers Press, 1998), 289.

73 Melvin Small, "The Impact of the Antiwar Movement on Lyndon Johnson, 1965–1968: A Preliminary Report," *Peace & Change* 10:1 (1984), 3.

74 Hall, *Rethinking the American Anti-War Movement*, p. 23; Rhodri Jeffreys-Jones, *Peace Now! American Society and the Ending of the Vietnam War* (New Haven: Yale University Press, 1999), 32.

75 As noted in Jeffreys-Jones, *Peace Now!* 101.

76 Ibid., 103–6.

77 Amy Scott, "Patriots for Peace: People-to-People Diplomacy and the Anti-war Movement," in Andrew Wiest, Kathryn Barbier, and Glenn Robins (eds.), *America and the Vietnam War: Re-examining the Culture and History of a Generation* (London: Routledge, 2010), 125.

78 Richard R. Lau, Thad A. Brown, and David O. Sears, "Self-Interest and Civilians' Attitudes Toward the Vietnam War," *Public Opinion Quarterly* 42:4 (1978), 464.

79 Wyatt, *When America Turned*, 49–50.

80 Mark Lorell and Charles Kelley, Jr. (with the assistance of Deborah Hensler), *Casualties, Public Opinion, and Presidential Policy during the Vietnam War* (Santa Monica: Rand, 1985), 25–27.

81 Cited in Tom Wells, *The War Within: America's Battle over Vietnam* (Berkeley: University of California Press, 1994), 123.

82 David F. Schmitz, *The Tet Offensive: Politics, War, and Public Opinion* (Lanham: Rowman and Littlefield Publishers, Inc., 2005), 53.

83 Hall, *Rethinking the American Anti-War Movement*, 88.

84 Sandra Scanlon, *The Pro-War Movement: Domestic Support for the Vietnam War and the making of Modern American Conservatism* (Amherst: University of Massachusetts Press, 2013), 87.

85 Penny Lewis, *Hardhats, Hippies and Hawks: The Vietnam Antiwar Movement as Myth and Memory* (New York: Cornell University Press, 2013), 164.

86 Nixon, *The Memoirs of Richard Nixon*, 350.

87 Ibid., 353–54.

88 Ibid., 399–401.

89 Ibid., 403.

90 Cited in the *New York Times*, November 4, 1969.

91 "Nixon declares 'silent majority' backs his speech," *New York Times*, November 4, 1969.

92 Cited in Hall, *Rethinking the American Anti-War Movement*, 40.

93 Hall, *Rethinking the American Anti-War Movement*, 40-42.

94 Nixon, *The Memoirs of Richard Nixon*, 410–12.

95 Hall, *Rethinking the American Anti-War Movement*, 42.

96 Ibid., 47.

97 Freeman, "Hardhats," 725.

98 As cited in John Dumbrell, *Rethinking the Vietnam War* (Basingstoke: Palgrave Macmillan, 2012), 144.

99 Cited in Gregory A. Daddis, "Mansplaining Vietnam: Male Veterans and America's Popular Image of the Vietnam War," *The Journal of Military History* 82:1 (2018), 191.

100 Lewis, *Hardhats, Hippies and Hawks*, 196.

101 See Hall, *Rethinking the American Anti-War Movement*, 137.

102 Ibid., 138.

103 Elegant, "How to Lose a War," 89.

104 Daniel Hallin, "The Media, the War in Vietnam, and Political Support: A Critique of the Thesis of an Oppositional Media," *The Journal of Politics* 46:1 (1984), 11.

105 Ibid., 20.

106 Small, "Influencing the Decision Makers," 195.

107 Gary Hess, *Vietnam: Explaining America's Lost War* (Oxford: Blackwell, 2009), 151–52.

Chapter 4

1 Enuga S. Reddy, "AAM and UN: Partners in the International Campaign against Apartheid," in the Anti-Apartheid Movement, *The Anti-Apartheid Movement:*

A 40-year Perspective, Symposium Report (South Africa House, London, June 25–26, 1999), 45.

2 Gregory Houston, "International Solidarity: Introduction," in South African Democracy Education Trust, *The Road to Democracy in South Africa, Volume 3: International Solidarity, Part 1* (Cape Town: UNISA Press, 2008), 1.

3 Audie Klotz, "Transnational Activism and Global Transformations: The Anti-Apartheid and Abolitionist Experiences," *European Journal of International Relations* 8:1 (2002), 50.

4 Cited in Houston, "International Solidarity," 1.

5 Håkan Thörn, "The Meaning(s) of Solidarity: Narratives of Anti-Apartheid Activism," *Journal of Southern African Studies* 35:2 (2009), 418.

6 Christabel Gurney, "'A Great Cause': The Origins of the Anti-Apartheid Movement, June 1959 – March 1960," *Journal of Southern African Studies* 26:1 (2000), 123–44.

7 "For God's Sake, Wake Up!" Letter from Trevor Huddleston, *The Observer*, August 30, 1953.

8 Cited in Gurney, "'A Great Cause,'" 123, 129.

9 Neta C. Crawford, "Trump Card or Theater? An Introduction to Two Sanctions Debates," in Neta C. Crawford and Audie Klotz (eds.), *How Sanctions Work: Lessons from South Africa* (Basingstoke: Macmillan, 1999), 15.

10 Ibid., 60.

11 Håkan Thörn, "Social Movements, the Media and the Emergence of a Global Public Sphere: From Anti-Apartheid to Global Justice," *Current Sociology* 55:6 (2007), 896–97.

12 Rob Skinner, *The Foundations of Anti-Apartheid: Liberal Humanitarians and Transnational Activists in Britain and the United States, c. 1919-64* (London: Palgrave, 2010), 6.

13 Wouter Goedertier, "The Quest for Transnational Authority: The Anti-Apartheid Movements of the European Community," *Revue belge de philologie et d'histoire* 3:4 (2011), 1256.

14 Gurney, "'A Great Cause,'" 133–35.

15 Christabel Gurney, "In the Heart of the Beast: The British Anti-Apartheid Movement, 1959-1994," in South African Democracy Education Trust, *The Road to Democracy in South Africa, Volume 3: International Solidarity, Part 1* (Cape Town: UNISA Press, 2008), 263–66.

16 Archive of the Anti-Apartheid Movement, Bodleian Library, Oxford: MSS AAM 13: Annual Report, 1969/70.

17 Louise Asmal, Kader Asmal, and Thomas Alberts, "The Irish Anti-Apartheid Movement," in South African Democracy Education Trust, *The Road to Democracy in South Africa, Volume 3: International Solidarity, Part 1* (Cape Town: UNISA Press, 2008), 418.

18 Tor Sellström, "Sweden and the Nordic Countries: Official Solidarity and Assistance from the West," in South African Democracy Education Trust, *The Road to Democracy in South Africa, Volume 3: International Solidarity, Part 1* (Cape Town: UNISA Press, 2008), 424.

19 Asmal, Asmal, and Alberts, "The Irish Anti-Apartheid Movement," 365–67.

20 Skinner, *The Foundations of Anti-Apartheid*, 80.

21 Lindsay Michie Eades, *The End of Apartheid in South Africa* (Westport: Greenwood Press, 1999), 84.

22 "Mr. Macmillan's Appeal to South Africans," *The Times*, September 4, 1960.

23 David Welsh and J. E. Spence, *Ending Apartheid* (Harlow: Longman, 2011), 160–61.

24 Eades, *The End of Apartheid in South Africa*, 86–87.

25 Gurney, "'A Great Cause,'" 136.

26 Cited in ibid., 136–39.

27 Ibid., 143.

28 Enuga Reddy, cited in Thörn, "The Meaning(s) of Solidarity," 426.

29 Klotz, "Transnational Activism and Global Transformations," 61.

30 Donald R. Culverson, "The Politics of the Anti-Apartheid Movement in the United States, 1969-1986," *Political Science Quarterly* 111:1 (1996), 136–37.

31 Goedertier, "Quest for Transnational Authority," 1260–61.

32 Gurney, "In the Heart of the Beast," 289–90.

33 Asmal, Asmal, and Alberts, "The Irish Anti-Apartheid Movement," 378.

34 Gurney, "In the Heart of the Beast," 333.

35 Goedertier, "Quest for Transnational Authority," 1263–64.

36 Eades, *The End of Apartheid in South Africa*, 86–88.

37 Culverson, "The Politics of the Anti-Apartheid Movement," 129.

38 Ibid., 146.

39 Ibid.

40 "What's Good for GM . . ." *The Guardian*, October 22, 1986.

41 The Anti-Apartheid Movement, *Manifesto for Sanctions* (January 1987), 10.

42 Stuart Hall, "The AAM and the Race-ing of Britain," in The Anti-Apartheid Movement, *The Anti-Apartheid Movement: A 40-year Perspective* Symposium Report (South Africa House, London, June 25–26, 1999), 54.

43 Victoria Brittain, "Western Media: Mirroring Whose Reality?" in The Anti-Apartheid Movement, *The Anti-Apartheid Movement: A 40-year Perspective* Symposium Report (South Africa House, London, June 25–26, 1999), 57.

44 Denis Herbstein, "Under Thatcher's Coattails," *Africa Report* (September–October 1986), 22.

45 Gurney, "In the Heart of the Beast," 335–36.

46 Meg Voorhes, "The US Divestment Movement," in Neta C. Crawford and Audie Klotz (eds.), *How Sanctions Work: Lessons from South Africa* (Basingstoke: Macmillan, 1999), 130.

47 Crawford, "Trump Card or Theater?" 11–12.

48 Ibid., 133–34.

49 Goedertier, "Quest for Transnational Authority," 1270–71.

50 Herbstein, "Under Thatcher's Coattails," 23.

51 Peter Hain, *Don't Play with Apartheid: The Background to the Stop the Seventy Tour Campaign* (London: George Allen & Unwin, 1971), 81–82.

52 Marc Keech and Barrie Houlihan, "Sport and the End of Apartheid," *The Round Table* 88:349 (1999), 112.

53 Malcolm Maclean, "Revisiting (and Revising?) Sports Boycotts: From Rugby against South Africa to Soccer in Israel," *The International Journal of the History of Sport* 31:15 (2014), 1833.

54 Gurney, "In the Heart of the Beast," 268.

55 Keech and Houlihan, "Sport and the End of Apartheid," 114.

56 Maurice Llewellyn, "Circumventing Apartheid: Racial Politics and the Issue of South Africa's Olympic Participation at the 1984 Los Angeles Games," *The International Journal of the History of Sport* 32:1 (2015), 58.

57 Maclean, "Revisiting (and Revising?) Sports Boycotts," 1836.

58 Fiona Skillen and Matthew L. McDowell, "The 1970 British Commonwealth Games: Scottish Reactions to Apartheid and Sporting Boycotts," *Journal of Sport History* 44:3 (2017), 372.

59 Gurney, "In the Heart of the Beast," 271.

60 Asmal, Asmal, and Alberts, "The Irish Anti-Apartheid Movement," 358.

61 Hain, *Don't Play with Apartheid*, 109.

62 Ibid., 110–11.

63 Peter Jenkins, "Putting in the Boot," *The Guardian*, November 11, 1969.

64 Hain, *Don't Play with Apartheid*, 115.

65 Ibid., 89.

66 Gurney, "In the Heart of the Beast," 288–89.

67 "Cricket hypocrisy," letter to *The Guardian* from the Right Reverend Ambrose Reeves, President of the Anti-Apartheid Movement, May 19, 1970.

68 Hain, *Don't Play with Apartheid*, 121.

69 Ibid., 123.

70 Ibid., 152.

71 John Arlott, "Progress – but only into a Cul-de-sac," *The Guardian*, December 19, 1969.

72 Peter Hain, *Outside In* (London: Biteback, 2012), 58.

73 "Isolating Apartheid," *New York Times*, May 27, 1970.

74 Peter Hain, "Away Defeat for the Springboks," *New Statesman*, October 25, 1996, 28.

75 Hain, *Don't Play with Apartheid*, 70.

76 Eric J. Morgan, "Don't Play Ball with South Africa: The United States, the Anti-Apartheid Movement, and the Davis Cup Protests," *The International Journal of the History of Sport* 34:3–4 (2017), 269.

77 Adrian Guelke, *Rethinking the Rise and Fall of Apartheid: South African and World Politics* (Basingstoke: Palgrave Macmillan, 2005), 193.

78 "South Africa Given Out," *The Guardian*, September 10, 1971.

79 Maclean, "Revisiting (and Revising?) Sports Boycotts," 1837.

80 Skillen and McDowell, "The 1970 British Commonwealth Games," 373; Bruce Kidd, "The Campaign against Sport in South Africa," *International Journal* 43 (1988), 655.

81 Morgan, "Don't Play Ball with South Africa," 272.

82 Cited in Kidd, "The Campaign against Sport," 646.

83 Ibid., 657.

84 Llewellyn, "Circumventing Apartheid," 59.

85 Kidd, "The Campaign against Sport," 646.

86 Ibid., 657.

87 Llewellyn, "Circumventing Apartheid," 67.

88 Keech and Houlihan, "Sport and the End of Apartheid," 119–20.

89 Kidd, "The Campaign against Sport," 646.

90 Ali Bacher, cited in Hain, "Away Defeat for the Springboks," 29.

91 Interview with Enuga S. Reddy, Secretary of the UN Committee Against Apartheid, by Håkan Thörn, June 21, 2000, reproduced on the Anti-Apartheid Movement Archives Committee Forward to freedom project website: https://www.aamarchives.org/interviews/e-s-reddy/file/5657-int16t-e-s-reddy.html (accessed April 4, 2019).

92 Enuga S. Reddy, "The United Nations and the Struggle for Liberation in South Africa," in South African Democracy Education Trust, *The Road to Democracy in South Africa, Volume 3: International Solidarity, Part 1* (Cape Town: UNISA Press, 2008), 105–6.

93 Gurney, "In the Heart of the Beast," 271.

94 The Anti-Apartheid Movement, *Manifesto for Sanctions*, 11.

95 Houston, "International Solidarity," 38.

96 Culverson, "The Politics of the Anti-Apartheid Movement in the United States," 142.

97 Thörn, "Social Movements, the Media and the Emergence of a Global Public Sphere," 901.

98 Ibid., 907.

99 Gurney, "In the Heart of the Beast," 304.

100 Ibid., 308–12.

101 Ibid., 312.

102 Asmal, Asmal, and Alberts, "The Irish Anti-Apartheid Movement," 400.

103 Ibid., 401–5.

104 Gurney, "In the Heart of the Beast," 324.

105 Cited in Crawford, "Trump Card or Theater?" 15.

106 Ibid.

107 Klotz, "Transnational Activism and Global Transformations," 65.

108 Culverson, "The Politics of the Anti-Apartheid Movement in the United States," 127.

109 Guelke, *Rethinking the Rise and Fall of Apartheid*, 196.

110 Eades, *The End of Apartheid in South Africa*, 89.

111 Ibid., 89.

112 Ibid., 89–90.

113 Welsh and Spence, *Ending Apartheid*, 183.

114 Eades, *The End of Apartheid in South Africa*, 88.

115 Guelke, *Rethinking the Rise and Fall of Apartheid*, 190.

116 Klotz, "Transnational Activism and Global Transformations," 51–52.

117 Thörn, "Social Movements, the Media and the Emergence of a Global Public Sphere," 898–900.

118 Gurney, "In the Heart of the Beast," 324.

119 Ibid., 326–27.

120 Thörn, "The Meaning(s) of Solidarity," 433.

121 Margaret Ling, cited in Thörn, "The Meaning(s) of Solidarity," 433.

122 Hilary Sapire, "Liberation Movements, Exile, and International Solidarity: An Introduction," *Journal of Southern African Studies* 35:2 (2009), 273.

123 Thörn, "Social Movements, the Media and the Emergence of a Global Public Sphere," 907.

124 Thörn, "The Meaning(s) of Solidarity," 426.

125 Tariq Mellet, cited in Thörn, "Social Movements, the Media and the Emergence of a Global Public Sphere," 910.

126 Welsh and Spence, *Ending Apartheid*, 157.

127 Ibid., 186–87.

128 Gurney, "In the Heart of the Beast," 327.

129 Ibid., 339.

130 Ibid., 340–42.

131 Interview with Jerry Dammers by Jeff Howarth, February 20, 2014, for the Anti-Apartheid Movement Archives Committee: https://www.aamarchives.org/interviews/jerry-dammers/file/10503-int31t-jerry-dammers-transcript.html (accessed April 4, 2019).

132 Interview with Victoria Brittain by Håkan Thörn, February 5, 2000, reproduced on the Anti-Apartheid Movement Archives Committee Forward to Freedom Project: https://www.aamarchives.org/interviews/victoria-brittain/file/7426-int17t-victoria-brittain.html (accessed April 4, 2019).

133 Christopher S. Wren, "Sweeping Revisions," *The New York Times*, February 3, 1990.

134 Guelke, *Rethinking the Rise and Fall of Apartheid*, 189.

135 Crawford, "Trump Card or Theater?" 9.

136 Houston, "International Solidarity," 38.

137 Gurney, "In the Heart of the Beast," 346.

138 Asmal, Asmal, and Alberts, "The Irish Anti-Apartheid Movement," 400.

139 Robert Price, *The Apartheid State in Crisis: Political Transformation in South Africa, 1975-1990* (New York: Oxford University Press, 1991).

140 Hermann Giliomee, "Democratization in South Africa," *Political Science Quarterly* 110:1 (1995), 86-7.

141 Timothy Sisk, *Democratization in South Africa: The Elusive Social Contract* (Princeton: Princeton University Press, 1995).

142 Voorhes, "The US Divestment Movement," 142.

143 Danny Schechter, cited in Thörn, "The Meaning(s) of Solidarity," 434.

144 Interview with Enuga S. Reddy, Secretary of the UN Committee Against Apartheid, by Håkan Thörn, June 21, 2000, reproduced on the Anti-Apartheid Movement Archives Committee Forward to freedom project website: https://www.aamarchives.org/interviews/e-s-reddy/file/5657-int16t-e-s-reddy.html (accessed April 4, 2019).

145 Thabo Mbeki's "Foreword," in the Anti-Apartheid Movement, *The Anti-Apartheid Movement: A 40-year Perspective* Symposium Report (South Africa House, London, June 25–26, 1999), 8.

Chapter 5

1 David Cameron, "EU Speech at Bloomberg," January 23, 2013: https://www.gov.uk/government/speeches/eu-speech-at-bloomberg (accessed April 2, 2019).

2 Nigel Farage, "'No Chance' Europe will Negotiate New Treaty," *The Telegraph*, January 23, 2013: https://www.telegraph.co.uk/news/worldnews/europe/eu/9820696/Nigel-Farage-no-chance-Europe-will-negotiate-new-treaty.html (accessed April 2, 2019).

3 Chris Roycroft-Davis, "Parliament Cannot Thwart the will of the British People," *The Daily Express*, October 12, 2016: https://www.express.co.uk/comment/expresscomment/720169/Parliament-vote-act-EU-Brexit-British-Westminster-MPs (accessed April 2, 2019).

4 Liesbet Hooghe, "What Drives Euroskepticism? Party-Public Cueing, Ideology and Strategic Opportunity," *European Union Politics* 8:1 (2007), 5.

5 Catherine de Vries, "Ambivalent Europeans? Public Support for European Integration in East and West," *Government and Opposition* 48:3 (2013), 437.

6 Christopher J. Anderson, "When in Doubt, Use Proxies: Attitudes Toward Domestic Politics and Support for European Integration," *Comparative Political Studies* 31:5 (1998), 570.

7   Russell J. Dalton and Robert Duvall, "The Political Environment and Foreign Policy Opinions: British Attitudes toward European Integration, 1972-1979," *British Journal of Political Studies* 16:1 (1986), 113.

8   Robert J. Shepherd, *Public Opinion and European Integration* (Farnborough: Saxon House, 1975), 1.

9   Leon Lindberg and Stuart Scheingold, *Europe's Would-be Polity* (Englewood Cliffs: Prentice Hall, 1970), 22.

10 Christopher J. Anderson and Jason D. Hecht, "The Preference for Europe: Public Opinion about European Integration since 1952," *European Union Politics* 19:4 (2018), 618–19.

11 Mark N. Franklin, Cees van der Eijk, and Michael Marsh, "Referendum Outcomes and Trust in Government: Public Support for Europe in the Wake of Maastricht," in Jack Hayward (ed.), *The Crisis of Representation in Europe* (London: Frank Cass, 1995), 102.

12 Lindberg and Scheingold, *Europe's Would-be Polity*, 62.

13 Ernst Haas, *The Uniting of Europe: Political, Social and Economic Forces, 1950-1957* (Stanford: Stanford University Press, 1958).

14 Shepherd, *Public Opinion and European Integration*, 48.

15 Stanley Hoffmann, "Obstinate or Obsolete? The Fate of the Nation-State and the Case of Western Europe," *Daedalus* 95:3 (1966), 909–10.

16 Richard Sinnott, "Bringing Public Opinion Back In," in Oskar Niedermayer and Richard Sinnott (eds.), *Public Opinion and Internationalized Governance* (Oxford: Oxford University Press, 1995), 15–16. See also Philippe Schmitter, "A Revised Theory of Regional Integration," in Leon Lindberg and Stuart Scheingold (eds.), *Regional Integration: Theory and Research* (Cambridge: Harvard University Press, 1971).

17 Lindberg and Scheingold, *Europe's Would-be Polity*, 277.

18 For more on this see Sinnott, "Bringing Public Opinion Back In," 29–31.

19 Anne Dulphy and Christine Manigand, "Introduction," in Anne Dulphy and Christine Manigand (eds.), *Les opinions publiques face à l'Europe communautaire: Entre cultures nationales et horizon européen* (Brussels: Peter Lang, 2004), 10.

20 Andrew Moravscik, "In Defence of the 'Democratic Deficit': Reassessing Legitimacy in the European Union," *Journal of Common Market Studies* 40:4 (2002), 606.

21 Dimiter Toshkov, "Public Opinion and Policy Output in the European Union: A Lost Relationship," *European Union Politics* 12:2 (2011), 170.

22 Ibid., 171.

23 Shepherd, *Public Opinion and European Integration*, 94.

24 Ronald Inglehart, "Cognitive Mobilization and European Identity," *Comparative Politics* 3:1 (1970), 67.

25 Shepherd, *Public Opinion and European Integration*, 94.

26 Ibid., 124, 156.

27 Paul Martin Gliddon, "The Labour Government and the Battle for Public Opinion in the 1975 Referendum on the European Community," *Contemporary British History* 31:1 (2018), 93.

28 Andy Mullen and Brian Burkitt, "Spinning Europe: Pro-European Union Propaganda Campaigns in Britain, 1962-1975," *The Political Quarterly* 76:1 (2005), 111–12.

29 European Commission, *Eurobarometer: Public Opinion in the European Community* [hereafter *Eurobarometer*] 9 (July 1978), 17.

30 *Eurobarometer*, 11 (May 1979), 4–7.

31 Commission des Communautés Européennes, *euro-baromètre: L'opinion publique dans la communauté européenne* [hereafter *euro-baromètre*] 13 (June 1980), 25.

32 Ibid., 30.

33 *Eurobarometer*, 41 (July 1994), 1.

34 Richard C. Eichenberg and Russell J. Dalton, "Europeans and the European Community: The Dynamics of Public Support for European Integration," *International Organization* 47:4 (1993), 529–30.

35 *Eurobarometer*, 43 (Autumn 1995), x (original emphasis).

36 See, for example, Christine Manigand and Anne Dulphy, "L'opinion publique française face à l'unification européenne: approche quantifiée," in Élisabeth du Réau (ed.), *Europe des élites? Europe des peuples? La construction de l'espace européen, 1945-1960* (Paris: Presses de la Sorbonne Nouvelle, 1999), 303.

37 Mark Franklin, Michael Marsh, and Lauren McLaren, "Uncorking the Bottle: Popular Opposition to European Unification in the Wake of Maastricht," *Journal of Common Market Studies* 32:4 (1994), 468.

38 *Eurobarometer*, 40 (December 1993), vi.

39 Toshkov, "Public Opinion and Policy Output in the European Union," 183.

40 Matthew Gabel and Harvey D. Palmer, "Understanding Variation in Public Support for European Integration," *European Journal of Political Research* 27:1 (1995), 3.

41 *Eurobarometer*, 40 (December 1993), x.

42 Toshkov, "Public Opinion and Policy Output in the European Union," 178.

43 Anderson and Hecht. "The Preference for Europe," 621.

44 Christine Manigand, "L'opinion publique française face aux élargissements," in Marie-Thérèse Bitsch, Wilfried Loth, and Charles Barthel (eds.), *Cultures politiques, opinions publiques et intégration européenne* (Brussels: Établissements Émile Bruylant, 2007), 135.

45 Anne Dulphy and Christine Manigand, "L'opinion française, vers l'euroconscience et le désenchantement," in Anne Dulphy and Christine Manigand (eds.), *Les opinions publiques face à l'Europe communautaire: Entre cultures nationales et horizon européen* (Brussels: Peter Lang, 2004), 25.

46 Shepherd, *Public Opinion and European Integration*, 70.

47 Anderson and Hecht, "The preference for Europe," 618.

48 Inglehart, "Cognitive Mobilization and European Identity," 62.

49 CPB Netherlands' Bureau for Economic Policy Analysis: SCP The Netherlands Institute for Social Research, *Europe's Neighbours: European Neighbourhood Policy and Public Opinion on the European Union*, European Outlook, 6 (The Hague, 2008), 33. Britain's struggle to accept the realities of the loss of Empire, and the impact of this on enthusiasm for European integration, has also been commented on by Oskar Niedermayer, in "Trends and Contrasts," in Oskar Niedermayer and Richard Sinnott (eds.), *Public Opinion and Internationalized Governance* (Oxford: Oxford University Press, 1995), 66.

50 Neill Nugent, "British Public Opinion and the European Community," in Stephen George (ed.), *Britain and the European Community: The Politics of Semi-Detachment* (Oxford: Clarendon Press, 1992), 178–79.

51 CPB Netherlands' Bureau, *Europe's Neighbours*, 33.

52 Niedermayer, "Trends and Contrasts," 53–59.

53 Ibid., 57–64.

54 Ibid., 67–71.

55 Ibid., 66.

56 Sebastian Lang-Jensen, "The Danish Left and European Integration, 1957-72," in Marie-Thérèse Bitsch, Wilfried Loth, and Charles Barthel (eds.), *Cultures politiques, opinions publiques et intégration européenne* (Brussels: Établissements Émile Bruylant, 2007), 104–5.

57 Michel Gehler, "L'opinion publique en Autriche et la construction européenne," in Marie-Thérèse Bitsch, Wilfried Loth, and Charles Barthel (eds.), *Cultures politiques, opinions publiques et intégration européenne* (Brussels: Établissements Émile Bruylant, 2007), 30.

58 Jürgen Elvert, "The Acession-Debate during the EU-Enlargements, 1973-1995: A Public Affair or a Closed Shop?" in Marie-Thérèse Bitsch, Wilfried Loth, and Charles Barthel (eds.), *Cultures politiques, opinions publiques et intégration européenne* (Brussels: Établissements Émile Bruylant, 2007), 171–72.

59 Gehler, "L'opinion publique en Autriche et la construction européenne," 46–47.

60 *Eurobarometer*, 53 (October 2000), 7.

61 Ibid., 26.

62 Toshkov, "Public Opinion and Policy Output in the European Union," 185–86.

63 Gehler, "L'opinion publique en Autriche et la construction européenne," 28.

64 *Eurobarometer*, 13 (June 1980), 35.

65 *Eurobarometer*, 18 (December 1982), 92.

66 James Adams and Lawrence Ezrow, "Who Do European Parties Represent? How Western European Parties Represent the Policy Preferences of Opinion Leaders," *The Journal of Politics* 71:1 (2009), 209.

67 *Eurobarometer*, 27 (June 1987) 34.

68 *Eurobarometer*, 34 (December 1990), 11.

69 *Eurobarometer*, 38 (December 1992), vii.

70 *Eurobarometer*, 27 (June 1992), 42.

71 *Eurobarometer*, 38 (December 1992), v.

72 Ibid., x.

73 *Eurobarometer*, 40 (December 1993), 35.

74 Alexander Reinfeldt, "British Public Opinion and European Integration: Supranational and Governmental Information Policies in Britain (1952-1973)," in Marie-Thérèse Bitsch, Wilfried Loth, and Charles Barthel (eds.), *Cultures politiques, opinions publiques et intégration européenne* (Brussels: Établissements Émile Bruylant, 2007), 111.

75 Marcel Machill, Markus Beiler, and Corinna Fischer, "Europe-Topics in Europe's Media: The Debate about the European Public Sphere: A Meta-Analysis of Media Content Analyses," *European Journal of Communication* 21:1 (2006), 58–59.

76 Ibid., 62.

77 Toshkov, "Public Opinion and Policy Output in the European Union," 172.

78 Erik Oddvar Eriksen, "An Emerging European Public Sphere," *European Journal of Social Theory* 8:3 (2005), 341.

79 Ignacio Sánchez-Cuenca, "The Political Basis of Support for European Integration," *European Union Politics* 1:2 (2000), 149.

80 Jürgen Habermas, *The Postnational Constellation: Political Essays*, translated and edited by Max Pensky (Cambridge: Polity, 2001), 110–11.

81 John Downey and Thomas Koenig, "Is There a European Public Sphere? The Berlusconi-Schulz Case," *European Journal of Communication* 21:2 (2006), 167.

82 Barbara Pfetsch, "Agents of Transnational Debate Across Europe," *Javnost – The Public: Journal of the European Institute for Communication and Culture* 15:4 (2008), 35–36.

83 Pfetsch, "Agents of Transnational Debate," 36.

84 Anderson, "When in Doubt, Use Proxies," 594.

85 *Eurobarometer*, 43 (Autumn 1995), x.

86 Phillip Schlesinger, "Changing Spaces of Political Communication: The Case of the European Union," *Political Communication* 16:3 (1999), 277.

87 Inglehart, "Cognitive Mobilization and European Identity," 45.

88 Ibid., 51.

89 Armen Hakhverdian, Erika van Elsas, Woueter van der Brug, and Theresa Juhn, "Euroscepticism and Education: A Longitudinal Study of 12 EU Member States, 1973-2010," *European Union Politics* 14:4 (2013), 523.

90 Ibid., 535.

91 Hooghe, "What Drives Euroskepticism?" 7.

92 *Eurobarometer*, 40 (December 1993), x.

93 *Eurobarometer*, 15 (June 1981), 54-6.

94 *Eurobarometer*, 18 (December 1982), 66.

95 *Eurobarometer*, 19 (June 1983), 76.

96 *Eurobarometer*, 45 (December 1996), 86.

97 *Eurobarometer*, 22 (December 1984), 48-9.

98 *Eurobarometer*, Special 30th Anniversary Edition (March 1987), 17.

99 *Eurobarometer*, 43 (Autumn 1995), x–xi.

100 Eriksen, "An Emerging European Public Sphere," 342.

101 See Habermas, *The Postnational Constellation*, 19.

102 Thomas Risse, *A Community of Europeans? Transnational Identities and Public Spheres* (Ithaca: Cornell University Press, 2010), 125.

103 Jan-Henrik Meyer, "Was there a European Public Sphere at the Summit of The Hague 1969? An Analysis of Discourses on the Legitimacy of the EC," in Marie-Thérèse Bitsch, Wilfried Loth, and Charles Barthel (eds.), *Cultures politiques, opinions publiques et intégration européenne* (Brussels: Établissements Émile Bruylant, 2007), 229.

104 Eriksen, "An Emerging European Public Sphere," 350.

105 Jørgen Bølstad, "Dynamics of European Integration: Public Opinion in the Core and Periphery," *European Union Politics* 16:1 (2015), 25.

106 Ibid., 38.

107 CPB Netherlands' Bureau, *Europe's Neighbours*, 39.

108 Menno Spiering, "British Euroscepticism," in Robert Harmsen and Menno Spiering (eds.), *Euroscepticism: Party Politics, National Identity and European Integration* (Amsterdam: Rodopi, 2004), 133–34.

109 Dulphy and Manigand, "Introduction," 10.

110 George Wilkes and Dominic Wring, "The British Press and European Integration: 1948-1996," in David Baker and David Seawright (eds.), *Britain For and Against Europe: British Politics and the Question of European Integration* (Oxford: Clarendon Press, 1998), 197.

111 Ibid., 199.

112 It has been noted the 1970s was a period in which the majority of British newspapers were pro-EC, implicitly if not always explicitly. It is clear that some right-wing papers, notably *The Sun* and *The Times* adopted a more stridently anti-EU stance into the 1990s. See CPB Netherlands' Bureau, *Europe's Neighbours*, 35.

113 Oliver Daddow, "The UK Media and 'Europe': From Permissive Consensus to Destructive Dissent," *International Affairs* 88:6 (2012), 1219.

114 Spiering, "British Euroscepticism," 139.

115 Wilkes and Wring, "The British Press and European Integration: 1948-1996," 195, 185.

116 Daddow, "The UK Media and 'Europe,'" 1232.

117 Ibid., 1236.

118 Machill, Beiler, and Fischer, "Europe-Topics in Europe's Media," 78–79.

119 *Eurobarometer*, 52 (April 2000), ii–iii.

120 Ibid., 58.

121 Sara B. Hobolt, "Ever Closer or Ever Wider? Public Attitudes towards Further Enlargement and Integration in the European Union," *Journal of European Public Policy* 21:5 (2014), 664–65.

122 Machill, Beiler, and Fischer, "Europe-Topics in Europe's Media," 80.

123 Shepherd, *Public Opinion and European Integration*, 157.

124 Franklin, Marsh, and McLaren, "Uncorking the Bottle," 471.

Conclusion

1   D. G. Boyce, "Public Opinion and the Historians," *History* 63:208 (1978), 225.

2   Cited in George Gallup, "Testing Public Opinion," *The Public Opinion Quarterly* 2:1 (1938), 14.

3   Cited in Laurence Fenton, *Palmerston and* The Times: *Foreign Policy, the Press and Public Opinion in Mid-Victorian Britain* (London: I.B. Tauris, 2013), 3.

4   Christina Twomey, "Framing Atrocity: Photography and Humanitarianism," *History of Photography* 36:3 (2012), 256.

5   Simon J. Potter, "Jingoism, Public Opinion, and the New Imperialism: Newspapers and Imperial Rivalries at the fin de siècle," *Media History* 20:1 (2014), 35.

6   Kenneth O. Morgan, "The Boer War and the Media (1899-1902)," *Twentieth Century British History* 13:1 (2002), 11.

7   Becker, "L'opinion publique: un populisme?", 96.

8   Thörn, "Social Movements, the Media and the Emergence of a Global Public Sphere," 901.

9   Douglas Foyle, "Foreign Policy Analysis and Globalization: Public Opinion, World Opinion, and the Individual," in Jean A. Garrisson (ed.), "Foreign Policy Analysis in 20/20: A Symposium," *International Studies Review* 5:2 (2003), 166.

10 Nancy Fraser, "Transnationalizing the Public Sphere: On the Legitimacy and Efficacy of Public opinion in a post-Westphalian World," *Theory, Culture & Society* 24:4 (2007), 8.

11 Herbst, "Critical Perspectives on Public Opinion," 307.

12 Ibid.

13 Pierre Bourdieu, "L'opinion publique n'existe pas," *Les temps moderne* 318 (1973), 1309. For more critical discussion about polls, see Loïc Blondiaux, "Ce que les sondages font à l'opinion publique," *Politix* 10:37 (1997), 117–36. For a strident defense of the polling industry, see Warren, *In Defense of Public Opinion Polling*.

14 Herbst, "Critical Perspectives on Public Opinion," 308–9.

15 Ibid., 313.

16 Jamie Bartlett, "You Can't Believe a Word Any of these People Is Saying – That's the 'Deep Fake' Era for You," *The Guardian*, June 16, 2019: https://www.theguardian.com/commentisfree/2019/jun/16/you-cant-believe-a-word-any-of-these-people-is-saying-thats-the-dep-fake-era-for-you (accessed July 15, 2019).

17 Foyle, "Public Opinion, Foreign Policy, and the Media: Toward an Integrative Theory," 667–69.

Bibliography

Archival, printed, televisual, online and periodical references are located in the book's citations.

Books

Almond, Gabriel, *The American People and Foreign Policy*. New York: Harcourt, Brace and Company, 1950.

Anderson, David L., *The Columbia Guide to the Vietnam War*. New York: Columbia University Press, 2002.

The Anti-Apartheid Movement, *Manifesto for Sanctions*. London, January 1987.

Audry, Colette, *Léon Blum ou la politique de la juste*. Paris: René Julliard, 1955.

Bardes, Barbara A. and Robert W. Oldendick, *Public Opinion: Measuring the American Mind*, 4th ed. Lanham: Rowman & Littlefield, 2012.

Baumont, Maurice, *La faillite de la paix, 1918–1939*. Paris: Presses universitaires de la France, 1946.

Berinsky, Andrew J., ed. *New Directions in Public Opinion*, 2nd ed. New York: Routledge, 2016.

Bernays, Edward, *Crystallizing Public Opinion*. New York: Liveright Publishing Corporation, 1923.

Black, Jeremy, *Debating Foreign Policy in Eighteenth-Century England*. Farnham: Ashgate, 2011.

Bloch, Marc, *L'étrange défaite: Témoignage écrit en 1940*. Paris: Société des Éditions Franc-Tireur, 1946.

Bouchard, Carl, *Le citoyen et l'ordre mondial (1914–1919): Le rêve d'une paix durable au lendemain de la Grande Guerre en France, en Grande-Bretagne et aux Etats-Unis*. Paris: Editions A. Pedone, 2008.

Bryce, James, *The American Commonwealth, Volume 1: The National Government* (London: Macmillan, 1888), and *Volume 2: The Party System*. London: Macmillan, 1891.

Carey, John, *The Intellectuals and the Masses: Pride and Prejudice Among the Literary Intelligentsia, 1880–1939*. Chicago: Academy Chicago, 2002.

Carr, Edward Hallett, *Conditions of Peace*. London: Macmillan, 1942.

Carroll, Eber Malcolm, *French Public Opinion and Foreign Affairs, 1870–1914*. London: The Century Co., 1931.

Ceadel, Martin, *Semi-Detached Idealists: The British Peace Movement and International Relations, 1854–1945*. Oxford: Oxford University Press, 2000.

Cohen, Bernard C., *The Public's Impact on Foreign Policy*. Boston: Little and Brown, 1973.

Cohrs, Patrick, *The Unfinished Peace after World War I: America, Britain and the Stabilisation of Europe, 1919–1932*. Cambridge: Cambridge University Press, 2006.

Corner, Paul, ed. *Popular Opinion in Totalitarian Regimes: Fascism, Nazism, Communism*. Oxford: Oxford University Press, 2009.

Crémieux-Brilhac, Jean-Louis, *Les Français de l'An 40, tome I: La guerre, oui ou non?* Paris: Gallimard, 1990.

D'Almeida, Fabrice, and Christian Delporte, *Histoire des médias en France de la Grande Guerre à nos jours*. Paris: Flammarion, 2010.

Davis, Richard, *Anglo-French Relations before the Second World War: Appeasement and Crisis*. Basingstoke: Macmillan, 2001.

Dell, Simon, *The Image of the Popular Front: The Masses and the Media in Interwar France*. Basingstoke: Palgrave, 2007.

Dumbrell, John, *Rethinking the Vietnam War*. Basingstoke: Palgrave Macmillan, 2012.

Duroselle, Jean-Baptiste, *Histoire diplomatique de 1919 à nos jours*. Paris: Dalloz, 1953.

Duroselle, Jean-Baptiste, *La décadence, 1932–1939*. Paris: Imprimerie Nationale, 1979. This is available in English as *France and the Nazi Threat: The Collapse of French Diplomacy, 1932–1939*. New York: Enigma Books, 2004.

Eades, Lindsay Michie, *The End of Apartheid in South Africa*. Westport: Greenwood Press, 1999.

Fenton, Laurence, *Palmerston and* The Times: *Foreign Policy, the Press and Public Opinion in Mid-Victorian Britain*. London: I. B. Tauris, 2013.

Finney, Patrick, *Remembering the Road to World War Two: International History, National Identity, Collective Memory*. London: Routledge, 2011.

Flandin, Pierre-Étienne, *Politique Française, 1919–1940*. Paris: Les Éditions Nouvelles, 1947.

Fleury, Alain, *"La Croix" et l'Allemagne, 1930–1940*. Paris: Les Éditions du Cerf, 1986.

Fry, Michael Graham, *And Fortune Fled: David Lloyd George, the First Democratic Statesman, 1916–1922*. New York: Peter Lang, 2011.

Géraud, André ('Pertinax'), *Les fossoyeurs: défaite militaire de la France*, 2 vols. New York: Éditions de la Maison française, 1943.

Glynn, Carroll J., Susan Herbst, Mark Lindeman, Garrett J. O'Keefe, and Robert Y. Shapiro, *Public Opinion*, 3rd ed. Boulder: Westview, 2016.

Guelke, Adrian, *Rethinking the Rise and Fall of Apartheid: South African and World Politics*. Basingstoke: Palgrave Macmillan, 2005.

Guieu, Jean-Michel, *Le rameau et le glaive: Les militants français pour la Société des Nations*. Paris: Presses de Sciences Po, 2008.

Haas, Ernst, *The Uniting of Europe: Political, Social and Economic Forces, 1950–1957*. Stanford: Stanford University Press, 1958.

Habermas, Jürgen, *The Postnational Constellation: Political Essays*, translated and edited by Max Pensky. Cambridge: Polity, 2001.

Habermas, Jürgen, *The Structural Transformation of the Public Sphere: An Inquiry into a Category of Bourgeois Society*. Cambridge: Polity, 1989.

Hain, Peter, *Don't Play with Apartheid: The Background to the Stop the Seventy Tour Campaign*. London: George Allen & Unwin, 1971.

Hain, Peter, *Outside In*. London: Biteback, 2012.

Halberstam, David, *The Powers That Be*. London: Chatto & Windus, 1979.

Hall, Simon, *Rethinking the American Anti-War Movement*. New York: Routledge, 2012.

Hallin, Daniel, *The "Uncensored War": The Media and Vietnam*. Oxford: Oxford University Press, 1986.

Hammond, William H., *Reporting Vietnam: Media & Military at War*. Lawrence: University Press of Kansas, 1998.

Herr, Michael, *Dispatches*. London: Pan Books, 1980.

Hess, Gary, *Vietnam: Explaining America's Lost War*. Oxford: Blackwell, 2009.

Hogan, J. Michael, *Woodrow Wilson's Western Tour: Rhetoric, Public Opinion, and the League of Nations*. College Station: Texas A & M University Press, 2006.

Holzer, Harold, *The War for Public Opinion: Lincoln and the Power of the Press*. New York: Simon & Schuster, 2014.

Hucker, Daniel, *Public Opinion and the End of Appeasement in Britain and France*. Farnham: Ashgate, 2011.

Jackson, Julian, *The Fall of France: The Nazi Invasion of 1940*. Oxford: Oxford University Press, 2003.

Jeanneney, Jean-Noël, *L'argent caché: Milieux d'affaires et pouvoirs politiques dans la France du XXè siècle*. Paris: Fayard, 1984.

Jeanneney, Jean-Noël, *Une histoire des médias des origines à nos jours*. Paris: Éditions du Seuil, 2001.

Jeffreys-Jones, Rhodri, *Peace Now! American Society and the Ending of the Vietnam War*. New Haven: Yale University Press, 1999.

Key, Valdimar Orlando, *Public Opinion and American Democracy*. New York: Alfred Knopf, 1963.

Kuhn, Raymond, *The Media in France*. London: Routledge, 1995.

Lacaze, Yvon, *L'opinion publique française et la crise de Munich*. Bern: Peter Lang, 1991.

Lewis, Penny, *Hardhats, Hippies and Hawks: The Vietnam Antiwar Movement as Myth and Memory*. New York: Cornell University Press, 2013.

Lindberg, Leon, and Stuart Scheingold, *Europe's Would-be Polity*. Englewood Cliffs: Prentice Hall, 1970.

Lippmann, Walter, *The Phantom Public*. Abingdon: Routledge, 2017 [1927].

Lippmann, Walter, *Public Opinion*. London: George Allen & Unwin, 1932 [1922].

Lloyd George, David, *Memoirs of the Peace Conference*, vol. 1. New Haven: Yale University Press, 1939.

Lorrell, Mark, and Charles Kelley, Jr. (with the assistance of Deborah Hensler), *Casualties, Public Opinion, and Presidential Policy During the Vietnam War*. Santa Monica: The Rand Coroporation, 1985.

Macmillan, Margaret, *Peacemakers: The Paris Conference of 1919 and Its Attempt to End War*. London: John Murray, 2001.

Margolis, Michael, and Gary A. Mauser, eds. *Manipulating Public Opinion: Essays on Public Opinion as a Dependent Variable*. Pacific Grove, CA: Brooks/Cole Publishing Company, 1989.

Martin, Benjamin F., *France in 1938*. Baton Rouge: Louisiana State University Press, 2005.

Martin, Benjamin F., *Years of Plenty, Years of Want: France and the Legacy of the Great War*. De Kalb: Northern Illinois University Press, 2013.

Mayer, Arno J., *Political Origins of the New Diplomacy, 1917–1918*. New Haven: Yale University Press, 1959.

Méadel, Cécile, *Histoire de la radio des années trente*. Paris: Anthropos/INA, 1994.

Melville, Cecil, *Guilty Frenchmen*. London: Jarrolds, 1940.

Micaud, Charles, *The French Right and Nazi Germany, 1933–1939*. New York: Octagon Books, 1972 [1942].

Monzie, Anatole de, *Ci-devant*. Paris: Flammarion, 1941.

Mueller, John E., *War, Presidents and Public Opinion*. New York: Wiley, 1973.

Mulligan, William, *The Great War for Peace*. New Haven: Yale University Press, 2014.

Nicolay, John G. and John Hay, eds. *Complete Works of Abraham Lincoln*, vol. V. New York: Francis D. Tandy Company, 1905.

Nicolson, Harold, *Diplomacy*. Washington DC: Institute for the Study of Diplomacy, 1988.

Nicolson, Harold, *Peacemaking, 1919: Being Reminiscences of the Paris Peace Conference*. Boston: Hougton Mifflin Company, 1933.

Nixon, Richard, *The Memoirs of Richard Nixon*. New York: Grosset & Dunlap, 1978.

Nord, Philip, *France 1940: Defending the Republic*. New Haven: Yale University Press, 2015.

Ober, Josiah, *Mass and Elite in Democratic Athens: Rhetoric, Ideology, and the Power of the People*. Princeton: Princeton University Press, 1989.

Oberdorfer, Don, *Tet! The Turning Point in the Vietnam War*. Baltimore: Johns Hopkins University Press, 2001.

Paxton, Robert, *Vichy France: Old Guard and New Order, 1940–1944*. New York: Columbia University Press, 2001 [1972].

Price, Robert, *The Apartheid State in Crisis: Political Transformation in South Africa, 1975–1990*. New York: Oxford University Press, 1991.

Puyaubert, Jacques, *Georges Bonnet (1889–1973): Les combats d'un pacifiste*. Rennes: Presses universitaires de Rennes, 2007.

Rearick, Charles, *The French in Love and War: Popular Culture in the Era of the World Wars*. New Haven: Yale University Press, 1997.

Réau, Élisabeth du, *Édouard Daladier, 1884–1970*. Paris: Fayard, 1993.

Renouvin, Pierre, *Histoire des relations internationales*. Paris: Hachette, 1958.

Riddell, George Allardice [Lord], *Lord Riddell's Intimate Diary of the Peace Conference and After, 1918–1923*. London: Victor Gollancz, 1933.

Risse, Thomas, *A Community of Europeans? Transnational Identities and Public Spheres*. Ithaca: Cornell University Press, 2010.

Scanlon, Sandra, *The Pro-War Movement: Domestic Support for the Vietnam War and the making of Modern American Conservatism*. Amherst, MA: University of Massachusetts Press, 2013.

Schmitz, David F., *The Tet Offensive: Politics, War, and Public Opinion*. Lanham: Rowman and Littlefield Publishers, Inc., 2005.

Shepherd, Robert J., *Public Opinion and European Integration*. Farnborough: Saxon House, 1975.

Shirer, William, *The Collapse of the Third Republic: An Inquiry Into the Fall of France in 1940*. London: The Literary Guild, 1970.

Sisk, Timothy, *Democratization in South Africa: The Elusive Social Contract*. Princeton: Princeton University Press, 1995.

Skinner, Rob, *The Foundations of Anti-Apartheid: Liberal Humanitarians and Transnational Activists in Britain and the United States, c. 1919–64*. London: Palgrave, 2010.

Sluga, Glenda, *Internationalism in the Age of Nationalism*. Philadelphia: University of Pennsylvania Press, 2013.

Small, Melvin, *Covering Dissent: The Media and the Anti-Vietnam War Movement*. New Brunswick: Rutgers University Press, 1994.

Spigel, Lynn, *Make Room for TV: Television and the Family Ideal in Postwar America*. Chicago: The University of Chicago Press, 1992.

Steiner, Zara, *The Lights That Failed: European International History, 1919–1933*. Oxford: Oxford University Press, 2005.

Streitmatter, Rodger, *Mightier Than the Sword: How the News Media Have Shaped American History*. Boulder: Westview, 2016.

Tabouis, Geneviève, *They Called Me Cassandra*. New York: Charles Scribner's and Sons, 1942.

Temperley, H. W. V., ed. *A History of the Peace Conference of Paris*, vol. 1. London: Hodder & Stoughton, 1920.

Thompson, James, *British Political Culture and the Idea of "Public Opinion", 1867–1914*. Cambridge: Cambridge University Press, 2013.

Unger, Irwin, and Debi Unger, eds. *The Times were a Changin': The Sixties Reader*. New York: Three Rivers Press, 1998.

Van Horn Melton, James, *The Rise of the Public in Enlightenment Europe*. Cambridge: Cambridge University Press, 2001.

Waley, Daniel, *British Public Opinion and the Abyssinian War, 1935–6*. London: Temple Smith, 1975.

Wardhaugh, Jessica, *In Pursuit of the People: Political Culture in France, 1934–39*. Basingstoke: Macmillan, 2009.

Warren, Kenneth F., *In Defense of Public Opinion Polling*. Boulder: Westview Press, 2001.

Weber, Eugen, *The Hollow Years: France in the 1930s*. London: Sinclair-Stevenson, 1995.

Wells, Tom, *The War Within: America's Battle Over Vietnam*. Berkeley: University of California Press, 1994.

Welsh, David, and J. E. Spence, *Ending Apartheid*. Harlow: Longman, 2011.

Werth, Alexander, *France in Ferment, 1933–1935*. London: Jarrolds, 1935.

Werth, Alexander, *The Twilight of France, 1933–1940*. New York: Howard Fertig, 1966 [1942].

Westmoreland, William C., *A Soldier Reports*. New York: Doubelday & Company, 1976.

Wyatt, David, *When America Turned: Reckoning with 1968*. Amherst: University of Massachusetts Press, 2014.

Yearwood, Peter, *Guarantee of Peace: The League of Nations in British Policy, 1914–1925*. Oxford: Oxford University Press, 2009.

Young, Robert J., *France and the Origins of the Second World War*. Basingstoke: Macmillan, 1996.

Zay, Jean, *Souvenirs et solitude*. Paris: René Julliard, 1945.

Articles and Book Chapters

Adams, James, and Lawrence Ezrow, "Who Do European Parties Represent? How Western European Parties Represent the Policy Preferences of Opinion Leaders," *The Journal of Politics* 71:1 (2009), 206–23.

Albert, Pierre, "La presse française de 1871 à 1940," in Claude Bellanger et al., eds. *Histoire générale de la presse française, tome III: de 1871 à 1940*. Paris: Presses Universitaires de France, 1972.

Almond, Gabriel, "Public Opinion and National Security Policy," *Public Opinion Quarterly* 20:2 (1956), 371–78.

Anderson, Christopher J., "When in Doubt, Use Proxies: Attitudes Toward Domestic Politics and Support for European Integration," *Comparative Political Studies* 31:5 (1998), 569–601.

Anderson, Christopher J. and Jason D. Hecht, "The Preference for Europe: Public Opinion About European Integration Since 1952," *European Union Politics* 19:4 (2018), 617–38.

Asmal, Louise, Kader Asmal, and Thomas Alberts, "The Irish Anti-Apartheid Movement," in South African Democracy Education Trust, ed. *The Road to Democracy in South Africa, Volume 3: International Solidarity, Part 1*. Pretoria: Unisa Press, 2008, 353–420.

Bauer, Wilhelm, "Public Opinion," in E. R. A. Seligman, ed. *Enyclopaedia of the Social Sciences*, vol. XII. New York: Macmillan, 1934, 669–74.

Becker, Jean-Jacques, "L'opinion publique: un populisme?" *Vingtième Siècle: Revue d'histoire* 56 (1997), 92–98.

Bernays, Edward, "Manipulating Public Opinion: The Why and the How," *American Journal of Sociology* 33:6 (1928), 958–71.

Best, Geoffrey, "Peace Conferences and the Century of Total War: The 1899 Hague Conference and What Came After," *International Affairs* 75:3 (1999), 619–34.

Bignon, Vincent, and Marc Flandreau, "The Price of Media Capture and the Debasement of the French Newspaper Industry During the Interwar," *The Journal of Economic History* 74:3 (2014), 799–830.

Blondiaux, Loïc, "Ce que les sondages font à l'opinion publique," *Politix* 10:37 (1997), 117–36.

Bølstad, Jørgen, "Dynamics of European Integration: Public Opinion in the Core and Periphery," *European Union Politics* 16:1 (2015), 23–44.

Bourdieu, Pierre, "L'opinion publique n'existe pas," *Les temps moderne* 318 (1973), 1292–309.

Bourdin, Janine, "Introduction," in René Rémond and Janine Bourdin, eds. *La France et les Français en 1938–1939*. Paris: Presses de la FNSP, 1978, 9–24.

Boyce, D. G., "Public Opinion and the Historians," *History* 63:208 (1978), 214–28.

Brittain, Victoria, "Western Media: Mirroring Whose Reality?" in Anti-Apartheid Movement Archives Committee, ed. *The Anti-Apartheid Movement: A 40-year Perspective*. London: AAM Archives Committee, 2000.

Carr, Edward Hallett, "Public Opinion as a Safeguard of Peace," *International Affairs* 15:6 (1936), 846–62.

Chalaby, Jean K., "Twenty Years of Contrast: The French and British Press During the Inter-War Period," *European Journal of Sociology* 37:1 (1996), 143–59.

Cohen, Bernard C., "The Relationship between Public Opinion and Foreign Policy Maker," in Melvin Small, ed. *Public Opinion and Historians: Interdisciplinary Perspectives*. Detroit: Wayne State University Press, 1970, 65–80.

Corner, Paul, "Fascist Italy in the 1930s: Popular Opinion in the Provinces," in Paul Corner, ed. *Popular Opinion in Totalitarian Regimes: Fascism, Nazism, Communism*. Oxford: Oxford University Press, 2009, 122–46.

Corner, Paul, "Introduction," in Paul Corner, ed. *Popular Opinion in Totalitarian Regimes: Fascism, Nazism, Communism*. Oxford: Oxford University Press, 2009, 1–13.

Crawford, Neta C., "Trump Card or Theater?' An Introduction to Two Sanctions Debates," in Neta C. Crawford and Audie Klotz, eds. *How Sanctions Work: Lessons from South Africa*. Basingstoke: Macmillan, 1999, 3–24.

Culbert, David, "Television's Visual Impact on Decision-Making in the USA, 1968: The Tet Offensive and Chicago's Democratic Convention," *Journal of Contemporary History* 33:3 (1998), 419–49.

Culverson, Donald R., "The Politics of the Anti-Apartheid Movement in the United States, 1969–1986," *Political Science Quarterly* 111:1 (1996), 127–49.

Daddis, Gregory A., "Mansplaining Vietnam: Male Veterans and America's Popular Image of the Vietnam War," *The Journal of Military History* 82:1 (2018), 181–207.

Daddow, Oliver, "The UK Media and 'Europe': From Permissive Consensus to Destructive Dissent," *International Affairs* 88:6 (2012), 1219–36.

Dalton, Russell J. and Robert Duvall, "The Political Environment and Foreign Policy Opinions: British Attitudes toward European Integration, 1972–1979," *British Journal of Political Studies* 16:1 (1986), 113–34.

Davies, Thomas, "France and the World Disarmament Conference of 1932–34," *Diplomacy & Statecraft* 15:4 (2004), 765–80.

Davis, Richard, "Le débat sur l'« appeasement » britannique et français dans les années 1930: Les crises d'Éthiope et de Rhénanie," *Revue d'histoire moderne et contemporaine* 45:4 (1998), 822–36.

Delporte, Christian, "The Image and Myth of the 'Fifth Column,'" in Valerie Holman and Debra Kelly, eds. *France at War in the Twentieth Century: Propaganda, Myth and Metaphor*. New York: Berghahn Books, 2000, 49–64.

Dodd, Lindsey, "Are We Defended? Conflicting Representations of War in Pre-War France," *University of Sussex Journal of Contemporary History* 12 (2008): http://eprints.hud.ac.uk/id/eprint/14675/, 1–13.

Downey, John, and Thomas Koenig, "Is There a European Public Sphere? The Berlusconi-Schulz Case," *European Journal of Communication* 21:2 (2006), 165–87.

Druckman, James N., "The Power of Television Images: The First Kennedy-Nixon Debate Revisited," *The Journal of Politics* 65:2 (2003), 559–71.

Dulphy, Anne, and Christine Manigand, "Introduction," in Anne Dulphy and Christine Manigand, eds. *Les opinions publiques face à l'Europe communautaire: Entre cultures nationales et horizon européen*. Brussels: Peter Lang, 2004, 9–20.

Dulphy, Anne, and Christine Manigand, "L'opinion française, vers l'euroconscience et le désenchantement," in Anne Dulphy and Christine Manigand, eds. *Les opinions publiques face à l'Europe communautaire: Entre cultures nationales et horizon européen*. Brussels: Peter Lang, 2004, 23–62.

Eichenberg, Richard C. and Russell J. Dalton, "Europeans and the European Community: The Dynamics of Public Support for European Integration," *International Organization* 47:4 (1993), 507–34.

Elegant, Robert, "How to Lose a War: Reflections of a Foreign Correspondent," *Encounter*, LVII:2 (August, 1981), 73–90.

Elvert, Jürgen, "The Acession-Debate During the EU-Enlargements, 1973–1995: A Public Affair or a Closed Shop?" in Marie-Thérèse Bitsch, Wilfried Loth, and Charles Barthel, eds. *Cultures politiques, opinions publiques et intégration européenne*. Brussels: Établissements Émile Bruylant, 2007.

Eriksen, Erik Oddvar, "An Emerging European Public Sphere," *European Journal of Social Theory* 8:3 (2005), 341–63.

Field, Mervin D., "Political Opinion Polling in the United States of America," in Robert M. Worcester, ed. *Political Opinion Polling: An International Review*. London: Macmillan, 1983, 198–228.

Finney, Patrick, "Introduction: What is International History?" in Patrick Finney, ed. *Palgrave Advances in International History*. Basingstoke: Palgrave Macmillan, 2005.

Foyle, Douglas C., "Foreign Policy Analysis and Globalization: Public Opinion, World Opinion, and the Individual," in Jean A. Garrisson, ed. "Foreign Policy Analysis in 20/20: A Symposium," *International Studies Review* 5:2 (2003), 163–202.

Foyle, Douglas C., "Public Opinion, Foreign Policy, and the Media: Toward an Integrative Theory," in Robert Y. Shapiro and Lawrence R. Jacobs, eds. *The Oxford Handbook of American Public Opinion and the Media*. Oxford: Oxford University Press, 2011, 658–74.

Franklin, Mark N., Cees van der Eijk, and Michael Marsh, "Referendum Outcomes and Trust in Government: Public Support for Europe in the Wake of Maastricht," in Jack Hayward, ed. *The Crisis of Representation in Europe*. London: Frank Cass, 1995.

Franklin, Mark, Michael Marsh, and Lauren McLaren, "Uncorking the Bottle: Popular Opposition to European Unification in the Wake of Maastricht," *Journal of Common Market Studies* 32:4 (1994), 455–72.

Fraser, Nancy, "Transnationalizing the Public Sphere: On the Legitimacy and Efficacy of Public Opinion in a Post-Westphalian World," *Theory, Culture & Society* 24:4 (2007), 7–30.

Freeman, Joshua B., "Hardhats: Construction Workers, Manliness, and the 1970 Pro-War Demonstrations," *Journal of Social History* 26:4 (1993), 725–44.

Fried, Amy, and Douglas B. Harris, "Governing with the Polls," *The Historian* 72:2 (2010), 321–53.

Gabel, Matthew, and Harvey D. Palmer, "Understanding Variation in Public Support for European Integration," *European Journal of Political Research* 27:1 (1995), 3–19.

Gallup, George, "Testing Public Opinion," *The Public Opinion Quarterly* 2:1 (1938), 8–14.

Garner, Scott Sigmund, and Gary M. Segura, "War, Casualties, and Public Opinion," *The Journal of Conflict Resolution* 42:3 (1998), 278–300.

Gehler, Michel, "L'opinion publique en Autriche et la construction européenne," in Marie-Thérèse Bitsch, Wilfried Loth, and Charles Barthel, eds. *Cultures politiques, opinions publiques et intégration européenne*. Brussels: Établissements Émile Bruylant, 2007.

Gili, Jean A., "Un élément constitutif de l'opinion publique: les actualités cinématographiques en France de 1914 à 1918," in *Opinion publique et politique extérieure en Europe, II: 1915–1940: Actes du Colloque de Rome (16 - 20 février 1981)*. Rome: École Française de Rome, 1984.

Giliomee, Hermann, "Democratization in South Africa," *Political Science Quarterly* 110:1 (1995), 83–104.

Gliddon, Paul Martin, "The Labour Government and the Battle for Public Opinion in the 1975 Referendum on the European Community," *Contemporary British History* 31:1 (2017), 91–113.

Goedertier, Wouter, "The Quest for Transnational Authority: The Anti-Apartheid Movements of the European Community," *Revue belge de philologie et d'histoire* 3:4 (2011), 1249–76.

Gottlieb, Julie V., "Neville Chamberlain's Umbrella: 'Object' Lessons in the History of Appeasement," *Twentieth Century British History* 27:3 (2016), 357–88.

Graham, Thomas W., "The Pattern and Importance of Public Knowledge in the Nuclear Age," *The Journal of Conflict Resolution* 32:2 (1988), 319–34.

Guillen, Pierre, "Opinion publique et politique extérieure en France, 1914–1940," in École Française de Rome (ed.), *Opinion publique et politique extérieure en Europe II: 1915–1940: Actes du Colloque du Rome (16–20 février 1981).* Rome: École Française de Rome, 1984.

Gunnell, John G., "Democracy and the Concept of Public Opinion," in Robert Y. Shapiro and Lawrence R. Jacobs, eds. *The Oxford Handbook of American Public Opinion and the Media.* Oxford: Oxford University Press, 2011, 269–83.

Gurney, Christabel, "'A Great Cause': The Origins of the Anti-Apartheid Movement, June 1959 – March 1960," *Journal of Southern African Studies* 26:1 (2000), 123–44.

Gurney, Christabel, "In the Heart of the Beast: The British Anti-Apartheid Movement, 1959–1994," in South African Democracy Education Trust, ed. *The Road to Democracy in South Africa, Volume 3: International Solidarity, Part 1.* Pretoria: Unisa Press, 2008.

Hakhverdian, Armen, Erika van Elsas, Wouter van der Brug, and Theresa Juhn, "Euroscepticism and Education: A Longitudinal Study of 12 EU Member States, 1973–2010," *European Union Politics* 14:4 (2013), 522–41.

Hall, Stuart, "The AAM and the Race-ing of Britain," in Anti-Apartheid Movement Archives Committee, ed. *The Anti-Apartheid Movement: A 40-year Perspective.* London: AAM Archives Committee, 2000.

Hallin, Daniel, "The Media, the War in Vietnam, and Political Support: A Critique of the Thesis of an Oppositional Media," *The Journal of Politics* 46:1 (1984), 2–24.

Harrisson, Tom, "What is Public Opinion?" *The Political Quarterly* 11:4 (1940), 368–83.

Henig, Ruth, "New Diplomacy and Old: A Reassessment of British Conceptions of a League of Nations, 1918–20," in Michael Dockrill and John Fisher, eds. *The Paris Peace Conference, 1919: Peace without Victory?* Basingstoke: Palgrave, 2001, 157–74.

Herbst, Susan, "Critical Perspectives on Public Opinion," in Robert Y. Shapiro and Lawrence R. Jacobs, eds. *The Oxford Handbook of American Public Opinion and the Media.* Oxford: Oxford University Press, 2011, 302–14.

Herbst, Susan, "The History and Meaning of Public Opinion," in Andrew J. Berinsky, ed. *New Directions in Public Opinion,* 2nd ed. New York: Routledge, 2016, 21–33.

Hobolt, Sara B., "Ever Closer or Ever Wider? Public Attitudes Towards Further Enlargement and Integration in the European Union," *Journal of European Public Policy* 21:5 (2014), 664–80.

Hoffmann, Stanley, "Obstinate or Obsolete? The Fate of the Nation-State and the Case of Western Europe," *Daedalus* 95:3 (1966), 862–915.

Holsti, Ole, "Public Opinion and Foreign Policy: Challenges to the Almond-Lippmann Consensus," *International Studies Quarterly* 36:4 (1992), 439–66.

Hooghe, Liesbet, "What Drives Euroskepticism? Party-Public Cueing, Ideology and Strategic Opportunity," *European Union Politics* 8:1 (2007), 5–12.

Houston, Gregory, "International Solidarity: Introduction," in South African Democracy Education Trust, ed. *The Road to Democracy in South Africa, Volume 3: International Solidarity, Part 1*. Pretoria: Unisa Press, 2008.

Hucker, Daniel, "British Peace Activism and 'New' Diplomacy: Revisiting the 1899 Hague Peace Conference," *Diplomacy & Statecraft* 26:3 (2015), 405–23.

Hucker, Daniel, "De 'quantité négligeable' au 'renouveau de la France': représentations de la France en tant qu'alliée militaire à la fin des années 1930," *Revue historique des armées* 264:3 (2011), 48–58.

Hucker, Daniel, "The French Media and the Forging of a Franco-British Alliance in the late 1930s," *Media History* 23:3–4 (2017), 330–44.

Hucker, Daniel, "French Public Attitudes Towards the Prospect of War in 1938–1939: 'Pacifism' or 'War Anxiety'?" *French History* 21:4 (2007), 431–49.

Hucker, Daniel, "International History and the Study of Public Opinion: Towards Methodological Clarity," *International History Review* 34:4 (2012), 775–94.

Hucker, Daniel, "'Our Expectations Were Perhaps Too High': Disarmament, Citizen Activism, and the 1907 Hague Peace Conference," *Peace & Change* 44:1 (2019), 5–32.

Hucker, Daniel, "Public Opinion, Policymakers, and the Munich Crisis: Adding Emotion to Diplomatic History," in Julie V. Gottlieb, Daniel Hucker, and Richard Toye, eds. *The Munich Crisis, Politics and the People*. Manchester: Manchester University Press, forthcoming.

Hurd of Westwell, The Right Honourable Lord, "The Rise and Fall of Morality in Peace Making," in Michael Dockrill and John Fisher, eds. *The Paris Peace Conference, 1919: Peace without Victory?* Basingstoke: Palgrave, 2001.

Hurwitz, Jon, and Mark Peffley, "How are Foreign Policy Attitudes Structured? A Hierarchical Model," *American Political Science Review* 81:4 (1987), 1099–1120.

Imlay, Talbot, "Paul Reynaud and France's Response to Nazi Germany, 1938–1940," *French Historical Studies* 26:3 (2003), 497–538.

Inglehart, Ronald, "Cognitive Mobilization and European Identity," *Comparative Politics* 3:1 (1970), 45–70.

Jackson, Peter, "French Intelligence and Hitler's Rise to Power," *The Historical Journal* 41:3 (1998), 795–824.

Jackson, Peter, "Post-war Politics and the Historiography of French Strategy and Diplomacy Before the Second World War," *History Compass* 4:5 (2006), 870–905.

Jentleson, Bruce W., "The Pretty Prudent Public: Post Post-Vietnam American Opinion on the Use of Military Force," *International Studies Quarterly* 36:1 (1992), 49–74.

Jentleson, Bruce W. (with Rebecca L. Britton), "Still Pretty Prudent: Post-Cold War American Public Opinion on the Use of Military Force," *The Journal of Conflict Resolution* 42:4 (1998), 395–417.

Kaiga, Sakiko, "The Use of Force to Prevent War? The Bryce Group's 'Proposals for the Avoidance of War,' 1914–15," *Journal of British Studies* 57:2 (2018), 308–32.

Keech, Marc, and Barrie Houlihan, "Sport and the End of Apartheid," *The Round Table* 88:349 (1999), 109–21.

Kershaw, Ian, "Consensus, Coercion and Popular Opinion in the Third Reich: Some Reflections," in Paul Corner, ed. *Popular Opinion in Totalitarian Regimes: Fascism, Nazism, Communism*. Oxford: Oxford University Press, 2009.

Kertzer, Joshua D. and Thomas Zeitzoff, "A Bottom-Up Theory of Public Opinion about Foreign Policy," *American Journal of Political Science* 61:3 (2017), 543–58.

Kidd, Bruce, "The Campaign Against Sport in South Africa," *International Journal* 43:4 (1988), 643–64.

Klotz, Audie, "Transnational Activism and Global Transformations: The Anti-Apartheid and Abolitionist Experiences," *European Journal of International Relations* 8:1 (2002), 49–76.

Knecht, Thomas, and M. Stephen Weatherford, "Public Opinion and Foreign Policy: The Stages of Presidential Decision Making," *International Studies Quarterly* 50:3 (2006), 705–27.

Lang-Jensen, Sebastian, "The Danish Left and European Integration, 1957–72," in Marie-Thérèse Bitsch, Wilfried Loth, and Charles Barthel, eds. *Cultures politiques, opinions publiques et intégration européenne*. Brussels: Établissements Émile Bruylant, 2007.

Lau, Richard R., Thad A. Brown, and David O. Sears, "Self-Interest and Civilians' Attitudes Toward the Vietnam War," *Public Opinion Quarterly* 42:4 (1978), 464–82.

Lentin, Antony, "'Appeasement' at the Paris Peace Conference," in Michael Dockrill and John Fisher, eds. *The Paris Peace Conference, 1919: Peace without Victory?* Basingstoke: Palgrave, 2001.

Llewellyn, Maurice, "Circumventing Apartheid: Racial Politics and the Issue of South Africa's Olympic Participation at the 1984 Los Angeles Games," *The International Journal of the History of Sport* 32:1 (2015), 53–71.

Lunch, William L. and Peter W. Sperlich, "American Public Opinion and the War in Vietnam," *The Western Political Quarterly* 32:1 (1979), 21–44.

Machill, Marcel, Markus Beiler, and Corinna Fischer, "Europe-Topics in Europe's Media: The Debate about the European Public Sphere: A Meta-Analysis of Media Content Analyses," *European Journal of Communication* 21:1 (2006), 57–88.

Maclean, Malcolm, "Revisiting (and Revising?) Sports Boycotts: From Rugby Against South Africa to Soccer in Israel," *The International Journal of the History of Sport* 31:15 (2014), 1832–51.

Manigand, Christine, "L'opinion publique française face aux élargissements," in Marie-Thérèse Bitsch, Wilfried Loth, and Charles Barthel, eds. *Cultures politiques, opinions publiques et intégration européenne*. Brussels: Établissements Émile Bruylant, 2007.

Manigand, Christine, and Anne Dulphy, "L'opinion publique française face à l'unification européenne: approche quantifiée," in Élisabeth du Réau, ed. *Europe des élites? Europe des peuples? La construction de l'espace européen, 1945–1960*. Paris: Presses de la Sorbonne Nouvelle, 1999.

Markel, Lester, "Opinion – A Neglected Instrument," in Lester Markel et al., eds. *Public Opinion and Foreign Policy*. New York: Harper & Brothers, 1949, 3–46.

Mbeki, Thabo, "Foreword," in Anti-Apartheid Movement Archives Committee, ed. *The Anti-Apartheid Movement: A 40-year Perspective*. London: AAM Archives Committee, 2000.

Meyer, Jan-Henrik, "Was there a European Public Sphere at the Summit of The Hague 1969? An Analysis of Discourses on the Legitimacy of the EC," in Marie-Thérèse Bitsch, Wilfried Loth, and Charles Barthel, eds. *Cultures politiques, opinions publiques et intégration européenne*. Brussels: Établissements Émile Bruylant, 2007.

Milza, Pierre, "Opinion publique et politique étrangère," in *Opinion publique et politique extérieure en Europe, tome I, 1870–1915: Actes du Colloque de Rome, 13–16 février 1980*. Rome: École Française de Rome, 1981, 663–87.

Minar, David W., "Public Opinion in the Perspective of Political Theory," *The Western Political Quarterly* 13:1 (1960), 31–44.

Moravscik, Andrew, "In Defence of the 'Democratic Deficit': Reassessing Legitimacy in the European Union," *Journal of Common Market Studies* 40:4 (2002), 603–24.

Morgan, Eric J., "Don't Play Ball with South Africa: The United States, the Anti-Apartheid Movement, and the Davis Cup Protests," *The International Journal of the History of Sport* 34:3–4 (2017), 266–82.

Morgan, Kenneth O., "The Boer War and the Media (1899–1902)," *Twentieth Century British History* 13:1 (2002), 1–16.

Mueller, John E., "Public Opinion, the Media, and War," in Robert Y. Shapiro and Lawrence R. Jacobs, eds. *The Oxford Handbook of American Public Opinion and the Media*. Oxford: Oxford University Press, 2011, 675–89.

Mueller, John E., "Trends in Popular Support for the Wars in Korea and Vietnam," *The American Political Science Review* 65:2 (1971), 358–75.

Mullen, Andy, and Brian Burkitt, "Spinning Europe: Pro-European Union Propaganda Campaigns in Britain, 1962–1975," *The Political Quarterly* 76:1 (2005), 100–113.

Müller, Tanja R., "The Long Shadow of Band Aid Humanitarianism: Revisiting the Dynamics between Famine and Celebrity," *Third World Quarterly* 34:3 (2013), 470–84.

Nicolson, Harold, "Modern Diplomacy and British Public Opinion," *International Affairs* 14:5 (1935), 599–618.

Niedermayer, Oskar, "Trends and Contrasts," in Oskar Niedermayer and Richard Sinnott, eds. *Public Opinion and Internationalized Governance*. Oxford: Oxford University Press, 1995.

Nugent, Neill, "British Public Opinion and the European Community," in Stephen George, ed. *Britain and the European Community: The Politics of Semi-Detachment*. Oxford: Clarendon Press, 1992.

Peters, John Durham, "Historical Tensions in the Concept of Public Opinion," in Theodore L. Glasser and Charles T. Salmon, eds. *Public Opinion and the Communication of Dissent.* New York: Guilford Press, 1995.

Peyrefitte, Christel, "Les premiers sondages d'opinion," in René Rémond and Janice Bourdin, eds. *Édouard Daladier, chef de gouvernement: avril 1938 – septembre 1939.* Paris: Presses de la FNSP, 1977.

Pfetsch, Barbara, "Agents of Transnational Debate Across Europe: The Press in Emerging European Public Sphere," *Javnost – The Public: Journal of the European Institute for Communication and Culture* 15:4 (2008), 21–40.

Potter, Simon J., "Jingoism, Public Opinion, and the New Imperialism: Newspapers and Imperial Rivalries at the fin de siècle," *Media History* 20:1 (2014), 34–50.

Powlick, Philip J., and Andrew Z. Katz, "Defining the American Public Opinion/ Foreign Policy Nexus," *Mershon International Studies Review* 42:1 (1998), 29–61.

Priest, Andrew, "Power to the People? American Public Opinion and the Vietnam War," in Andrew Johnstone and Helen Laville, eds. *The US Public and American Foreign Policy* (London: Routledge, 2011.

Reddy, Enuga S., "AAM and UN: Partners in the International Campaign Against Apartheid," in Anti-Apartheid Movement Archives Committee, ed. *The Anti-Apartheid Movement: A 40-year Perspective.* London: AAM Archives Committee, 2000.

Reddy, Enuga S., "The United Nations and the Struggle for Liberation in South Africa," in South African Democracy Education Trust, ed. *The Road to Democracy in South Africa, Volume 3: International Solidarity, Part 1.* Pretoria: Unisa Press, 2008.

Reinfeldt, Alexander, "British Public Opinion and European Integration: Supranational and Governmental Information Policies in Britain (1952–1973)," in Marie-Thérèse Bitsch, Wilfried Loth, and Charles Barthel, eds. *Cultures politiques, opinions publiques et intégration européenne* Brussels: Établissements Émile Bruylant, 2007.

Reynolds, David, "International History, the Cultural Turn and the Diplomatic Twitch," *Cultural and Social History* 3 (2006), 75–91.

Rich, Paul, "Reinventing Peace: David Davies, Alfred Zimmern and Liberal Internationalism in Interwar Britain," *International Relations* 16:1 (2002), 117–33.

Robbins, Keith, "Lord Bryce and the First World War," *The Historical Journal* 10:2 (1967), 255–78.

Robbins, Keith, "The Treaty of Versailles, 'Never Again' and Appeasement," in Michael Dockrill and John Fisher, eds. *The Paris Peace Conference, 1919: Peace without Victory?.* Basingstoke: Palgrave, 2001.

Sánchez-Cuenca, Ignacio, "The Political Basis of Support for European Integration," *European Union Politics* 1:2 (2000), 147–71.

Sapire, Hilary, "Liberation Movements, Exile, and International Solidarity: An Introduction," *Journal of Southern African Studies* 35:2 (2009), 271–86.

Schlesinger, Phillip, "Changing Spaces of Political Communication: The Case of the European Union," *Political Communication* 16:3 (1999), 263–79.

Schmitter, Philippe, "A Revised Theory of Regional Integration," in Leon Lindberg and Stuart Scheingold, eds. *Regional Integration: Theory and Research*. Cambridge: Harvard University Press, 1971.

Scott, Amy, "Patriots for Peace: People-to-People Diplomacy and the Anti-War Movement," in Andrew Wiest, Kathryn Barbier, and Glenn Robins, eds. *America and the Vietnam War: Re-examining the Culture and History of a Generation*. London: Routledge, 2010.

Sellström, Tor, "Sweden and the Nordic Countries: Official Solidarity and Assistance from the West," in South African Democracy Education Trust, ed. *The Road to Democracy in South Africa, Volume 3: International Solidarity, Part 1*. Pretoria: Unisa Press, 2008.

Shapiro, Robert Y. and Benjamin I. Page, "Foreign Policy and the Rational Public," *The Journal of Conflict Resolution* 32:2 (1988), 211–47.

Sinnott, Richard, "Bringing Public Opinion Back In," in Oskar Niedermayer and Richard Sinnott, eds. *Public Opinion and Internationalized Governance*. Oxford: Oxford University Press, 1995.

Skillen, Fiona, and Matthew L. McDowell, "The 1970 British Commonwealth Games: Scottish Reactions to Apartheid and Sporting Boycotts," *Journal of Sport History* 44:3 (2017), 367–83.

Small, Melvin, "The Impact of the Antiwar Movement on Lyndon Johnson, 1965–1968: A Preliminary Report," *Peace & Change* 10:1 (1984), 1–22.

Small, Melvin, "Influencing the Decision Makers: The Vietnam Experience," *Journal of Peace Research* 24:2 (1987), 185–98.

Sohlberg, Jacob, Peter Esaisson, and Johann Martinsson, "The Changing Political Impact of Compassion-Evoking Pictures: The Case of the Drowned Toddler Alan Kurdi," *Journal of Ethnic and Migration Studies* 45:13 (2019), 2275–88.

Soucy, Robert J., "French Press Reactions to Hitler's First Two Years in Power," *Contemporary European History* 7:1 (1998), 21–38.

Speier, Hans, "Historical Development of Public Opinion," *American Journal of Sociology* 55:4 (1950), 376–88.

Spiering, Menno, "British Euroscepticism," in Robert Harmsen and Menno Spiering, eds. *Euroscepticism: Party Politics, National Identity and European Integration*. Amsterdam: Rodopi, 2004.

Strebble, Elizabeth Grottle, "Political Polarisation and French Cinema, 1934–39," in Nicholas Pronay and D. W. Spring, eds. *Propaganda, Politics and Film, 1918–45*. London: Macmillan, 1982.

Taylor, Edmond, "Democracy Demoralized: The French Collapse," *Public Opinion Quarterly* 4:4 (1940), 630–50.

Terrou, Fernand, "L'évolution du droit de la presse de 1881 à 1940," in Claude Bellanger et al., eds. *Histoire générale de la presse française, tome III: de 1871 à 1940*. Paris: Presses Universitaires de France, 1972.

Thörn, Håkan, "The Meaning(s) of Solidarity: Narratives of Anti-Apartheid Activism," *Journal of Southern African Studies* 35:2 (2009), 417–36.

Thörn, Håkan, "Social Movements, the Media and the Emergence of a Global Public Sphere: From Anti-Apartheid to Global Justice," *Current Sociology* 55:6 (2007), 896–918.

Toshkov, Dimiter, "Public Opinion and Policy Output in the European Union: A Lost Relationship," *European Union Politics* 12:2 (2011), 169–91.

Touchard, Jean, and Louis Bodin, "L'état de l'opinion au début de l'année 1936," in Pierre Renouvin and René Rémond, eds. *Léon Blum: Chef de gouvernement, 1936-1937.* Paris: Presses de la FNSP, 1981.

Trachtenberg, Marc, "Reparation at the Paris Peace Conference," *The Journal of Modern History* 51:1 (1979), 24–55.

Trachtenberg, Marc, "Versailles after Sixty Years," *Journal of Contemporary History* 17:3 (1982), 487–506.

Twomey, Christina, "Framing Atrocity: Photography and Humanitarianism," *History of Photography* 36:3 (2012), 255–64.

Verba, Sidney et al., "Public Opinion and the War in Vietnam," *The American Political Science Review* 61:2 (1967), 317–33.

Voorhes, Meg, "The US Divestment Movement," in Neta C. Crawford and Audie Klotz, eds. *How Sanctions Work: Lessons from South Africa.* Basingstoke: Macmillan, 1999.

Vries, Catherine de, "Ambivalent Europeans? Public Support for European Integration in East and West," *Government and Opposition* 48:3 (2013), 434–61.

Wardhaugh, Jessica, "Crowds, Culture and Power: Mass Politics and the Press in Interwar France," *Journalism Studies* 14:5 (2013), 743–58.

Wardhaugh, Jessica, "France in the Blue Light of Munich: Popular Agency, Activity, and the Reframing of History," in Julie V. Gottlieb, Daniel Hucker, and Richard Toye, eds. *The Munich Crisis, Politics and the People.* Manchester: Manchester University Press, forthcoming.

Watson, Mary Ann, "Television and the Presidency: Eisenhower and Kennedy," in Gary R. Edgerton, ed. *The Columbia History of American Television.* New York: Columbia University Press, 2010.

Wilkes, George, and Dominic Wring, "The British Press and European Integration: 1948-1996," in David Baker and David Seawright, eds. *Britain For and Against Europe: British Politics and the Question of European Integration.* Oxford: Clarendon Press, 1998.

Wilson, Francis G., "James Bryce on Public Opinion: Fifty Years Later," *Public Opinion Quarterly* 3:3 (1939), 420–35.

Young, Robert J., "The Use and Abuse of Fear: France and the Air Menace in the 1930s," *Intelligence and National Security* 2:4 (1987), 88–109.

Index